Weldon Nisly

WITHOUT THE LOSS OF ONE

Although Don, Mildred, and Titus Bender were lead authors of this book, Hilda Bender Swartz was the author of one chapter and provided significant editorial refinements. In addition, all nine Bender siblings and their spouses contributed in various ways to the development and completion of the project.

WITHOUT THE LOSS OF ONE

Don Bender, Mildred Bender, and Titus Bender

Foreword by Melodie M. Davis
Afterword by Joan K. King

DreamSeeker Books
TELFORD, PENNSYLVANIA

an imprint of
Cascadia Publishing House

Copublished with
Herald Press
Scottdale, Pennsylvania

Cascadia Publishing House orders, information, reprint permissions:
contact@CascadiaPublishingHouse.com
1-215-723-9125
126 Klingerman Road, Telford PA 18969
www.CascadiaPublishingHouse.com

Without the Loss of One
Copyright © 2005 by Cascadia Publishing House.
Telford, PA 18969
All rights reserved
DreamSeeker Books is an imprint of Cascadia Publishing House.
Copublished with Herald Press, Scottdale, PA
Library of Congress Catalog Number: 2005015180
ISBN: 1-931038-31-7
Printed in the United States by GBCS, Logan Township, NJ
Book design by Cascadia Publishing House
Cover design by Gwen M. Stamm

The paper used in this publication is recycled and meets the
minimum requirements of American National Standard for Information Sciences—
Permanence of Paper for Printed Library Materials, ANSI Z39.48-1984.1984

Library of Congress Cataloguing-in-Publication Data
Bender, Don, 1940-
  Without the loss of one : the story of Nevin and Esther Bender and its implications for the church today / Don Bender, Mildred Bender, and Titus Bender ; afterword by Joan K. King.
    p. cm.
  Includes bibliographical references and index.
  ISBN 1-931038-31-7 (trade pbk. : alk. paper)
  1. Bender, Nevin, 1892-1975. 2. Bender, Esther, 1898-1967. 3. Amish Mennonites--United States--Biography. 4. Conservative Mennonite Conference--Bishops--Biography.   I. Bender, Mildred, 1934-   .
II. Bender, Titus, 1932-   . III. Title.
BX8129.C69B46 2005
289.7'092'2--dc22
[B]
                                                              2005015180

11 10 09 08 07 06 05   10 9 8 7 6 5 4 3 2 1

Contents

Foreword by Melodie M. Davis   7
Preface   11
Preface to the First Edition   17

PART ONE: THE CONVERGING PATHS, 1892-1925
1 Nevin's Path: He Always Stood Straight · 21
2 Esther's Path: She Put First Things First · 39
3 Marriage: What God Has Joined Together · 47

PART TWO: THE GREENWOOD YEARS
4 Becoming Family:
   Won't We Be Happy When Tuesday Comes! · 55
5 Growing Up: We Have Each Other · 77
6 Economic Life: Is There Any More Back? · 97
7 Education: The More I Learn,
   the More There Is to Learn · 115
8 Church Life: All You Preach Is Love, Love, Love · 125

PART THREE: WITNESS IN MISSISSIPPI
9 A Major Move: There Is an Open Door · 151
10 Facing Violence: The Lord Has Given Grace · 170
11 Esther's Passing: O for a Faith That Will Not Shrink · 183

PART FOUR: SOJOURN AND RETURN TO GREENWOOD
12 Year in Beirut:
   O Healing River, Send Down Your Waters · 201

13 Transitions: The Times, They Are a Changin' · 211
14 Return to Greenwood: Going Home · 225

Afterword by Joan K. King   243

APPENDIX 1: REFLECTIONS
Thoughts on the Day My Father Died, by Paul Bender   247
*My Grandpa and Grandma Bender—and the Meaning of Faith,
   by Daryl J. Swartz   248*
Refugees, by Jean Bender   251
"You Have Considered," by Phyllis Benner   252
To Mother, by Mildred Bender   253
My Garage Buddy, by Beth Myers   255
A Tribute to Nevin from His Daughter, by Miriam Jantzi   256
Nevin's Final Family Circle Letter, by Nevin Bender   258

APPENDIX TWO: DOCUMENTS
School Children Must Salute Flag or Suffer Suspension   261
*Consulting the Church
   Regarding Issues Current in 1958   262*
The Journey to Egypt   263
Our Journey to Palestine: Part 1   264
Our Journey to Palestine: Part 2   265
Talk Given by Nevin at Near East School of Theology   268

The Authors   271

FOREWORD

*T*HE TELLING OR WRITING OF FAMILY STORIES is crucial to me; that's why I agreed to write this foreword. This is a simply written, straightforward, but captivating book, even for people not in the Bender family—and that is the whole point. The story of Nevin and Esther Bender has enough touch points with U.S. culture and recent history to have universal application for many of us. Moreover, it has enough specific similarities to thousands of Mennonite families growing up in the 1930s, '40s, '50s and '60s that I have no doubt many will find the simple (although formally written) pages quite compelling.

    The beauty of this book is that it was originally conceived and written by family, for family. But almost anyone born in the larger Mennonite faith family in the 1950s or earlier will find points of identification with the Bender story. In fact, I was amazed at how many experiences my family shared, even though we grew up in Indiana, in a much smaller farm family of three girls and one boy, in an (Old) Mennonite (not Conservative Conference) church, with Dad "just" a deacon and not a bishop.

    The stories of Nevin's youth reminded me of similar stories I heard and the issues we faced in our church and family, such as a child run over by horses; young Titus left behind all alone at home; jumping dangerously off of barn beams; canning together; children asking forgiveness for an alleged wrongdoing they couldn't recall; stories of Dad being chosen by the "lot"; spending Sunday mornings and evenings plus Wednesday evenings exactly as we did in our family (always at church, always kneeling for prayer Wednesday evenings).

Where the Bender story intersects with the larger cultural and historical story of the U.S. experience, I found my interest piqued even more: Here was a family that actually challenged the state rulings on reciting the pledge of allegiance, resulting in children being suspended from school and the formation of the very first Mennonite elementary school in the U.S., Greenwood Mennonite School, Delaware. Here was a son who lived just four blocks from Ebenezer Baptist Church in Atlanta, where he heard Martin Luther Jr. preach frequently and became an integral part of the civil rights movement.

Then came the years when the Benders experienced the pain of the civil rights movement, in part at least for their beliefs in the equality of all people, including the original Native Americans. A church they founded in ministry with the Choctaw peoples in Mississippi was burned and rebuilt not once but three times. This was at the time of similar racially incited burnings all over Mississippi. The Bender family story intersects with and perhaps even subtly impacts the national story—probably more than most of our stories do.

But the overall larger impact of this story and book is the way Nevin models, at least in this telling, the grace of a conservative Mennonite leader growing older, wiser, mellower, and able to embrace not being able to figure out every single aspect of Christian faith. While Esther plays a key supportive and loving role as wife, mother, and helpmeet, the book and its authors do not pretend she had a leadership role she didn't have, since this was a different time in history.

I appreciated the insights into my own faith heritage brought by this family story, such as the major difference between Amish and other Anabaptist groups being the Amish insistence on a bishop's authority versus the Anabaptist understanding of the importance of the "priesthood of all believers" in decision-making. This key understanding became critical in one of the main crises of Nevin's life, when he was essentially asked as a leader to coerce the wearing of the plain coat and he was not inclined to do so. Eventually Nevin basically recommended that a new bishop take over to break the impasse, and the Benders wisely moved on to new areas of service and challenge in God's kingdom.

Perhaps this book will also inspire other families to in some way write or record part or all of their family stories. Like the Benders, you will find that you will come to new insights, understandings, and serendipities—and that your family will be changed even in the process of gathering, writing, and reading. If so, then the circle of inspiration will be complete.

—*Melodie (Miller) Davis is a writer/producer for Mennonite Media in Harrisonburg, Virginia, and editor of the* Together *and* Living *periodicals for Shalom Foundation publications. She is the author of eight books and the "Another Way" syndicated column.*

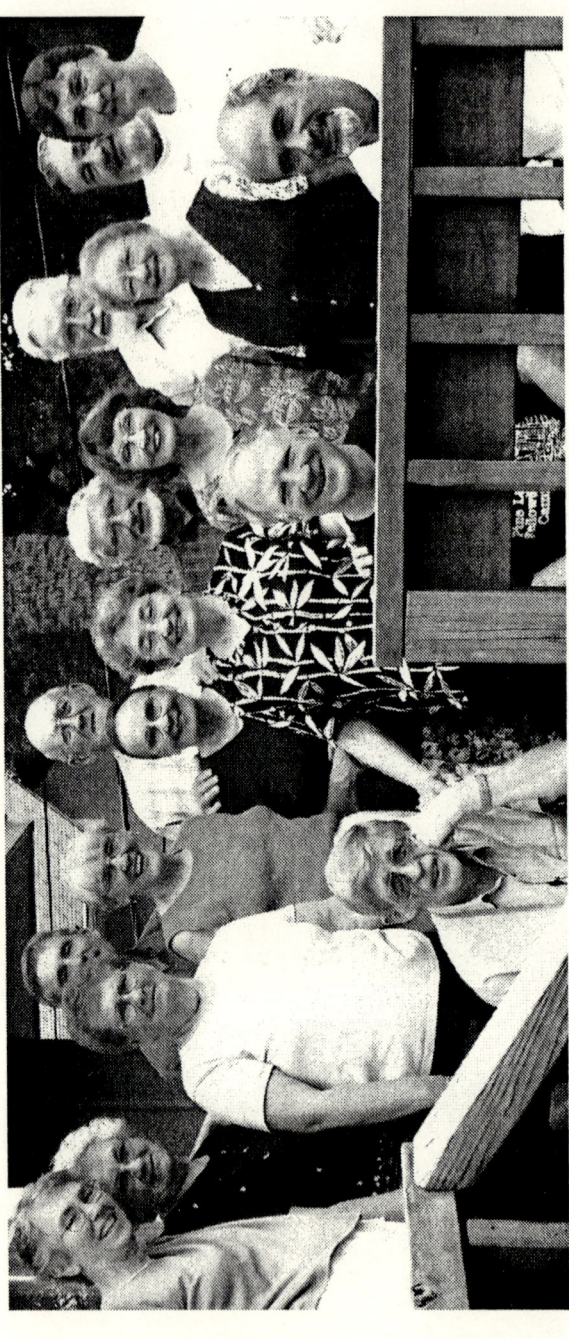

This photograph was taken at a gathering of the 17 members of the Bender family on October 10, 2004 at Tybee Island, Georgia. At this gathering the Preface was affirmed by all 17 members. From left to right those pictured are as follows: Judith Bender (spouse of Don), Ann Bender (spouse of Titus), Virginia Bender (spouse of Paul), Nevin Bender, Lourene Bender (spouse of Nevin), Miriam Jantzi, Elmer Jantzi (spouse of Miriam), Hilda Swartz, Titus Bender, Emma Myers, Millard Benner (spouse of Lura), Lura Benner, Paul Bender, Mildred Bender, front row Merlin Swartz (spouse of Hilda), Glenn Myers (spouse of Emma), and Don Bender

PREFACE

*A Personal Statement from
Nevin and Esther Bender's Children and Their Spouses*

NEVIN AND ESTHER BENDER FOUND THE CHURCH a place of intense joy and, occasionally, of painful disappointment. For Mennonites and Amish, or any people who take their community of faith seriously, this community can be loving arms of support or a smothering embrace that stifles an honest search for truth. For Nevin and Esther and their family—and for so many others then and now—the church became a combination of these two experiences.

During his teenage years Nevin Bender was known as "a hickory," according to his cousin Ezra Bender. A hickory in that Springs, Pennsylvania, community in the early 1900s meant he was adventurous and not easily squeezed into a mold. Ironically, Nevin later became a minister and bishop in the newly formed Amish Mennonite Conference, where pushing people to fit in was seen by many as a necessary virtue in a bishop. Even after a profound spiritual experience in his mid-20s, ordination to the ministry, and being chosen for the office of bishop, he found himself suspect among certain kinds of leaders. This young hickory turned minister and bishop is our father. The love of his life, Esther, is our mother. She left us in 1967 and he in 1975. Yet in many ways they are still with us.

In Nevin's Amish Mennonite Conference, fear of change caused many pastors of congregations to demand conformity to rules. These rules were generally a reflection of the leader's beliefs and those of an inner core of men. (Neither women nor youth played key roles in decision making in this conference during the early years.) The rules were based on Scripture, parishioners were assured.

Nevin faced a growing inner tension. On the one hand, Nevin's peers, many Amish Mennonite Conference leaders, reflected fear of a dangerous drift toward "worldliness" by the larger Mennonite church. ("Worldliness" in that era focused on giving up distinctive clothing.) On the other hand, Nevin was developing a growing uneasiness that people with questioning minds were being isolated from the church.

In retrospect it seems clear the most important distinction between Nevin and some of his more conservative fellow conference ministers was not related to the specific church traditions being considered. He had respect for the depth of convictions about these traditions. However, for Nevin, a higher priority was creating active dialogue with church members during the process of considering change. He believed church members could grow in trust and respect for each other if they talked with rather than past each other.

Nevin and Esther Lauver were married in 1925. They were lifelong partners in his church leadership efforts. Through any stretch of the imagination they were not co-pastors by today's standards. Esther never felt comfortable in the public limelight, but she had a humanizing influence through her personal relationships. For her there was no such reality as class difference. Her sense of justice was instinctive and deep. She reached out not only to trusted friends but also to those who were different from her. No one doubted the humanity and compassion with which she related to others. As children we sensed her keen disappointment when a person, any person, was excluded. We never saw her try to hurt anyone, even those in an adversarial role with her spouse.

♦

Esther's relationship to Nevin had a profound impact on his ministry. She was his lover in the deepest sense of the word—a trusted confidant and a lens through which he could view the world as he and Esther moved toward increasing acceptance of a wide variety of persons as daughters and sons of God. (We must hasten to say that our mother would have been embarrassed to call our father her lover in front of her children. Their deepest intimacy was too private for that. Yet Esther was obviously pleased when Nevin's playfulness and affection occurred in the presence of their children. Her children remember Nevin reaching out as Esther passed by and pulling her into his lap on numerous occasions. She always cooperated with a pleased and bashful expression on her face.)

Nevin had risen rather quickly from being a teenage hickory to being trusted by influential leaders in the Amish Mennonite Conference. These leaders had parted from the Amish tradition, yet many tended to mistrust the larger Mennonite church. Nevin was increasingly invited to preach in those Mennonite circles. He was finding the mistrust of Mennonites by many of his Amish Mennonite colleagues divisive. When Nevin was ordained, many of the major leaders who had begun the new conference were emphasizing the role of "church discipline" in avoiding "worldliness." This meant keeping a clear-cut distinction between their church members and everyone else in the community.

An influential player in the new Amish Mennonite movement was Mike Zehr. He took Nevin under his wing and had a conservative effect on him during his early years as a minister. One time Zehr, an older church leader, small in stature but stout of heart, became quite ill with asthma and was advised by his physician to move to Arizona. Illustrating their close relationship, he asked Nevin to accompany him by train. Gladly Nevin made this trip with him—one he would always remember. He never lost his deep respect for Mike and his camaraderie with him.

Hearing the opinions and concerns of a wide variety of people was a trademark of Nevin's ministry. His ears were open to his fellow Amish Mennonite leaders such as Mike Zehr and other conference colleagues. He maintained dialogue with a variety of people in the Mennonite church, welcoming the voices of women and youth. What seemed to some a gift of listening seemed to others a danger to tradition. In sermon notes among the files his children have kept is the constant concern to recognize those beliefs which are based on unchanging principles, maintaining traditions which stand the test of time. He opened his ears and heart to a wide variety of people to an extent that was unusual in his Amish Mennonite Conference.

During the 1940s and early 1950s, Nevin Bender reached a place of considerable influence in the conference, now calling itself the Conservative Mennonite Conference. Nevin had been active in this name change. As a member of the Executive Committee with responsibilities to mediate dissension in congregations, he increasingly urged church leaders to "take the voice of the church." He believed members should be involved in finding peaceful solutions. To those oriented toward top-down decision making, this was dangerous. Nevin had become a "square peg in a round hole" in the eyes of a number of increasingly conservative conference leaders.

Why did Nevin and Esther not simply walk away into the larger Mennonite church? For Amish and Mennonites this is more complex than it seems, especially for those who have deep roots in either tradition.

When an Amish or Mennonite family finds its beliefs out of step with its church there is inescapable pain. Church is seldom a casual experience, especially for those whose roots, both doctrinal and genealogical, run deep in this faith community. Far more than a creed binds us together. We experience ourselves as a family that stands together, a community of faith in which each looks out for the other. Church is about taking Jesus seriously when he said, "Follow me," as he refused to hurt or destroy people. It is about being misunderstood for nonviolence, especially during times of armed conflict when anger toward "the enemy" abroad creates less patience for those who disagree at home.

There is a downside to this glue that holds Amish or Mennonites together. When people suffer because of unjust institutions, the temptation for some Mennonites is to look the other way and leave such problems to "the world." This keeps our hands cleaner but gives "heartburn" to those who see this as dishonest. The church that provides a context for vibrant togetherness can carry this protective shield so far that some of its members find it "hard to breathe" and necessary to search for a vigorous relationship to persons and institutions outside its own circle. When change is essential to faithfully meet the challenges of a new day there can be a heavy price to pay for not fitting in. Unless a Mennonite is on the periphery of the community, walking away can be a painful option. Nevin and Esther's roots were deep in the conference in which they served. They tried to stay even when Nevin's approach to church discipline became a minority view.

In the local Greenwood Conservative Mennonite church where Nevin was pastor, the bond of mutual trust between most of the members and Nevin and Esther remained strong during their entire ministry. When tension increased through voices of dissent that were alarmed about the "worldly drift," the result was to draw the nine children and their spouses into greater respect for their parents and each other. Probably we are not fully aware of the extent to which each of our journeys has been shaped by this mixture of painful and exhilarating times together as our family sensed impulses within the church against inclusiveness toward those who differed. For us there was always our family. Here we experienced love and faith. There was vigorous dialogue that made clear we were not carbon copies of each other. There was questioning and laughter—always laughter. It is clear that the spouses that came into the Bender family each brought valuable experiences to our family from their own family traditions and enriched ours. For this we are grateful.

Today nine siblings and eight spouses get together regularly. These are "The Seventeen" who all participated—to varying degrees—in this story of our parents/parents-in-law, *Without the Loss of One*. We believe there is no degree of tension that can ever tear us apart. In this book we share with you the story of our parents.

PREFACE TO THE FIRST EDITION

This is the Preface to the first "family edition" of 1993. That edition, published by Nevin and Esther's nine children, was intended primarily for Nevin and Esther's grandchildren.

THIS IS A STORY ABOUT THE LAUVER-BENDER family, conceived, birthed, and nurtured by Nevin and Esther Lauver Bender and remembered in this book by their children. It is a story about our family, for us and by us. It is a story about what has made our family unique and considers the myth that has guided our lives.

It is a story for our children and their children. Some of them did not know Mother and Dad—their grandma and grandpa. They have asked questions and we want to claim the gift that is ours, as honestly as possible.

Aunt Lucy (Schrock) reminded us that "to whom much has been given, much is expected." We are fortunate to have a legacy of seeking education, respecting the ideas and dignity of others, and opening ourselves to new truth. It is a legacy of including all people in our circle and drinking deeply as we celebrate life. We grew up in a community where authoritarian attitudes, rigidity, exclusion, and somberness were also present, so we do not take our family's legacy for granted.

This story is an effort which began as a weekend gathering in a mountain retreat center in Syria, Virginia, in July, 1986. The nine siblings and their spouses gathered to remember. We laughed and cried as we listened to each other and to our own hearts. The story is a dynamic one and even as it was being told, it was unfolding, changing, being shaped. As we gathered for communion the final night, we dealt with the feelings resulting from our brother Nevin's life-changing aneurism in 1979 and our efforts to respond to that event. We realized that a deep healing was happening among us. Telling our story was changing us, even as our story was changing in the telling.

The story of this family began with the marriage of Nevin and Esther on October 13, 1925, a Tuesday afternoon. They were married in Juniata County, Pennsylvania, Esther's home, then moved to Greenwood, Delaware, Nevin's home, to begin their own home and family. Over the next 16 years their union created ten children, the last of whom was stillborn. It is this family's life together that this book describes.

What were the threads of central purpose that gave this family its specific flavor? One phrase with which Nevin ended most of his prayers lingers in the minds of his children, that when we are finished here, God would receive us unto himself "without the loss of one." This circle of inclusiveness broadened in the hearts of Nevin and Esther (and in the hearts of their children) as the years went by. It became a central paradigm for the way Nevin, Esther, and their family came to understand the heart and work of God. "Without the loss of one," as an understanding of God's intention, stood in contrast to exclusive attitudes the family sometimes encountered in a variety of communities.

To consider who Nevin and Esther were, we begin with the background of their separate paths before marriage.

Part One

The Converging Paths

One

NEVIN'S PATH

He always stood straight.

—Aunt Lucy's statement about her brother Nevin.

NEVIN V. BENDER WAS BORN OCTOBER 27, 1892, in the rocky, hilly farming country of Springs, Pennsylvania, near the Maryland border. His father Valentine ("Feldy") Bender was the son of Wilhelm Bender, who had come to that area from Germany as a teenager in 1830 to avoid military service. His mother was Caroline Gingerich, whose family came from Negro mountain, a nearby area.

Nevin was the third child and oldest son of the thirteen children born to Feldy and Caroline Bender. Savilla and Cora were his older sisters. The younger siblings were Amelia, Savannah, Nanna, Lucy, Earl, Lester, Hilda, and Pauline. There were also two stillborn children, a son and a daughter.

Nevin was deeply affected by the deaths of three of his siblings. In Pennsylvania, 16-year-old Nevin felt keenly the death of Lester, his two-year-old brother. Earl at four and Lester at two were playmates and loved coming out to meet their big brother when he came home from work. The day Earl came out without Lester, and Nevin discovered that his seriously ill brother was dying, was a day he would never forget. Nine years later, Cora, who was particularly close to Nevin, died while he was in camp, refusing military service. She had been recently married and was three months pregnant with her first child. She wrote him a letter of encouragement shortly before her death, which Nevin kept for many years. In it she said that the light was needed where there was darkness, not where there was already light. Her letter was an encouragement to Nevin, a newly ordained minister, in his difficult days in camp as a conscientious objector.

A year later his sister, Hilda, at age 12, developed an illness that lasted some weeks and to which she finally succumbed. Nevin at 26, a new pastor, ministered to his own parents in this experience. They had lost babies, Lester and two stillborn, but now it was their fun-loving 12-year-old, and so soon after the death of their second oldest daughter, Cora. Nevin comforted his family, especially his mother, even as he experienced his own profound grief for Cora.

Nevin's father, Feldy, was a large and very strong man with a beard. Nevin describes him as a businessman, a conciliator, a good song leader and an emotional speaker (although somewhat limited with words). Feldy and his family had changed to a more progressive wing of the Amish church when Nevin was a small child. Later, when Nevin was 20, this group became a part of the newly formed Conservative Amish Mennonite Conference. The word *Amish* was dropped from its name by the 1950s, but the conference continued to have a blend of Amish and Mennonite characteristics. Feldy was a leader in the movement from Amish to progressive Amish to Amish Mennonite. He continued to be a progressive voice in the new Conservative Amish Mennonite Conference. As an entrepreneur, he operated a woolen mill, three saw mills, and a coal mine in the Springs, Pennsylvania, area. Feldy was also active in the larger community which was unusual for an Amishman.

Caroline Bender is remembered as a quiet bulwark of stability. Raising eleven children was a huge task, and she also at times cooked for many more than her own family. Nevin recalled that when the Standard Oil pipeline was being laid in their area, his mother would often cook for twenty extra people and even as many as forty. She later became a familiar and important person in the lives of Nevin and Esther's children.

Nevin attended a one-room school during his early grades. Later he went to a two-room school with primary grades on the first floor and grammar school on the second. When his class was called to the front for their reading recitation, the students sat on two benches, girls on one and boys on the other. The boys competed for the inside seat next to the girls. One time as Nevin got to the preferred seat and prepared to sit down, another boy slid under him and Nevin, unintentionally, sat on his lap. As punishment the teacher had them stay in for recess and read a book without looking up, with the threat that if they looked up they would get a spanking. This made a lasting impression on Nevin. In telling the story, he clearly felt that the punishment was unfair since he had not intentionally caused any disturbance.

Nevin's favorite subject was math, in which he and two other boys would work ahead. When they completed the book the teacher gave them challenging problems to solve. One he remembered was to calculate the area a cow could cover if she was tethered to the corner of a 25-foot square barn with a 100-foot rope.

Nevin and his siblings walked a mile and a half to school and in the winter went by sled. Sledding was a favorite winter sport, using both bobsleds and small sleds. The favorite sledding spot was the hill from the Upper Tub to the Lower Tub (later known as Upper Springs and Lower Springs). The first name originated from the tubs which were placed at the springs to catch water.

Aunt Lucy recalled her big brother as rather daring. Once he rode his bike as fast as he could down a hill until he lost control and flew over the handlebars. On another occasion his parents had bought a lamp shade which was advertised as nonbreakable. Nevin tried dropping it on the floor as the directions stated one could do. It didn't break. Still not convinced that the advertisement was true, he then tried dropping it in a different way, and this time it did break. He was taken outside to receive his punishment. Aunt Lucy remembered Nevin often getting more punishment than his sisters, but always out of their sight.

When Nevin was 15 years old he became tired of school, evidently feeling unchallenged, and he often missed school to work. One of the first jobs he did was to bring chunks of limestone by sled from the top of Negro Mountain to the farm. After a large pile was accumulated, it was burned to use on the land. Later, when Standard Oil laid an eight-inch pipeline across their land, Nevin pulled large sections of the pipe from the railroad to the end of the line with two teams of horses. He also worked as a water boy for the construction crew for 20 cents a day. This was a time when Nevin's mother boarded pipeline workers and cooked for large groups of men.

Although Nevin joined the church at age 15, apparently this did not seriously curb his fun-loving and daring nature. Later, at the age of 25, he made a more substantial commitment.

Feldy Bender served as the pipeline road master in his area and hired a crew to do the work. Nevin worked on that gang for a while but found the men to be extremely crude and felt they were a negative influence on him. Lucy recalls him complaining to his parents about the language of the men. He also said later that he felt their influence gave him internal struggles. Although he never said so explicitly, one could imply that he was referring to lewd and disrespectful conversation about sex.

When Nevin was 21 years old (January 1, 1914), their family moved to Delaware. One of the motivations for the move was that his father apparently felt quite constrained by the church. The Casselman Congregation in Northern Maryland where Feldy's family were members, had moved from being

Amish to Amish Mennonite and was considered progressive in relation to some of the other churches in the area. For example, they placed more value on education. However the progress was not enough for Feldy, who was interested in missions and also wanted an active young people's program for his children. These interests were opposed by many of the conservative people in the Maryland church they attended. Also motivating the move was Feldy's dislike of the rocky, hilly farmland of Pennsylvania.

No doubt, another reason for the move was Feldy's adventurous spirit. After looking at a number of locations he bought a farm in Bay Minette, Baldwin County, Alabama, in 1912. Caroline, however, objected to this move so far from home and the search turned to the Eastern Shore. He and his brother-in-law, Will Tressler, finally decided on Delaware because of the availability of flat and inexpensive land. At his father Wilhelm's request, Feldy delayed making the move to Delaware until after his father died.

Feldy Bender and Will Tressler were married to sisters, Caroline and Barbara Gingerich. The two families moved to Delaware together and soon other families joined them there. The Bender family, partly because of its size and partly to its gregarious nature, was the gathering place for Mennonite young people and also community people. The new arrivals met for worship in homes, but the young people also often met with the Brethren Church at Owens Station (the present location of the Tressler Mennonite church).

The young people attended community box socials which were sometimes followed by a dance. The Mennonite youth did not participate in the dance, however, because it was not considered an appropriate Christian activity. Lucy could not recall that Nevin dated non-Mennonite girls from the community although a few Mennonite youth did.

New families were invited to move to Delaware through promotion in an Amish newsletter called *The Budget*. Feldy bought more land, cleared the timber, and sold the land to new people who wanted to relocate there. His daughter Lucy said that he tried to sell at prices people could afford. Although he did not make much money from this, some accused him of taking advantage of people. This charge she considered unfounded.

In the aftermath of their son Lester's death, Feldy and Caroline decided to adopt another boy. Eight years after Lester's death, when Nevin was 23 years old, they felt the time was right so Caroline traveled by train to the Grantsville Children's Home to see about securing a child. She had decided to take three-year-old, curly haired William Welfly when John Embleton (who, at 12, had become somewhat familiar with the Benders) said, "I always thought that Pop Bender would give me a home." When Caroline called Feldy to tell him she had found a boy, she also related John's remark. Feldy was moved and urged that they also give John a home. Caroline agreed, though with some reservation about taking in two children.

Because the two boys had very different personalities, this was not an easy transition for Earl, who was the same age as John. Earl was rather quiet and did not enjoy being associated with the more aggressive boys. He remarked that he was more of a Gingerich (Caroline's side, which he saw as being more quiet and reserved) than a Bender (Feldy's side, which he saw as more gregarious and assertive).

Earl later became disillusioned with the Mennonite church. His sister, Lucy, mentioned that Earl observed one of their ministers, while in a store, take some candy without paying for it. He also felt that some of the young people were wild and crude but were accepted by the church because they obeyed the rules. It was a number of such perceptions and experiences which led him to reject the Mennonite church. Nevin later expressed strongly that he wished he had listened more carefully to his younger brother's concerns and challenges.

In Germany it had been customary to serve alcohol in the home. Feldy felt that this was acceptable, although others in the church disagreed. Feldy apparently changed his view when John and Earl got into his supply one day and became intoxicated. Since some Bender relatives through the years had problems with alcohol, Nevin developed a cautious attitude toward it and later the Greenwood Church forbid its use.

After moving to Delaware, Nevin attended normal school, as teacher education programs were then called, for three summers and became qualified to teach. In the years preceding his ordination he taught in the public school system. During these years as a student and then as a teacher, Nevin was considered a "sport," as his cousin Ezra Bender, put it. He rode a motorcycle—rather wildly according to a shaken fellow teacher who expected a quiet ride with this plainly dressed young man. Nevin's numerous spills were documented by scars on his legs which he later showed to his children when given enough encouragement.

At the age of 25, Nevin, who was teaching at the time, went through a profound inner change which proved to be a turning point in his life. Ezra Bender recognized the spiritual change at this time. As part of that inner transformation, Nevin began to feel a call to the ministry, but without any clarity as to what form that ministry should take. He could not have known how soon this new direction and calling would begin to take shape.

In spring of 1918 Nevin was chosen by lot to become the new minister at Greenwood. The *lot* was a traditional Mennonite and Amish method of selecting ministers. All the men receiving a minimum number of votes were in the lot. Songbooks equal to the number of men in the lot were placed before them. One of the songbooks contained the "call," a slip of paper with the message that the person receiving it was the new minister. At the direction of the officiating minister, each candidate would choose a songbook. The songbooks were then opened one by one until the one containing the call was reached. The person who had chosen the book containing the call became the new minister. Congregations participated in such ordination services in a spirit of prayer, knowing that much rested on the outcome.

At this ordination, Nevin was the next-to-last person to choose a book. He started to pick up the book next in line on the table and then instead felt led to pick up the other remaining book. The man who took the last book, who would have received the call if Nevin had stayed with his first inclination, apparently felt betrayed. A very conservative man, he often opposed Nevin through the years.

In the Mennonite church at that time, the ministry was a primary place for a man to receive recognition. It could be an influential role, especially since some believed that the ministers, and particularly the bishop, had the authority to set the rules of the church, with or without the consent of the congregation. While people were usually careful about openly seeking ministerial roles, there could be subtle efforts toward being chosen, and parents often pointed with satisfaction to the number of their sons who were ministers.

Nevin's relationship with the man not chosen in 1918 was problematic through the years, simmering and coming to a boil from time to time. Almost 40 years later, in 1955, it boiled over at the ordination of this man's son. In giving the charge at the ordination of this son, Nevin and the officiating minister put their hands on his head. The father rose from the congregation to demand of Nevin, "Take your hands off my son!" Nevin kept his hands on, though the other minister tried to soften the matter by saying, "Well, I'm giving the charge." Later in the service, this man stood to assert that Nevin's refusal to listen to him would serve to "widen the breach" between them.

As Nevin describes developments in some of his notes, six ministers and three lay brethren met several days later at the home of this man, to consider the situation. At the close of the meeting, the man agreed to make a confession before the church. Nevin acknowledged at that same public meeting that there were times when he had failed, for which he expressed grief. While differences continued to exist, the relationship between the two men finally became less strained after that incident was resolved.

In this relationship as well as others, it is helpful to interpret these church controversies, at least in part, as a power struggle for the role of minister and more particularly for the more powerful role of bishop. This is in no way to detract from the sincerity of Nevin or those who took issue with him. In his role as minister and then bishop, Nevin was at the center of influence in the church and the community and thus at the center of controversies. In light of the potential for use (or abuse) of power in the position of bishop, it seems significant that Nevin's journey in this position steadily moved him toward taking seriously the members of the church, including those who were less powerful, in "finding God's will" for the church. It was this journey which created the most intense controversies between him and a minority of men who wanted him to assert more authority to keep the church from making changes of which they did not approve.

In August 1918, shortly after being ordained a minister, Nevin was drafted to enter the military. As a conscientious objector to war, he was placed in a tough position because there was no regular provision for "COs" at that time. His account of this experience follows in his own words.

NONRESISTANCE UNDER TEST

The year 1918, a time when the United States entered the war against Germany and her allies, was a time of testing for many young men who believed in and who purposed in their hearts to follow Jesus, the Prince of Peace. It is significant to notice that William Jennings Bryan, who was Secretary of State during the Wilson Administration, resigned in 1915 because of his fears of the U.S. entering World War I, which took place in 1918.

A number of our Mennonite leaders were sent to Washington by General Conference to make contacts with the Washington officials concerning the position of the Conscientious Objectors. They found a Mennonite Confession of Faith open on the desk of one of the officials. While the officials took an open attitude, there was at this time no arrangement that could provide for draftees who had a conscience against war. The plan at that time was that the COs when drafted should go into the army camp along with other draftees and face the situation in the army camp.

There were a number of tips that our Mennonite leaders gave to the young men that proved very valuable. One was a statement with President Wilson's signature to the effect that COs would not be required to take military training, would not be required to wear the army uniform, and would not be required to carry weapons. This was published in small print in the *Gospel Herald*. This I clipped and saved for the time when I would need it. A second tip was that young men, upon going to camp, should write a letter addressed to the Captain, clearly stating one's position and firm decision to be true to the teachings of Scriptures, while expressing the willingness to cooperate in every way possible.

Having been recently ordained to the ministry, I was rather surprised when I received my notice for induction. I was to be taken with other young men to Camp Meade, Maryland. Before going, I became very conscious of the seriousness of what might lie ahead. I recognized that in my going to camp I might be facing severe trials and that it was quite possible that I might never return. It led to a deepening of my Christian experience. I wanted to be sure that I had peace with God and that I was prepared for what might come. For me, the decision was made that no matter what I would need to face in the army, I would be true to the Lord.

Answering the Draft

The morning when I was to answer the call, Father called the family together in the yard for a period of Scripture reading and prayer. As a family, I believe we realized very keenly what was at stake. We implored God for direction and strength, then proceeded to Georgetown where with others I boarded the train for Camp Meade. It would be hard to describe the feelings that I had as the train carried us toward our destination. On the way I addressed a letter to the Captain. After reading it, he (the Sergeant) told me to keep it until the next morning at which time he would call for it and take it to the Captain.

The next morning the Sergeant spoke to me, stating that they were going out into the field to give first instructions and advised me to go along. He promised that he would take my letter to the Captain when we returned at noon. I decided to trust him and went. When we returned to our barracks at noon, the Sergeant asked me for my letter and took it to the Captain. He returned after 15 minutes, stating that the Captain wanted to see me. Thus I had a private interview with the Captain.... After a period of questioning and some threats, he stated that there was no possibility for me to expect to take this kind of a position in the army. Finally, I drew the clipping from my pocket with President Wilson's signature and handed it to him. After reading it, he recognized that I was informed and stated that I would not need to wear the uniform, or drill, or carry weapons, but he added, "You will want to be a good boy." This interview proved to be quite helpful to me later.

The next morning my Sergeant assigned me to the task of cleaning the latrine. I was aware that some COs, when they went into camp, were given small tasks at first, then larger tasks, and finally found themselves engaged in military service, but I decided to avoid disobeying my Sergeant until I would have the opportunity of talking to him, so I cleaned the latrine. When I met him at noon, I mentioned that I did what he had requested because I did not want to disobey his orders before I could talk it over with him. I told him, however, that I couldn't conscientiously perform duties under the military arm of the government and that if he would ask me again I would need to disobey. He then stated that he would like to talk with me. We arranged for an interview which lasted for an hour or two. During this time he questioned me carefully about my faith and took a very considerate attitude toward me. At the close of our conversation he said, "You and I will have no trouble, but you would better not be in the barrack during the day and you would better not be out in the field. It might be all right for you to walk on the road." He then added, "You can go where you want to, only make sure that you are back to report for meals and bed." It seemed as though he felt that it would be best for me to keep out of sight.

One morning, perhaps the next one, I strolled quietly out along the road quite some distance until I was outside of the camp and saw the mountains in the distance. Noticing an abandoned log cabin, I entered and spent the forenoon alone in meditation and prayer. It was a precious forenoon because the Lord was very near. When the noon hour approached, I started back to report for the noon meal. As I walked toward the camp, I was startled and completely baffled when a truck approached and two Military Police jumped out and came toward me, calling me to halt. After some questioning they stated, "You're under arrest." I then learned from them that I had been sent for that forenoon for further examining. When the Sergeant was unable to tell them where I was, two M.P.'s were sent to find me. They took me back to my barrack where my Sergeant gave them a receipt that the prisoner was returned and then they left. After the M.P.'s were gone the Sergeant said, "I wish those fellows would mind their own business. I knew you would be back."

After a number of days I was transferred to another barrack where I found myself with a new group of men and with another Sergeant with whom I had had no previous contact. The young men in this barrack were an extremely rough group. During my first weekend in this group, the Sergeant went home to visit his sick wife. That Sunday I found seclusion in an abandoned dugout which had earlier been used in drilling practices. My time of communion with my Heavenly Father was especially meaningful that day. I experienced a deep sense of peace and confidence, and yet I was filled with such a strange sense of foreboding. I reported for meals as usual.

When evening came, I went back to retire. I tried to go as quietly and unnoticed as possible and lay down on my couch with my face down. I soon heard conversations that chilled me. I caught snatches of their coarse, brutal talk as they discussed what they would like to do to me. What was a fellow like me doing in the army, they wondered? Soon I heard many footsteps, and I realized that I was being surrounded. The thought gripped me, maybe this is it. A broom stick was thrown at me. A moment later one of the men kicked the head end of my couch and it went to the floor. Fearing that the fellows would soon be on me with their feet, I stood up. As if on cue, the fellows on one side of the circle where I stood gave me a shove, and as I came to the other side I was shoved back. Sensing that I might be stomped to death if I fell, I breathed a prayer and began to plead with them. Their accusations came back bitterly and forcefully.. Why wasn't I wearing the army uniform? At this point my earlier contact with the Captain proved valuable. I informed them that the Captain had told me that I would not need to. This started a controversy among the fellows. Some wanted to finish me off, while others began to pull back. I can still see the faces of two fellows who were on opposite sides as the group argued and threatened. One big fellow finally seemed to be persuading the rest that they had no right to harm me. "He has a right to his conscience the same as the rest of us," he argued. I sank on my couch with weakness and deep gratitude when the crowd gradually began to disperse. I was left alone, and finally fell asleep.

Another incident stands out in my mind. One evening some of the men informed me that they had the ropes ready, my grave was dug, and by the next morning I would be buried. I remember answering, "I will be in Heaven that much more quickly." That turned out to be an empty threat, again aimed at making me surrender in fear.

In the C.O. barrack

After being interrogated by the last judge before whom I needed to appear, I was taken to the CO Barrack. I found myself in company with about 120 COs, half of whom were religious objectors and the other half political objectors. This was my first opportunity to fellowship with fellow COs in camp. The men in this CO Barrack took care of the work of planning and cooking meals, washing dishes, cleaning the barrack, latrine, the outside, and so forth I remember very vividly the scene in that barrack every morning and night. The religious COs would be found on their knees in communion with God. Bible study and fellowship helped us find a common strength. Young men were brought together from many denominations and lived together as brothers because of their deep commitment to a God of Love and Peace. I remember quite clearly one young Methodist man of sterling character and purpose whose parents and pastor rejected his position as a CO He felt unable to accept a farm furlough but chose instead to be sent to the Federal prison where he suffered many humiliating experiences.

On furlough: Alternative service

After arrangements came through from Washington, the COs were offered farm furloughs as an alternative to army service. These arrangements had been worked out by government officials in consultation with church officials. I was assigned to a job on a large farm known as the former estate of Charles Carroll of Carrolton. Mr. Carroll had been the last man to give his signature to the Declaration of Independence. This farm was close to Ellicott City, Maryland, just off of old Route 40. I helped in taking care of a large dairy herd of short-horn cows. I enjoyed the early hours before daylight, bringing in the cows and caring for them. I was rarely allowed to attend worship services or even go to town.

Later an opportunity developed for me to be transferred to a Friends (Quaker) farm near Rosedale, Pennsylvania, where I again took care of a dairy herd. I was very grateful for the privilege I had here of attending worship service quite freely.

One of the saddest experiences that came to me while I was in camp was at a time when I was expecting a visit from my sister Cora who was two years older than me and who had been especially close to me. She and her husband had sold their farm and were preparing to move to Delaware. They were planning to drive through Ellicott City on their way to Delaware, when just two weeks before this expected visit, I received the sad message of her sudden death due to a complication of the German flu at a time when they were looking forward to the birth of their first child. This was a heartbreaking experience for me. At the time of my ordination, which was less than a year earlier, since Cora felt unable to express her sentiment to me, she sent a copy of a poem she had read, as an expression of her testimony to me:

A faithful witness
    His lamp am I, to shine where he shall say.
    And lamps are not for sunny rooms, nor for
        the light of day,
    But for the dark places of the earth
    Where shame and wrong and crime have birth,
    Or for the murky twilight gray
    Where wandering sheep have gone astray,
    Or where the light of faith grows dim
    And souls are groping after him.
    And sometimes a flame we find clear
        shining through the night
    So bright we do not see the light but
        only see the flame.
    So may I shine, his life the flame
    That men may glorify his name.

Life seems to hold suffering and pain mingled with deep, peace and joy, which is possible alone through union with the Prince of Peace. It was a time of rejoicing when I was given a discharge so that I could return to my home after being in service a little more than six months.

(Reprinted by permission from a booklet issued under the same name by the Conservative Mennonite Board of Missions and Charities)

For several years the new Greenwood congregation had been meeting in a public building called the Carlysle School. As a result of World War II, anti-German sentiment was high. The Mennonites were of German descent and, furthermore, as pacifists refused to participate in the war. Due to community sentiment, the Carlysle School was no longer made available to them, so they bought the site where the Greenwood Mennonite Church stands as of the writing of this book. A frame building,

30 feet by 40 feet, was built and dedicated on July 4, 1920. Twenty-seven years later a new Brick Church was built.

At the time the new building was being constructed in 1920, Nevin returned from his alternative service. Around this time the two older and more conservative ministers, who had opposed the purchase of the new church site and who apparently sensed a more progressive direction on the part of the church, left the community, leaving Nevin as the only minister. Nevin's brother-in-law, Eli Swartzentruber, was ordained by lot in 1921, and they served together until Nevin's resignation in 1960.

Nevin was a gifted speaker and counselor. His quiet manner of speaking contrasted with the emotional style of many of his contemporaries. It was a time when a "hellfire" style was popular, but Nevin's positive emphasis on love and respect was particularly well received by young people and he was much in demand as a speaker throughout the Mennonite church.

During this early ministry Nevin encountered his first church controversy. It had been customary for men of the congregation to wear hooks and eyes on their coats. Buttons were considered "adornment" by some of the older and more conservative men. Nevin had developed a side service of measuring men for traditional Amish and Mennonite "plain suits" which he ordered from Perkasie Uniform Company. When at their request he ordered for some men coats with buttons, he was considered an accessory to a sinful act by those who felt wearing buttons was wrong. Eli Swartzentruber backed up Nevin on this first adjustment to modernity as did 75 percent of the congregation, with most of the rest on some middle ground. Eventually the conference decided the Greenwood congregation could wear buttons. This adjustment was accepted but led to countless discussions as to where the church should "draw the line."

As demand for Nevin's speaking increased, he traveled more widely. On one such trip he met Esther Lauver.

Two

ESTHER'S PATH

She put first things first.

—How Mary Ferster Graybill, Esther's best childhood friend, described Esther after both had grown to adulthood.

Esther Mae Lauver, the first daughter of Jacob and Emma Lauver, was born on June 4, 1898, in the beautiful Susquehanna Valley near Evandale, Pennsylvania. She had an older brother, William. Esther was second followed by four sisters. She and her sister, Lura were considered the older girls. The younger girls were Mary and Alma. Gladys, the "baby" was five years younger than Alma.

Their father, Jacob Lauver, who farmed all his life in the Evandale and Cocolamus area of Pennsylvania, was an ordained deacon in the Mennonite church. He did not see himself as a good public speaker and was not a forceful public figure. He was more comfortable in a role as a trustee, taking care of the church building and property. His leadership was characterized by a deep sensitivity, a quality which endears him even today in the memory of his many descendants. He was seen as a more humorous, less serious person than Esther's mother. Alma's daughter, Orpha, thought the humor for which the Lauver family was famous came from the father's influence.

Esther's mother, Mary Emma (called Emma), had a rather forceful personality. Her father, William Graybill, was a minister in the Mennonite church. While he was a strong leader, he was also flexible. For example, when a man, Leroy Pellman transferred his membership to the Mennonite church from the Church of the Brethren, he said that he expected that he would have to begin wearing the plain coat. Minister Graybill said that he should do that only if he wanted to. The wearing of the plain clothes was a new movement in the 1920s and 1930s and by 1940 the situation had gotten a bit tense with some pressure for a more rigid enforcement of the wearing of plain clothes. In this context, William Graybill represented a more flexible approach.

Esther's mother, Mary Emma, was considered a serious and deeply spiritual person according to her daughter, Gladys. Her granddaughter, Orpha, spent much time with her grandmother growing up because her grandparents who lived on the adjacent farm had electricity and a phone before Orpha's parents, Michael and Alma, did. Orpha would go to her grandmother's house to iron and use the phone, and often enjoyed having deep spiritual discussions with her.

Mary Emma joined the Mennonite church before getting married, which was unusual for Mennonite youth in the Juniata County area. After going to a Brethren evangelistic service when she was 16, she wanted to join the church. Her father agreed and her example led to more youth becoming church members before they were married. Esther's father, by contrast, did not join the church until after his marriage. Mary Emma is remembered as a worrier, a trait she apparently inherited from her father, who worried about many issues, including how he would ever pay the loan on his farm.

An interesting contrast between the Graybill and Lauver families was that in Jacob's family, only he and his brother Will remained in the Mennonite church, according to Lloyd Guengerich. (Lloyd is the husband of Esther's niece, Orpha.) Staying in the Mennonite church was crucial to the many Mennonites who saw their church as being the most faithful to the teachings of the Bible. The Graybill children by contrast to the Lauver family all remained in the Mennonite church. Jacob had grown up in a family of 12 (six boys and six girls) but three of the girls died at an early age. Jacob was next to the oldest. Mary Emma was the third of seven children.

Esther developed more of her father's traits. She also was not a strong public person but did her best work in small groups or one on one. Esther had a contagious sense of humor and was unusually accepting of people, just as they were. This showed itself early, and certainly in her attitude through the years of her ministry with Nevin, toward the unusually diverse people who entered their lives.

Jacob and Emma Lauver, after first setting up housekeeping with Emma's parents, moved to a house next to the Lauvers' church where their oldest son, William, was born. They soon moved just across the road to a house that their family shared with their Grandpa and Grandma Lauver, and this is where Esther and all her sisters were born. The house was divided into two sides but Esther's family's side was very small. In 1909, when Gladys, the youngest, was one year old, and Esther was 11, they moved to the adjacent farm. Soon after the move, Emma's mother came to live with them after becoming widowed and stayed until her death in 1927.

In 1914, after their Grandpa Lauver died, Grandma Lauver also moved in with the family and was there until her death in 1920. She had first moved in with her daughter, Amanda, but at Grandma Lauver's request, Amanda brought her to the Lauver family, without advance notice. Grandma Lauver had spent much time in the attached house next to her son and daughter-in-law and apparently felt more comfortable with them. The two grandmothers, now living with the Lauver family, apparently got along well and provided companionship for each other.

The Lauvers were an extended family with grandparents in the home most of the time the children were growing up. Esther learned much from this aspect of family life. No doubt this was her early learning in relating to all ages and kinds of people and the beginning of her ability to pick up the conversation with anyone who was in her presence.

Esther's cousin Mary Ferster (later Graybill) lived nearby and was a good friend. In fact, they were later married in a double wedding. Since Grandma Lauver, with whom Esther lived, was also Mary's grandma, Mary would often visit. Mary recalled that she and Esther, along with other children, would take their grandpa's two-wheeled cart to the top of the hill and then take turns riding down. Other favorite games were blind man's bluff and jacks. Esther was a very dutiful daughter and, as the oldest child, she accepted responsibility early. Thus she did not have as much time to play as her younger siblings.

Mealtimes and good food played a central role in the life of the Lauver family. They excelled in the preparation of food and the meals were great family social occasions. Saturdays, particularly, were days of preparing for the weekend and even for the following week.

Mary Graybill recalled an incident involving Esther's mother, Emma, and her Aunt Mary from Altoona. They were making noodles in the summer house and hanging them over the backs of chairs to dry. The children, who were running in and out, left the door open. All of a sudden, one of them exclaimed, "The chickens have the noodles!" They chased away the chickens, rescued the noodles, and brushed off those that were left. Having labored all morning, they wanted to salvage as much of the results of their work as possible, even at the expense of the high standard of cleanliness, which usually prevailed.

Another time they were baking cookies when a big three-seat automobile filled with people came driving in. By the time the guests left, the cookies were gone and the children good-naturedly complained as they had to start baking all over again.

Esther was sometimes kidded because she always enjoyed baking cookies and her favorite thing was to make corn starch pudding along with sugar cookies for their guests.

Gladys remembers that Esther's brother William, older by 14 months, waited a year so he and Esther could start school together. They walked to the one-room Red Bank School which was in sight of the Lauver homestead. Always a quick learner, Esther enjoyed school, especially subjects related to language, such as reading, writing and spelling. The children were not encouraged to attend high school at McAlisterville High. Esther decided to take the eighth grade a second time because she enjoyed school so much. A 1914 photograph of the Red Brick School group shows twenty-seven students and two teachers. The photograph includes all six of the Lauver children. Esther later attended a Bible school term at Eastern Mennonite School (now Eastern Mennonite University).

Esther's sister Gladys recalls that in the winter they traveled by sled pulled by a team of horses to school, revival meetings, and church. On Sunday mornings they picked up those who were walking, often arriving at church with a sled packed with people. Once Esther's mother was unceremoniously dumped into the snow after the sled tipped over. In response to Jacob's "Are you hurt?" she testily replied, "No, but I'm all snowy!"

Esther was baptized into the church along with her sister Lura on December 18, 1910. Esther, throughout her life, was not one to engage in pious conversation but was deeply spiritual. Her beliefs were deep and personal and she lived her faith in her hospitality, her warmth, and her ministry to her children, as well as to the host of people passing through her life.

During her teen-age years, Esther did housework for other people. She worked alongside the mother of the home, doing the regular household duties. Besides the cleaning, she helped with cooking, laundry, and the other domestic tasks. In the summer she tended the garden and helped to can and dry fruits and vegetables for the winter. She worked in five or six different homes, some for two weeks on the arrival of a new baby, and others for a summer or an entire year.

One of these homes was her Uncle Will's. Another was for the parents of Roy Graybill, who later married her cousin Mary. Roy said that his mother was pleased with her work and "the way she got along with us." He remarked, "She just knew what to do about the work." Roy's wife, Mary, said that she never knew Esther to get angry, and speaking of her later as a young mother, added, "She was so patient and she just had a way of doing things. She wasn't fast, she wasn't slow, but she'd get it done somehow without any fuss. She didn't sputter around but just kept at it and got it done. She was so patient." Perhaps her greatest compliment was, "She knew how to put first things first." This was one of the qualities which later endeared her to her children.

Gladys, as her baby sister, remembers that Esther was willing to do more than her share of the work and that, in fact, she could be imposed on. Gladys said that Esther was very kind to her mother and doesn't remember her ever being curt with her mother as daughters can be at times. Gladys also has fond memories of sitting in her big sister's lap.

Even in her periods of working in the community, Esther, as the oldest daughter, carried much of the practical responsibility for the family during the times she was at home. She worked hard and was deeply respected, though she was considered to be less talented than her sister, Lura, in areas of leadership and more public gifts. Esther's cousin, Mary, speaking after Esther's death, said that people had the impression that Lura outshone Esther. Lura was more at ease in speaking. When Lura went to the Altoona mission, where her Uncle Abe and Aunt Mary were leaders, she became active in leadership in the church program. When Esther came later, it was to do the housework at her Uncle Abe's. It was easy to underestimate her—and many did. While Esther, like her father, stayed in the background, there was a quiet strength to her character. When it came to developing relationships and getting into other people's shoes, nobody could outshine Esther.

In 1917, Esther's brother, William, was chosen by lot to the ministry, a few days before he was 21. This event had a strong impact on the family. From that time on, they had family devotions with Bible reading and prayer every day. Grandma Graybill, whose husband had been a minister, evidently took this ordination to heart in such a way that she could hardly make peace with it. She became very agitated after the ordination, and for the remaining ten years of her life was on medication to calm her nerves. The seriousness with which such ordinations were approached is very striking. Being a minister or missionary was often referred to as "full-time Christian service" and such work carried with it a sense of heavy responsibility.

William was a minister and the only son to help his father on the farm but that did not prevent him from being drafted in 1918. Gladys said that there was a draft board member in Mifflintown, who seemed determined that he go. William was apparently the only conscientious objector in the group in which he was drafted. The war was winding down, however, and shortly after the train began its trip to Camp Mead in Maryland, the war ended and the train was stopped and returned to Mifflintown with the young men. William married Florence in 1920 and the following year they left for Argentina where they spent the next 25 years as missionaries.

One event in this family proved to be both a traumatic and a good experience in the meaning of community. The Lauver family's barn burned in June 1923. Esther's father had just brought in a load of hay when lightening struck the barn and it was ablaze immediately. He had time to get the horses out but not much more. Before the summer was over, the neighbors, in the grand Amish and Mennonite tradition of barn raising, got together and built a new barn. The men did the construction and the women put out spreads of food which were more like banquets.

In 1927, after Alma and Esther were married, the Lauvers moved to the house, where they lived until both parents died. The Lauvers had one cow for their milk, an apple orchard with yellow apples, and they raised corn and wheat. As an example of neighborly cooperation, Jacob had one horse and the adjacent Leister family also had one horse. They took turns using both horses as a team. Esther's single sisters Mary and Gladys lived in this house for 61 years. A creek flowed behind it, which later was a favorite spot for the Bender children when they visited. They remember wading and fishing for minnows in this creek and have many other fond memories associated with visiting their Grandpa and Grandma Lauver.

Three

MARRIAGE

What God has joined together.
—From the Bible

Nevin and Esther met at the Mennonite mission in Altoona, Pennsylvania, where Esther was helping in the home of her Uncle Abe, a leader in the mission. Nevin, who was already in demand as a visiting minister, probably went to the mission on a speaking engagement. Nevin's sister, Nanna, was living there with her husband Laban. This family connection probably influenced his first visit to the mission which occurred before Esther arrived in Altoona. At that time Nevin met Lura, Esther's younger sister, and asked to date her. Since she was already dating someone else she did not accept the invitation, which disappointed Nevin, according to his sister, Lucy.

In spring 1924, he met Esther who had arrived by this time to help in the mission and she and Nevin began a courtship. On their first date, Nevin walked Esther home from church on a Sunday evening to her Uncle Abe's house, about four blocks away. She didn't invite him in because she was self-conscious and concerned that her Uncle Abe would tease her. As the relationship developed, this self-consciousness disappeared.

Later when Lura's relationship with her boyfriend ended, Esther thought that Nevin might still wish to date Lura. Always self-effacing and unselfish, she told him that if he did prefer Lura and wanted to ask her out again, he should feel free to do that. She would not stand in the way. Nevin let Esther know beyond any doubt that she was the one that he wanted!

Nevin's sister Lucy remembers first meeting Esther when she went to the Altoona mission to help Nanna after the birth of their first baby. Esther took Lucy, who was 22, and her friend over to Uncle Abe's house and Lucy remembers her first impression of Esther as being "so pleasant and easy."

The courtship of Nevin and Esther apparently occurred mostly while she was away from home, as her sisters Gladys and Mary did not recall Nevin visiting much at their home until Esther returned from Altoona to prepare for the wedding. During their courtship, in January 1925, Esther spent a six-week term at Eastern Mennonite School (EMS), in Harrisonburg, Virginia, along with her cousin Mary. During that term Clayton Kauffman, who was the boyfriend of Esther's sister Mary, was also at EMS. He became ill after visiting one of the caverns in the area and died following a two-week illness. Esther and her cousin Mary were there to console sister Mary when she arrived on January 31 for the funeral.

While Esther was at EMS, she and Nevin were becoming quite serious in their relationship. During that term, Nevin was at Pigeon River, Michigan, teaching Bible school. The other girls would tease her by asking whether the pigeons were fluttering. Despite this growing seriousness, a letter dated January 19, 1925, from Nevin to Esther hardly reads like a love letter. He refers to the heavy snow and having a sleigh ride with the young people, as well as the difficulty of traveling. Many of the cars got stuck so that travel was limited to sled or sleigh. He also mentions at length the need not to take credit for the success of the Bible school. For example, he writes, "The Lord has truly been blessing the work. All honor is due him for it is he who. . .

is giving. I wish. . . that we may hide completely beneath the shadow of the cross. For we can only honor him when we disappear ourselves." This tone was also characteristic of the rest of the letter.

In the fall of the year, Esther returned home to prepare for their double wedding with her cousin Mary (Ferster) and Roy Graybill, who was also a first cousin from her mother's side of the family.

Nevin and Esther Bender were married in a double ceremony with Mary and Roy Graybill on October 13, 1925, a Tuesday afternoon. Bishop John L. Mast was the officiating minister for Nevin and Esther, while Bishop William Graybill married Roy and Mary. Bishop Graybill was the father of Roy. Weddings of that time were very simple affairs and there were no attendants. Aside from the theme of the service and the making of vows, the service was a typical Mennonite worship service with congregational singing and a sermon.

Nevin's sister Lucy remembers crying at the event because Nevin would now be leaving home. Esther's sisters asked her why she was crying, since Nevin and Esther would be living in Greenwood, near his home and family. They felt it was they who had reason to feel sad, since their sister was moving 200 miles away from home to be with her new husband.

The two couples, now the Benders and the Graybills, went on their honeymoon together to Niagara Falls. Such a trip was considered rather far for a honeymoon, but it was the place that they all had agreed on. Nevin, who had traveled fairly extensively for his speaking engagements, was the source of information about places they might consider, but the decision was made by consensus. As Nevin, together with Roy and Mary Graybill, recalled that decision many years later, he was pleased to remember that the decision had been made by consensus. He perhaps feared that, considering those times, he might have weighed in too heavily in the decision, or that the two men might have made the decision.

The first night, the honeymooners drove to Liberty, Pennsylvania, to a tourist home. The next day, the two couples discovered that a similar saga had unfolded in their two bedrooms the night before. The two women, extremely modest, were both anxious to get into bed before their new husbands. As they prepared to dress for bed they discovered that someone, apparently their sisters, had sewn the legs and arms of their night clothes shut—both theirs and the men's. Also their sisters had packed them a lunch, which they opened to discover onion sandwiches. Such pranks were apparently not unusual for the siblings of a bride or groom in their community at that time.

Nevin had an appointment to preach at a Sunday evening service in Clarence Center, New York, near the end of the honeymoon. As they were on their way to the service, they passed through Williamsville, a town with which Nevin was familiar. Since the time of his last visit a traffic light had been installed in the main intersection at an inconspicuous height, according to Nevin. The light was apparently red when they came to the intersection, but they did not see it. Less than a mile out of town they were stopped by an officer who had seen them run the red light. Nevin tried to explain the situation and that they were running late for a speaking engagement. The officer was not impressed and finally said, "The longer you talk, the madder I get!" He then asked them to follow him back into town, and it seemed to the honeymooners that he drove as slowly as possible.

When they arrived at the police station the officer began filling out the paperwork. Soon the chief entered the room, saw Nevin's plain coat, and asked if they were Mennonites. When Nevin answered that they were, the chief recommended that the officer let them go, saying, "I know these people and I don't think they intended to disobey the law."

The delay caused them to arrive about an hour late at the church. As they came in, the man who had apparently been leading a discussion to fill the time, abruptly closed his Bible and announced that Nevin Bender had arrived and would now preach.

The four also recalled their visit to the zoo in Toronto. They had to get a taxi to the boat which would take them to the zoo. The taxi driver said they would have to rush to catch the boat, and he proceeded to take them on a speedy ride which left them breathless and praying for their safety. They did arrive safely and on time.

At Niagara Falls, the two couples wanted to see everything there was to see. They went on the "Maid of the Mist" boat ride and what was referred to as the "hurricane deck." On the Canadian side they went to a space where visitors could go behind the falls. This trip was later discontinued, apparently due to its lack of safety.

After his marriage, as he had before, Nevin traveled widely and for some extended periods of time, both for preaching and teaching. In the summer before their first daughter Lura was born, Esther wrote him a letter in Lancaster, New York. She was very expressive saying, "I am like a child counting the days, guess the hours, after while." She also noted from looking at the program that he was speaking that morning and said, "I am thinking of you in a special way." A year after they were married and soon after Lura was born, Nevin had a series of speaking engagements in New York. At one point Esther wrote, "Over half the time has already passed," and later she wrote, "If all goes well and the Lord spares our lives, there sure will be a happy little family in Delaware in a little over a week. Once in a while I just think I must see you but now it won't be long anymore."

Once Esther chided Nevin for signing his full name to his letters. She wrote, "It makes me feel as though it was a letter . . . from someone that is not as near and dear to me as you are." She added, however, "Now if you have [something] to say to me concerning mine, [letters] I shall be glad to have you do so."

Nevin's letters spoke of how the meetings were going, how he missed Esther, and of practical advice. He asked Esther to remind Willie, the hired man, not to neglect keeping salt with the horses and cows. He suggested that if Esther didn't have enough money she should get some from Ted or Eli (Nevin's brothers-in-law) until the milk check came and reminded her to endorse the check before sending it to the bank. On a similar topic from Baden, Ontario, he wrote, "If all checks [clear], there will be only about $1.40 [left in the account]. It might cost $.50 if it is all taken out."

As one trip neared an end, Nevin wrote that he planned to arrive Tuesday noon at the train station and said, "Say, won't we be happy when Tuesday afternoon comes."

PART TWO

THE GREENWOOD YEARS

Four

BECOMING FAMILY

Won't we be happy when Tuesday comes!

—From a letter written by Nevin to Esther looking
forward to returning from an extended preaching engagement

Nevin was almost 34 and Esther 28 when their first child, Lura, was born in 1926, ten and one-half months after their marriage. They were, as new parents, older and more mature than was usual for those times, and they were both looking forward to becoming family together. They both wanted a large family and opened themselves to the children that God—and love—would give them. They did not plan to use birth control; this was a conviction that felt right for them. Nursing each baby for about one year, as Esther did, provided a kind of built-in birth control. As Esther was carrying each child there was always at least one or two sisters or sisters-in-law, and sometimes three or four, who were also pregnant.

The shared experience of pregnancy was no doubt at its height in 1926 when seven babies were born to the Bender and the Lauver clans. Esther was carrying Paul, while her sister Lura was carrying John Mark. Her sister Alma had given birth to Alene in January. On the Bender side, Savilla was pregnant with twins, Mark and Luke; Lucy was pregnant with their first child, Betty; and Earl and Katie were awaiting the birth of their first, Marilyn. It is impossible to fully comprehend the tremendous feeling of support this must have given to these women as they prepared for the births of their babies.

As the years passed, the large Bender family included the "big girls," Lura and Miriam; the "big boys," Paul and Titus; the "little girls," Mildred and Emma; and the "little boys," Nevin James and Donald. Hilda, though fourth in line, was in many ways the "middle child. Even though this large family must have felt quite big, even too big at times, each of the children carried a deep sense that they were wanted, unique, and special to "Mama and Papa."

Some of that assurance came from the anticipation the children felt from their parents when a new baby was expected, then joy on the birth of that little one. One of Mildred's most poignant memories is of a summer evening in 1941 when Esther was pregnant with their tenth child (who was stillborn that September). The children were playing outdoors as dusk was falling, chasing fireflies and playing games.

Mildred recalls running up to the porch where her parents were relaxing and talking together as they watched their children and interacted with them now and again. As Mildred leaned against her father for a moment to catch her breath he asked, "Which do you think you would like—a baby sister or a baby brother?" She was surprised because she had not been fully aware that there was to be a new baby. While Mildred thought this over, he added, "Wouldn't a little brother be nice? Then we'd have five girls and five boys." Mildred remembers well the joy and warmth she sensed in his voice.

When the baby was stillborn several months later, Esther and Nevin grieved for this little son they would never know. She spoke to her daughters later of a friend who had tried to comfort her by saying she still had a baby (Donnie was only 17 months old) and all her other children. That was true, she told her daughters, but it didn't soften the loss of this child she sensed would be her last. It was this genuine wanting and welcoming, this special love for each child, this feeling that there were never too many, that each of the nine Bender siblings still carries today.

The task of caring for this family through the Great Depression must have felt overwhelming at times. There often wasn't enough time for some of the long one-on-one chats that probably both parents and children wished for. They were too busy with survival always to be aware of sibling interactions, or that a "big one" might be taking advantage of a "little one." Sometimes a more introverted child felt lost in the family group and unsure of his or her own unique gift or specialness. But always the love was deep and unconditional, there was a strong sense of loyalty, and each one knew beyond any doubt that he or she "belonged."

Nevin and Esther's love for each other was the root of their love for their children. They had a hard time tolerating fighting among their children, and both were known to wonder aloud how their children could fight when they as parents loved one another so deeply. In fact, Lura remembers her father explaining to his quarreling children one day that, since he and Mama loved each other so much, he thought the children should be able to settle their differences in a peaceful manner.

The memories of the older children begin with the four-room, two-story house that Esther and Nevin moved into right after they were married. Located near Grandpa and Grandma Bender, they lived there until 1933, after Titus was born. This house was moved into the woods across the road in 1937 and became the permanent home for the Bender family.

Lura remembers the night Hilda was born as she lay on the floor with Miriam and Paul beside the stairwell, with their heads hanging out over the steps. "I suppose I told the others what was happening. Finally we heard the baby cry! Papa let us come down to see the baby and share in the excitement." She also recalls Titus' birth and the beautifully arranged trays of food that Mrs. Hatfield, who lived across the road from the Benders, brought especially for her mother—after both births. "There were delicacies on those trays we had never seen before," Lura says. "Mama shared them with us."

Lura, Miriam, and Paul will never forget several of their childhood pranks. Miriam recalls the time they turned on the kerosene faucet. "We were outside playing and saw the kerosene tank with the faucet on it. In those days a faucet was a pretty unusual thing. We didn't have a faucet in our house, just a pump. It was a lot of fun to turn it on and off and watch the kerosene flow freely to the ground. Papa came on the scene and saw what we were doing. We got spankings."

Another warm day the same three siblings decided to run among the newly washed sheets hanging on the line. (One wonders who the ring-leader was in these threesome-escapades!) Miriam says, "Wash day was a big day. We didn't have it handy. Once the sheets were clean, that was an accomplishment. As we ran back and forth, we got them dirty, very dirty." This time they were given the choice: a spanking or an hour in bed in the middle of the day. Lura chose the spanking, while Miriam and Paul chose bed. "When Lura's spanking was over she came upstairs, peeked around the corner at Paul and me, and laughed at us" Lura has admitted since that she probably deserved two spankings that day!

From 1933 until 1937 the Bender family lived in the Powell Place, or the "red house," as they called it, located several miles from the church and the school.

An early memory at the red house stands out starkly in the minds of all the older children. Emma was run over by a team of horses soon after her first birthday. This story has become something of a legend in the family. Miriam, aged nine, remembers putting Emma in a little wagon and taking her out the lane alongside the field where eight-year-old Paul was harrowing with the horses. Thinking Paul's work looked more exciting than her own, she told Hilda, aged six, to take care of

Emma. "I wanted to go out and help Paul," she explains. "The first thing I did was to tell the horses, 'Get up! Get up!' And get up they did. They took off and went gallivanting down the field, over the lane and right over Emma in the little wagon."

Hilda was in charge of caring for Emma but was not able to protect her. As she was pulling her in the wagon, she heard Miriam yelling, "Get Emma out of the way!" Totally panicked, Hilda began to pull her to the side of the road. She remembers jumping over the ditch as the horses galloped toward them, but the horses caught Emma and pulled the wagon over on top of her. Emma was unconscious and the children were afraid she might be dead as they watched their father pick up her little limp body and carry her in to the pump where he put water on her face. The older children went upstairs to pray. Soon they heard Emma crying and knew that she was alive. "Nothing can compare to the sense of relief we all felt," Hilda says. She remembers the family getting together in the living room after her parents had returned from the hospital or doctor where they took Emma to have her checked. They prayed and talked about how they would feel if Emma had been killed. Although no guilt was placed or even hinted at, both sisters dealt with feelings of guilt which lingered a long time for Hilda.

Another poignant and never-to-be-forgotten event for the older children—but most of all for Titus—occurred during the "red house" years. One Sunday morning as the family was rushing around trying to get everyone ready for church on time, Titus, just a little tot, was out chasing chickens and was left behind when the car headed for church. When the family discovered that Titus was not with them they rushed home to search for him. The speed limit and timely arrival at church both took second place in importance that day. They found Titus standing inside the screen door, sobbing quietly and waiting for his family's return.

Since the red house was several miles from the schoolhouse, the older children remember many long walks to school. There was a log bridge over a big ditch and then the walk through the woods, often in the company of the Lorenzo Schlabach children. Those walks were sometimes cold ones during the winter, but the memories are mainly pleasant.

The older children remember the very earliest Christmases and the simple, special way they were celebrated. Lura recalls, "Mama and Papa would come to the top of the stairs and sing a Christmas carol or two. Then we'd gather around the wood heater and enjoy our small gifts, arranged on a plate with an orange and some candy. Often the gift was an item of needed clothing, but it could also be a toy which we treasured. The meaning of Christmas was never forgotten as Papa read the Christmas story to us." Gradually there were slight changes in these celebrations, but the memory of being sung awake (although most were already awake!) on Christmas morning—often with "Silent Night"—is a treasured memory for all of the children. That did not change, nor did the joy of receiving simple presents given with such love.

The move to the woods and the farm that is still in the family took place in 1937. The house the family moved into was actually the same one they had lived in until their move to the "red house" in 1933. Now it was moved across the road and into the woods. All of the children, down to Mildred, remember parts of that move. It was a big undertaking, but Nevin had set his heart on creating a permanent home in this woods he deeply loved on land he had bought from his father.

Lura describes the details of moving this four-room house from its location across the road to the spot where it stills stands today at the edge of the woods, though the house was enlarged and made more than twice as big about five years after the move. "I remember the beams the house rested on and the skids for it to slide on. I remember what Papa called a 'dead man' with a pole attached. A horse was hitched to the pole and he walked round and round, winding a cable attached from the house to the 'dead man'. Slowly the house moved over the skids.

At the proper time, the skids over which the house had been pulled and the 'dead man' were moved ahead and the procedure continued." Moving this house was a community event with many of the uncles, as well as other men, helping.

Hilda remembers that "it was exciting to move to a different house and to be able to dash across the field for school at the last minute." Some memories at this new location include "climbing up on the chicken house and jumping into Papa's arms—a thrill difficult to describe—(he never dropped anyone!) and being pushed high into the trees in a swing which he had hung from a branch of the big oak tree at the edge of the yard."

This fun-loving father may be stronger in the memories of the older children than of the younger ones. Later he was away from home more, and at times was quite weighed down with the difficulties at the Greenwood Church, as well as broader conference responsibilities. Yet all of the children remember their father's playfulness. After returning from a trip he often would be down on all fours giving "horsey rides" to the younger ones. He frequently demonstrated his ability to stand on his head, balancing himself with his hands. Later his children learned from folks they had never met before that he had demonstrated this skill to them also. It was this lack of inhibitions, among other qualities, which endeared him to his children and to many other people.

Playtime was limited on the farm. There were cows to milk and other daily chores year round. There was school in winter and planting, harvesting, gardening, canning, and freezing in the spring and summer. Still the children found time to play and had a lot of fun together, especially during the long summer evenings. For small children there were games and pastimes such as hopscotch, hoop and T, balancing on and rolling metal drums or barrels, hide and seek, and a great favorite, kick the tin can. With a large family, there didn't need to be visitors to have enough kids for a good game, but additional cousins and friends added excitement. There was also stilt-walking. Don remembers that Nevin James was particularly daring with the five-foot stilts which he had to put on by sitting on the porch roof. Nevin's stilts were substantially taller than those anyone else in the community dared to wear.

There were ordinary activities—and some not so ordinary—that only farm kids would dream up. Emma recalls going up into the hayloft with her siblings and jumping from the cross beams into the hay, both at home and also at Uncle Ted's with their cousins. Don remembers when the grain was stored in the loft, jumping from the cross beams into the grain bin. This was a particularly exhilarating and frightening experience. But with half a dozen of one's peers looking on, there was no alternative but to swallow one's terror and jump!

There was also the door of the imagination, which could be—and was—opened to add to the breadth and enchantment of their world. The sisters remember many fun evenings in "the girls' room," the bedroom in which all five slept after the move, until the house was enlarged and three more bedrooms were added upstairs. The sisters have fond memories of their crowded bedroom, much of the space being taken with the big double beds. Lura, always a prolific reader with a great imagination, loved to tell continued stories almost as much as her younger sisters loved to hear them. No doubt using a combination of the stories she had read and the ones her fantasy made up with a little real life thrown in, Lura would usually leave her sisters wondering what in the world would happen the next night when the story would be continued.

Miriam's antics and sometimes imitation of serious situations often sent her sisters, as well as herself, into peals of hilarious laughter. Her unique sense of humor was especially irresistible because she so totally enjoyed her own jokes. A "goodnight ritual," partly copied from the occasional end-of-day confessional that occurred for awhile at the Mennonite school, went like this, in Miriam's version, with just the right cadence: "I forgive everybody! Everybody forgive me? Goodnight, everybody! Here's a kiss for everybody!" Sometimes each sister would take her own turn in making sure she was right with her sisters—and with the universe!

Esther had to be, and truly was, an efficient homemaker as she dealt with nine children, assorted guests, and a husband much in demand away from home. She had to be organized to keep even a reasonable level of order and some semblance of a schedule. Some who were used to "apple-pie-clean" houses were sometimes critical of her housekeeping, but as her friend and cousin, Mary Graybill, said, "The way I see it, she knew what was important." What was important was unlimited time to counsel and console, to nurse and to hear confessions, and simply to love. Titus remembers that when her children achieved, their mother would caution them not to be proud, but when they experienced self-doubt, she made them feel how wonderful they were. Paul recalls times that his mother was the only one he trusted enough to unburden his soul to.

As the older children reached their teens and even before, they began to assume more responsibility and take some of the load from their mother. Lura learned to sew at about age 12 or 13. She had a natural gift for it and basically taught herself. She soon took over making the "prayer coverings" for her mother and sisters. This was quite delicate sewing, and Lura learned to do it so neatly that it was difficult for her sisters to be satisfied with anyone else's efforts. She started to make her own and Miriam's dresses and gradually she began sewing for her other sisters, with Miriam helping on the dresses for the little girls. It's interesting to note that an hour after making three or four coverings or a dress, Lura might be out plowing on the tractor, work she probably enjoyed more.

Miriam had a great gift for cleaning, as well as for getting and keeping things organized. She meticulously kept track of everything. Not even a scrub rag could disappear without her watchful eye noticing and finding it. Her passion for a clean house was matched by her willingness to work hard and to teach her younger sisters the skills needed to have a place they could be proud of, especially after the enlargement and renovation of the house in the early 1940s. Mildred will never forget being shown carefully how to scrub the stairs leading to the second floor which was done every week (and often waxed, as well) or how to clean every fixture in the bathroom. The sisters often laughed in later years and decided that their family must have been either extremely clean or extremely dirty to warrant such a thorough cleaning of the whole house every week. But Miriam's standards were high, and, interestingly, no one questioned her authority. Perhaps some compensation for the chaos of the earlier years was taking place.

At a young age, Miriam also began to take responsibility for overseeing the weekly baths and head-washings of the younger children, as the big tub was pulled out each week and water was heated on the stove. Miriam also loved to have some of the little ones sit with her in church, to make it easier for her mother. A familiar sight was Miriam walking into church with Donnie on her hip with his cute curl of which she was immensely proud, and a couple little ones following behind.

It was not until Lura and Miriam were married that Hilda was the unchallenged "big sister." Don remembers her as a counselor/friend with whom a younger sibling could share deepest thoughts. He particularly remembers a long conversation with her at night in the front yard under the hickory trees. "She assumed no authority from her age status but related as an equal, sharing her thoughts and feelings and listening with understanding to those of her youngest brother."

Mildred remembers that Hilda made delicious pies. She had both the skill and the art for making the crusts exactly right. Mildred remembers replacing her sister in a family she worked for in Greenwood when Hilda went into nurses' training in Milford. This job included practical nursing as well as cooking and taking care of the house and two grandchildren.

Mildred felt she could never quite measure up, even in ways other than the cooking and baking.

Paul also had an important effect on the younger boys, particularly in the early years. After watching his father plant corn in long straight rows he decided one day he, too, could plant corn. While his father was occupied, Paul, with the assistance of a younger brother, planted a couple short rows crosswise at one end. Success seemed inevitable until the corn came up and his father saw what had happened. He called Paul over to explain. Nothing short of the truth could possibly explain the corn that had gotten out of its row.

The same sort of adventure led Paul to get his private airplane pilot's license at age 19. Once while landing in a pasture field on the Beachy farm, he narrowly avoided crashing into the woods by swerving the plane at the last minute and sliding sideways, wing first into a tree. In his ideas as well, Paul did not accept traditional ways of seeing things without thinking them through for himself. His impulses for daring and celebration influenced his younger brothers, who tended to be more serious in their early years.

From the earliest days the Bender home often included more than family. Bill Stoneburner, an orphan, came to live with the family and helped with the farm work in the early days when Nevin was often gone. There were other "hired men" along the way. Anna Bontrager was a young woman who found in Esther such total acceptance that she loved to come to help take care of the children. The little girls especially enjoyed her. In the next decade she made her home with the Benders for periods of time, renting a room or parking her trailer nearby in the woods simply because she felt loved and accepted and enjoyed being a part of this family. A mystery surrounding Anna that intrigued the little girls was her age. They tried literally every way they knew to trick her into divulging this great secret, but they never succeeded. It's true that Anna, with her big heart and the inner wounds she carried, seemed ageless.

Later on, as the older children were in their teens, numerous cousins and others came to find work in the area and to make the Bender home their own for a few months or even much longer. Alene Wert, the first of the Wert cousins to come, along with Fern Hepner, began this trend. They were from Juniata County in Pennsylvania where Esther had grown up. Gladys Wert would often come for the weekend when she and Hilda were students at Lancaster Mennonite School. Another cousin, Mary Lou Lauver, made her home with the Benders on her days off when she worked in Delaware for a summer. Freda Wert also was there for awhile, attending Greenwood Mennonite School. The three Wert sisters found their husbands in Greenwood, and two settled in the area to raise their families.

Everyone who came seemed to fit right into the household and became a real part of the family. With so many lively teenagers and young adults around, the house fairly danced with energy, with laughter, and with work accomplished, especially in the summer. No one escaped without helping with the humongous amount of canning and freezing that took place in the Bender home each summer. Mary Lou, particularly, will probably never forget canning tomato juice, hundreds of quarts, and cleaning up the "tomato slurp" after a day in the kitchen! The Bender-Lauver sense of humor that permeated the kitchen—and the whole house—when these cousins were together helping "Aunt Esther" made the most tedious and messiest tasks feel like fun, or at least, palatable.

Many other people lived in the Bender home for a while. Some were folks who had been pushed to the margins of society. The family remembers Mr. Murphy, an alcoholic from Wilmington, who decided he wanted to change his life. Nevin and Esther brought him home one weekend, hoping that work on the farm and a wholesome family life would help. He even went forward at an evangelistic meeting. Apparently the change was too difficult to maintain, and after a few days he left. But he departed having experienced that willingness on the part of Nevin and Esther to offer a chance and provide a place of love and acceptance, whether it could be received or not.

Acceptance, hospitality, and a place of welcome for whomever might want to experience it for even one meal, or a night—this was a way of life. It was not at all unusual for one or two carloads of people who knew and loved Nevin to arrive unannounced. These were people whom he had met on one of his speaking engagements and whom, no doubt, he had invited to stop and visit if they ever got in the area. They were sure he would be delighted to have them for dinner and overnight. He was.

And Esther and the family always rose to the occasion, although it constantly called for great flexibility. The house was quite chaotic at times, not exactly prepared to receive guests. In all honesty, there were also those times that the underlying feelings of the children to these unexpected visitors were not totally congruent with the friendliness they tried to extend (or sometimes didn't). Perhaps it was expecting too much. Some of the children feel there was also a down side to this hospitality that failed to give them enough freedom of choice not to invite someone hoping for an invitation, when that might have been the most honest thing to do.

Emma remembers a carload of guests arriving late one afternoon amid working out the details for a spontaneous swimming trip to Denton. When the guests gladly accepted the invitation to stay for supper and overnight, Emma knew the Denton trip was off. She could not really express her resentment with company there, but she acknowledges, "I remember I wasn't very gracious to our guests that night!" The children will not presume to speak for Esther, as she welcomed a great variety of guests through the years. Certainly, the warmth with which she unfailingly received guests, expected or not, came from her very heart.

It was not easy to plan ahead in such an open household. Not tightly organized, the household was characterized by a wonderful spontaneity which bordered often on the joyful, and sometimes on the chaotic. All the children had the highest regard for their family and, Don was convinced, shared an unspoken feeling that everyone, given a choice, would want to stay in their home! In fact, an observation by son-in-law Glenn some years later seems to bear this out. At a family gathering, he told of some of his first impressions: "One of the things that really attracted me in being with the family was the way you treated each other and the nieces and nephews, just talking to them like they were adult, and treating the children like they had worth and had something good to say. So it was this sort of acceptance of people, the specialness, the love, the caring—and I thought, 'What better place to get a wife?'"

Meals were an important time in the life of the family, perhaps starting as early as Esther and Nevin's days as newlyweds. Both of them enjoyed sharing the story of some of their very special breakfasts together, sitting on either side of the corner of their lovely new wood cook stove, frying a couple of Esther's famous buckwheat cakes on the griddle. They would eat them hot off the griddle as the next two were frying, then on to the next two. Nevin was sure that it had been decreed in heaven for hot food to be as absolutely hot as possible, whether it was coffee, oyster stew, or pancakes! They reveled in those breakfasts for two in the early days.

The family's most important meal of the day was the evening meal or supper, as it was usually called. This was true even during the Depression, when feeding a family of growing children was no easy task. Some of the meals were very simple. One of these remembered by Hilda and others was simply called "cornstarch," a vanilla or chocolate pudding laced with milk and added sugar. Another was banana soup—bread, milk and sugar mixed together with bananas or another fruit. A simple but favorite meal was Esther's marvelous apple dumplings, served with milk already flavored with sugar. Perhaps this was done for the sake of simplicity in serving as well as to monitor the amount of sugar, but for the little ones it simply made the apple dumplings more delicious.

Oyster stew provided a feast. This was a sumptuous meal because these were no ordinary oysters. Nevin would pick up a bushel of fresh ones near the Chesapeake and shuck them himself. He even introduced his children to raw oysters, which at least some of them pretended to like, but when made into stew, there was no need to pretend. Although oyster stew was a family favorite for most, Miriam was not afraid to be the lone dissenter. She refused to eat the oysters, but she did enjoy the stew. There was absolutely nothing like that first bowl of piping hot stew with oyster crackers. In fact, a number of the spouses of the Bender siblings had their introduction to oyster stew around the Bender family table.

Because these oysters were freshly shucked, sometimes an orange crab was found. For some bizarre reason, Hilda loved these crabs. It became routine that if one were found in the stew, it was passed over to her. She still remembers that delicious, crunchy taste.

The Benders have always been a family of seafood lovers, no doubt because of regularly eating fresh fish, in addition to the oysters, from the nearby ocean or bay. A fisherman came to the house in a pickup truck, carrying bushels of freshly caught trout, which were bought, cleaned, and fried as only Esther could fry them. There were, of course, many meat-potatoes-vegetable meals as well. During the summer the garden always provided fresh vegetables. Much of the meat was also grown on the farm and butchered at Uncle Milts.

When the children were little, their parents made sure that each child ate his or her food (even asparagus and spinach!) and that some degree of order was maintained amid the high energy and sometimes boisterous exchanges around the table. The children learned early that bread crusts helped to make you healthy and gave you rosy cheeks, so hiding them under the rim of the plate was not acceptable! Two rules were: that only one person talk at a time while the others listened (or didn't listen), and even if you don't like something, eat a little bit. The second rule worked quite well as there is probably not one picky eater among the Bender siblings today.

The first rule was, quite frankly, a losing proposition. But getting excused from the table for a few minutes to "think it over" helped more than one child to observe the rule for at least a few minutes after being allowed back. Needing to leave the table temporarily was a punishment/reminder used for numerous other infractions such as getting into arguments at the table or being rude to a sister or brother. But that wasn't always needed. Just receiving a stern look from Papa with the culprit's name spoken firmly had a way of working instantly. This father was very gentle and kind, but also strict—probably more so as a young father.

A memory shared by most of the siblings was Titus' question, as a little boy, when he sat down to one of his favorite meals. Usually a number of serving dishes were filled and put on the table family style, with the big ones also helping the little ones. The serving dishes were passed to the left (another understanding). As Titus would help himself and then see the food rapidly disappearing as it went around the table, he would look at his mother and ask anxiously, "Is there any more back?" Perhaps he remembered some of the more frugal times when there wasn't "any more back." But usually there was more being kept warm on the stove.

The Sunday noon meal, served after a whole morning spent in church and Sunday school, was usually a large spread which often included "Sunday potatoes" (home fries) and usually roast beef or chicken. It was a meal that, quite honestly, felt "earned"! That, and the weekday evening meals, were the social times as the children grew older. Conversation was usually very spontaneous and often animated and extended. Sometimes the conversation had everyone in uproarious laughter. One image remembered by all of her children is of Esther laughing until her whole body shook, wiping her face with her apron as tears rolled down her cheeks. On other occasions there would be a vigorous debate of church or political issues. These were sometimes quite serious, even painful.

Sometimes the teenage children had to leave for other activities after the evening meal, but on those occasions when there was an open evening, Don remembers that the dinner discussion could be quite extended. "The conversation would sometimes carry on into the washing of dishes," he recalls. "While the women and girls bore the brunt of the cleanup, the boys often helped as well."

He also recalls the very lively exchange that took place on the rare but exciting evenings when churning homemade ice cream became an event in which everyone loved to participate. As the ice cream became harder, churning was more of a challenge and tasting became an absolute necessity if perfect texture and hardness were to be achieved! The Benders usually had a two-gallon freezer, larger than the four- or six-quart ones that some of their cousins had. In this, as in many areas, Nevin never did things halfway.

A specific memory of the younger siblings during their middle and late teens and even when home from college on holiday, is a particular late-night snack—a real specialty. No one is sure of the origin of the famous fried-onion-and-egg sandwiches, usually served with catsup. This was definitely an activity that needed sharing; one seldom did it alone. It was meant for late night, often after their parents were in bed. Someone would get the urge—sister or brother—and would always have one or two takers. It was not only delicious but also a natural invitation to late night confidences and discussions around that much-used dining room table. It was an activity even worthy of inviting a date to join.

After dishes were done on weeknights there was often an attempt to have family devotions, a time for Bible reading and spontaneous prayer. There was some resistance to this since family members had already logged an impressive number of hours in religious activities. Conflicting and active evening schedules also made the attempt less than successful. As the family got smaller there was more experimentation, usually in the direction of brevity, with Scripture reading before the evening meals or before breakfast.

Almost everyone remembers the Bible stories that were told by both parents. Lura recalls listening to her father's stories, even amid chores, when she was quite little. "I remember the stories Papa told us as we sat on the sill behind him while he was milking. I don't think he missed any except the one about Jepthah's daughter in Judges 11. I asked him years later why he didn't tell us that one. He said, 'I didn't like it very much.'" (It's the story of a father who sacrificed his daughter's life to keep a vow to God.)

Others remember that their father's stories tended to be more dramatic than their mother's. He would get into acting them out, at times. Also, because she was always at home, their mother told more stories, often when she was very tired. The younger children remember her dozing off in the middle of a story. They realized what was happening as a sentence would suddenly wander off in a strange direction. That always added spice to storytelling time as it ended in hilarious laughter.

Another event often went with the milking, a tradition that Nevin seemed to enjoy as much as his children. Hilda remembers three or four children standing near their father with tin cups as he was milking, and at the right moment handing them over, one at a time, to be filled with warm milk foaming at the top. Certainly no milk ever tasted better! Watching their father squeeze the swollen teats and send that milk in steady streams into their cups with such obvious enjoyment and patience made it taste twice as good. He reveled in giving his children these small childhood pleasures.

Perhaps the single greatest event of the year was the trip to Juniata County to see "Grandpa Lauvers" which naturally included Aunt Mary and Aunt Gladys, the cousins, and other aunts and uncles. As one of the older children, Paul remembers these trips from his earliest days. "We held our Lauver family in high regard, and we eagerly welcomed these trips which were at least annual events. Anticipation would build as the big day approached. Dad would prepare the car for the trip. As the family increased in size, so did the preparations. A board was bolted from the front fender to the rear fender on the right side of the car to provide a secure place on the running board for numerous suitcases and boxes. Sleep came slowly the night before we were to leave on that long-awaited trip, while wake-up time came quickly, sometimes as early as 1:00 or 2:00 a.m."

Miriam recalls the preparations the older girls and their mother would make. "We spent days picking out our wardrobe for the trip," she says, which of course also meant planning for each of the younger children.

Packing into the car in the wee hours of the morning, the little ones continued sleeping or fell back to sleep. The younger ones sat on the laps of the older children and some sat on stools. Paul says, "By trading places and stopping at selected ice-cream stores for bathroom breaks, as well as the usual stop at the roadside spring between Amity Hall and Cocolamus (a treasured ritual) we managed to endure the long trip which often ended near breakfast time at Grandpa and Grandma Lauvers. Hugs and kisses, ham and eggs, endless love and sharing with Grandpa, Grandma, Aunt Mary and Aunt Gladys, Uncle Michael's and our other uncles, aunts, and cousins were a heady experiences that lasted two or three glorious days." Miriam recalls the shyness the cousins experienced initially when they met: "We'd always be afraid of each other at the beginning, then we'd loosen up and have lots of fun."

On the Bender side of the family Grandma Bender stands out as an important part of the daily lives of the Bender children, while the Bender cousins were simply a part of the ongoing life of school and church and, therefore, taken somewhat for granted. All of them lived in the Greenwood area during most of their growing up years except Uncle Earl and Aunt Katie's family who lived in Indiana.

Since Grandpa had died when Lura was only seven and Mildred a baby, little is remembered of this grandparent. One treasured piece of information about their grandpa that the children learned from their Aunt Savannah was a tidbit that Mildred got while traveling with her uncle and aunt. When Nevin first brought Esther home to meet his family, according to Aunt Savanna, Grandpa knew that his son had found a real gem of a woman. (He was obviously a man of keen discernment and insight!) He was deeply impressed with her and remarked, "If Nevin gets Esther, he can lick his arms clear up to his elbows!" The children were not sure just what licking his arms had to do with it, but they were delighted, in hindsight, that their father did indeed "get Esther," even though Grandpa was able to enjoy her as a daughter-in-law for less than nine years.

Grandma survived her husband by 20 years and lived less than a half-mile up the road with the children's Uncle Ted and Aunt Pauline. She was indeed important to her grandchildren and they eagerly looked forward to her weekly visits. What a familiar sight to see Grandma come walking in the long lane, usually with her cane! She preferred to walk, but often liked to be driven home in the afternoon. Frequently she came for the whole day and helped Esther with mending, especially torn overalls or jeans, and with other sewing. Such work was also a social activity. The conversation flew as rapidly as the needles, often a mixture of Pennsylvania Dutch and English. The children hung around to get the benefit of the conversation. And almost always Grandma had her little stash of hard, round candy, both white (peppermint) and pink (wintergreen) in a pocket of her Amish type apron. She carried these with her even to church on Sundays and was generous in giving them out.

Often the visits went the other way. Going to visit Grandma, alone or with a sibling, was a real treat, especially since Aunt Pauline and Uncle Ted were favorites and great fun to visit. The Beachy cousins were always welcoming. They raised popcorn and often popped an abundance of it on Sunday afternoons.

Grandma Bender was a lively and quite humorous conversationalist in private. In public, she maintained a lower profile, as conservative Mennonite women were expected to do. She was a very warm and loving person and she and Esther enjoyed a close relationship. Esther once remarked that if all mothers-in-law were like Caroline, there would be no in-law problems. Grandma Bender died in 1954 at the age of 85 years. She had over 50 great-grandchildren at the time of her death. As long as she lived, her children and their families gathered in Greenwood, usually in the summer, for a family reunion. Uncle Earl and Aunt Katie and their family came from Indiana. This was a special time for relating to the Bender cousins.

Aunt Lucy, who was a registered nurse at a time when this was quite unusual in the Greenwood Mennonite community, was an important part of the family's "medical system" as well as that of the whole community. She was the first "doctor" to be called in an emergency, as the time when Nevin began to bleed internally from his ulcer in 1952.

Mildred will never forget speeding up to Uncle Eli Schrock's after her father fainted and her mother phoned Aunt Lucy. Her aunt was waiting for her, her medicine bag ready, and within minutes she was able to alleviate the fears of the family. She was also ready to serve as Nevin's private duty nurse when it was discovered he needed surgery. She was always amazingly available, and certainly at tremendous cost to her own family at times. Her husband Eli deserves great credit for making her available in the community. Aunt Lucy helped to deliver each of the nine Bender children at home. (Esther needed to go to the hospital with her last, stillborn son.) During the worst of the Depression days Aunt Lucy delivered several of the babies without the doctor's assistance.

The two extended families, the Lauvers and the Benders, were such an integral part of the children's growing up years, that it would have been impossible to imagine life without them. However, the time was approaching when the Bender's nuclear family of 11—two parents and nine children—would itself become an "extended family." To help their children grow into mature, responsible, and happy adults, Nevin and Esther took seriously the discipline and teaching of their growing brood. But it was not only discipline that mattered, although that was certainly considered crucial. Nevin, who both reveled in life and took it very seriously, and Esther, whose laughter and tears, whose anxiety and trust, lived together in her sometimes overburdened heart, did their best to prepare their children for a life that would, no doubt, be very different from their own. How different, they could never have dreamed.

Five

THE FAMILY GROWING UP

We have each other.

—Response of Mildred, daughter of Nevin and Esther, after a painful discussion between Nevin and those who felt his approach to church discipline was not authoritarian enough.

Discipline was generally strong in German Mennonite homes and the Bender home was no exception. The heart of that discipline was in teaching, in talking things over, and always with both parents setting an example. Nevin and Esther tried to be clear in their expectations. Encouragement was given, as well as affirmation, when these expectations were met. When they were not, some form of punishment could be expected, or sometimes simply a "tough and tender" talking to. Spanking was one form of punishment resorted to when either parent deemed that necessary, since even the Bible taught that sparing the rod would spoil the child. Yet, even with this punishment, teaching and talking over the misdeed would be a part of it. Lura remembers that, when she was spanked, "Papa always held me afterward and talked awhile. It was very difficult for Mama to spank me. Her tears and gentle smacks I'll never forget."

All of the Bender children remember Esther spanking, but immediately embracing them as she wept. Spanking was an action she evidently felt she should take at times, but it clearly went against her nature. The younger siblings were told that the older ones were spanked or punished more often than the younger ones. This was hard for the younger siblings to refute since they had no independent data on the earlier practices.

Besides punishment, and even before punishment, there was ample opportunity in the Bender home for the children to think through their own actions and take responsibility for them; not just when they got caught. They were encouraged to come and talk things over when something was bothering them. In fact, Don recalls his parents' bedroom as "an always open counseling center." It wasn't unusual for one of the children to walk into their parents' bedroom late at night to confess some remembered wrongdoing. Tender consciences, rasped by the hell-fire sermons of visiting evangelists, were soothed by these talks. Emma remembers one night, after numerous trips to her parents' bedroom, being gently told by a patient but weary mother, "Emma, if you remember anything else tonight, just remember that I forgive you." A few minutes later another "sin" came to her mind, but she refrained from going back into their bedroom the rest of that night.

Hilda recalls convincing Mildred to go with her one evening to make a confession for a supposedly shared wrongdoing. She wanted Mildred's moral support. Hilda must have been very persuasive because her younger sister obediently went with her, even though she could not remember the alleged wrongdoing.

But far more than guilt and confession are remembered in the family life of the Benders. Memories that even today evoke excitement and joy, just in the recalling, are the beach trips—one of Nevin's greatest loves. Esther loved the ocean, as well, but just to sit and contemplate (not possible when the children were small). In fact, their unique characteristics were never more evident than on a family day at the beach, a special treat that they made sure would happen at least several times each summer through the years, despite their busy life on the farm. Rehoboth was their favorite beach, because the waves were higher and more fun for jumping. Nevin, always ready for adventure, played in the waves with his children. He taught all of the children to swim and he watched over them in the water. Esther, who did not swim and had no desire to learn, was the check-in point on the beach, and her eyes and fingers kept continuous count to make sure all nine children and her husband were accounted for. Often the littlest children played in the sand and the shallow water near her.

The children later recognized what a courageous and loving act it was for their mother to go along with those "beach days" with her husband, and help them to happen, when deep down she felt anxiety about keeping all of the family safe. After days at the beach, she was always relieved to be heading home with all their children. She knew that every single member of her family enjoyed the ocean immensely, and so she chose to take in stride her part as the matriarch of this clan.

Beach attire for plain Mennonites was always a challenge. Conventional bathing suits were considered immodest by some Mennonites, and improvised wear such as jeans for boys and dresses for girls, while less than satisfactory, was the usual dress in the 1930s and early 1940s. In the late 1940s it was gradually accepted in the Bender family for both the girls and the boys to wear ordinary swimming suits of the most modest variety. Not all in the church approved of these changes or even of "mixed bathing" (a mixture of boys and girls).

Some activities that the Bender young people engaged in were a cross between religious and recreational and are covered under church life. Church life was totally absorbing, particularly in Nevin's time. The children felt some resentment and disappointment that their father was often away for church functions and did not have more time to spend at home. This put more stress on Esther and the family. Later in life, he acknowledged that one of his regrets was that he had not spent more time with his family. He wondered if he should not have limited his speaking engagements more than he did. Emma remembers that it was healing for her to hear him say that.

There was an irony in these choices that Nevin and Esther felt compelled to make. It would be hard to find a father anywhere who so genuinely enjoyed his children and being with his family. At the same time, his love for the church and commitment to his work as a minister was the guiding passion of his life. He was increasingly in demand as a speaker and was away more frequently as the younger children were growing up. His children were pleased that he was a talented speaker and a widely respected leader in the church. Still, his absences were keenly felt and his returns were events to be celebrated. His younger sons, particularly, probably needed their father more than he was available, not only to give guidance in the farm work, which they handled quite remarkably with Millard's help, but also to offer more guidance and support in the task of growing up and becoming men.

Yet when Nevin was at home he was totally there. Esther remarked about this often, how present and helpful he was when he was able to be at home. She acknowledged that she could not have carried her heavy load if he had he not been as supportive and involved as a father. Millard, the first to enter the family through marriage, was keenly aware of this. "When he was there, he was totally present," he observed. Millard, who was also farming, became a most supportive and helpful big brother.

One of Nevin's joys as the children grew older and Esther was more free was to take his wife and the younger children along on teaching or preaching trips, especially for short or even longer weekends, when the older ones could take care of the chores. The five youngest remember several such special treats. On one trip to Canada for a conference, they took in Niagara Falls, the honeymoon site for their parents many years before.

The older children also remember taking trips with their father when they were small or nearing their teen years. It was not unusual for one or two to accompany him for a weekend of special meetings. They were pleased at his enjoyment in having them with him. Paul remembers going along with his father to meetings in churches in Pennsylvania. On one such trip, they visited Grandpa and Grandma Lauver en route to the Susquehanna church. Nevin felt a real sense of pride, although he would not have called it that, in his children—he was "pleased" with them.

After the children had all left home, he seldom went anywhere without Esther. They were constant companions, finally free to travel and minister together.

In summer 1948, Nevin was away in Canada for an unusually long six weeks. With its near catastrophes, it was a summer the family never forgot and certainly never wanted to live through again. Nevin James, just turning ten, was nearly electrocuted when he went barefoot into the basement to pull a plug from a receptacle. The plug was hooked to a pump which was getting rid of the water in the basement. He pulled on the wire, forgetting that he was standing in water. Jolted by the strong shocks, he started to holler, so Miriam went down to help him and saw that he couldn't get loose. She began pulling on him and got shocked herself. She says to this day she's not quite sure what she did, or how, but she knows she pulled the plug out, "and Nevin was free and I was free."

Not only was young Nevin nearly electrocuted during these six weeks, but Paul also had an accident that could have proved fatal. He overturned a tractor, injuring his groin, on a weekend trip to Springs, Pennsylvania, negotiating hills he was not used to in flat Delaware. Thankfully he survived the ordeal, although the severe injury caused him a lot of pain later in life. Also during these weeks Mildred was diagnosed with rheumatic fever. Esther assured her husband on the phone that she and the children could handle it all. Emma remembers that her mother counted the days until Nevin returned and was much relieved when the halfway point came. His homecoming in late July was the cause for much celebration. The guardian angels of the Bender family must have been extraordinarily busy that summer.

After weeks of going to doctors and trying to discover the cause of her severe joint pain, Mildred's diagnosis of rheumatic fever had a direct impact on the whole family. Not only was there one less person to help with the work, but there was also someone to care for, as well as added medical expense. Told by the doctor that she should plan on four to six weeks of bed rest to recover, neither Mildred nor anyone else dreamed that it would be 21 months before she could be up and able to resume her normal life.

Next to Mildred herself, Esther was most affected by this illness, as she gave loving care to her 14-year-old daughter. The whole family rallied round, and learned to deal with the inconvenience of the large living room also serving as a bedroom. This couldn't help but affect the dating habits of the older sisters and brothers. The living room was no longer available for private times, unless they wanted an eavesdropper on all conversations! They generally dealt with this quite graciously. Emma, as the younger sister, did much of the waiting on Mildred, generously trying to be available for different needs.

All of the brothers and sisters were supportive and helpful as Mildred struggled with her disappointment when months went by with hopes raised and then dashed as her temperature fluctuated and blood tests revealed a continued inflammation. Titus remembers, as does Mildred, how he often came in and sat on the bed, simply to talk and joke and cheer up his sister. And Nevin James, younger by six years, recalls climbing onto his big sister's bed and trying to hold her and make her feel better.

There was the time after many months of monthly blood tests and home visits by Dr. Fitchett that Esther, unknown to Mildred, went through a time of near despair, with hopes raised and dashed so often. She expressed her frustration to the doctor. Why was her daughter not getting better? Why was progress so very slow? The doctor's response was quite sobering and held out the possibility of Mildred's never returning to full health unless great care continued to be taken. Worried and subdued, Esther simply continued with her patient nursing.

Finally, in fall of the second year, Mildred was allowed to begin her high school studies; this gave a tremendous boost to her spirits. Emma faithfully brought home the assignments each day and offered invaluable help. And then toward spring, after Mildred's sixteenth birthday and just when it seemed that this way of life might never change, Dr. Fitchett arranged for a thorough examination and tests with a heart specialist in Wilmington. The report was good, the tender loving care and patience of the family was finally rewarded, and Mildred could resume her normal life again. The whole family was relieved and grateful. The living room was available once more for normal dating and general family functioning.

Dating was an important part of the Bender family life and the source of much teasing. All of the Bender siblings did most of their dating with young people from outside the Greenwood community, and those who married eventually chose spouses from a distance. Still, almost all the Benders first dated Greenwood young people. Most of them met their spouses at Eastern Mennonite College or High School, or at Fairview Bible School in Michigan. Since many of the courtships were carried on long distance by letter and many weekend visits, it became a rather familiar sight through the years to have one or two (or more) of the siblings, sitting at the dining room table in the evening with a picture of the special person in their life in front of them, writing that important "love letter." It was not uncommon to have a younger sibling trying to catch snatches of the writing or begging to read the last letter received.

The event of a girlfriend or boyfriend of their older brothers and sisters visiting from out of town was a time for the younger children to help tidy up the grounds and thoroughly clean the house. (The younger ones had to do most of their own tidying up, when the time came—but things in general were in better condition by then.) The dating couple usually got the living room, if they weren't going out or when they'd return, although that changed during the months that Mildred was battling rheumatic fever. Even when a couple thought they had privacy, there was no guarantee they really did, since there was a high stump outside the living room window where some of the younger ones were known to perch for a view. Still, it was a rather unrewarding effort, as dating relationships were quite reserved in that time.

One concern of those who brought dates home was the state of the area in front of the house. At certain times of the year the cows were walked past the house to go to the front pasture and they seemed to prefer to drop their "cow pies" in transit. The cows were usually hustled along to avoid this indiscretion, but generally there needed to be some follow-up with a scoop. Failure to do the follow-up resulted in some unpleasant brotherly or sisterly confrontations as stepping in "something" did not add to the romantic mood of a date. Family members usually had opinions about the dates their siblings chose and weren't shy about voicing them. Fortunately, those who were eventually chosen all received good reviews!

Nevin and Esther showed a deep trust in their children, and in numerous ways let them know they had confidence in them. Even when the children were small, this was evident. "I remember one of my first years in school when Sister Irene stood me in a corner because she said I had stuck out my tongue at her," Lura recalls. "I really hadn't, and when Papa asked me about it I told him the truth—that I was just licking my lips. He believed me."

This trust and respect, this core belief in their daughters and sons as well as in the spouses they married, was one of the greatest gifts Nevin and Esther could have given their children, a fact recognized to this day. There was the time in 1960 when Merlin and Hilda made the decision for Merlin to study at Harvard and get his PhD in Middle Eastern Studies. Esther and Nevin were not only at peace with this decision, but were strongly encouraging. However, not long afterwards when Esther visited her sisters in Pennsylvania, a great deal of concern was expressed that Harvard was a place where scholars often "lost their faith." They urged Esther to try to get Merlin and Hilda to change their minds or at least to consider another option. They were genuinely concerned and felt strongly that something must be done.

Esther's reply was one still treasured by her family. In effect she said, "We simply have to trust our children and their decisions. We don't know what's best for them. They know what they need to do. We'll pray for them, but it's their decision and we trust them." Esther was clear and her sisters let it rest.

Merlin later said that he felt trust and confidence from his mother-in-law from the very beginning. In his words, "She was a very special person. Her gentleness, her sensitivity, and her confidence were terrific."

In his different decisions throughout the years, Nevin James remembers this confidence he felt from both his parents. At the time that Titus left for college and seminary, in Nevin's middle teens, he felt a special trust from his father when he and Don began to carry major responsibility for the farm. He experienced it again several years later when he decided that seminary needed to be his direction. His father was very affirming and was pleased as this son, who carried his name, began to minister after his ordination in some of the same circles (especially in Pennsylvania) where he himself had served through the years.

Still later, in the early 1970s when Nevin Jr. took a leave of absence from pastoring and began to relate to troubled, high-risk children as a social worker, he recalls that his father really wanted to understand this choice and they talked at length together about it. Even if he could not completely understand, Nevin gave his son and Lourene his full support and blessing.

Through the years Esther and Nevin exhibited this spirit of trust time and again, even as they saw their children make some very different choices from their own. Of course, there were times when that trust became a bit fragile, when it seemed that confidence was not fully earned or given. But always their basic attitude as parents was one of respect and trust, recognizing that their children, as they grew up, were separate human beings who had to become responsible for their own lives and make their own choices—and their own mistakes. They felt that their task as parents was to love and to pray, to be available to talk, to give counsel when asked or when needed, and to be free to challenge. They then supported their children wholeheartedly in their choices and directions.

Still the Bender siblings struggled to gain the approval of their parents, especially their father, and dealt with feelings of competitiveness and wondering if they were measuring up. Many of the perceived expectations were unspoken and experienced differently and uniquely by each sibling. Nevin Jr. speaks of his own internal struggle in this regard. "I recall the expectation that we were to 'hold up' the family name. We were expected to excel in what we did, either because of our parents or perhaps from within ourselves. I remember the unconscious competitive spirit I had in trying to outdo my older siblings, who were setting an example I couldn't always reach. The ministry was always looked up to in our home, partly because of the example we had in Dad. I knew I was going to go to seminary and be a preacher."

It was when he went to Eastern Mennonite College in preparation for seminary that Nevin says he experienced some of his greatest disappointments—perhaps in part because he was following three older siblings there. One deep disappointment, he says, was "not being chosen for Collegiate Chorus, the elite singing group. Somehow I felt that the family was let down by my not getting in. It was so hard to follow the footsteps of my elders—because they were so big." His older siblings had no idea how significant this was to Nevin. They wish they had known. Nevin's feeling of not adequately measuring up to his older siblings changed through the years as he gained confidence and found his own directions.

Often he has remarked that he is grateful to be part of a supportive and caring family. That appreciation took on added meaning when he and Lourene and their children faced profound changes in their lives after Nevin's aneurism and brain surgery in 1979. The need of a tender and compassionate God and a supportive family ready to give unconditional love was crucial. No one in the family came through this experience unchanged as they realized their own vulnerability as well as strength. The love and family spirit nurtured by Nevin and Esther through the years became even deeper.

As new sons and daughters came into the family through marriage the family dynamics changed. There were adjustments and there was added richness as well as complexity. The relationship of each of the spouses with their newly acquired parents was certainly unique and found its own expression. One of Esther's characteristics that Glenn and Ann, among others, have remarked on was her concern that her children treat their spouses well—with deep love and respect. These new daughters and sons felt totally supported and loved by their mother-in-law, as well as their father-in-law. As Hilda has said about her mother, "I think she was more concerned that we were the right kind of people than that we got the right kind. She really wanted us to be good husbands and wives; if she ever felt we weren't doing that, she really got after us!"

Glenn remembers with some humor his experience of asking Nevin and Esther for their daughter Emma's "hand in marriage." He was nervous, but assumed it was just a formality; he understood it was the thing to do in this family. He was not quite prepared for Nevin's searching question: "Do you realize what a big thing you're asking?" Well . . . yes, he thought he did! However, they all survived the awkward moment and Nevin, as well as Esther, was obviously satisfied with Glenn's response. Glenn felt that Esther sensed some of his insecurity and vulnerability in a unique way, and her support and trust through the years helped him to develop into a more sensitive and confident person.

Ann believes that many of her ideas about courtship and family were formed through Nevin's influence when he would come to Ohio for weekends of teaching and other meetings. In fact, she was quite taken with his "soft-spoken, kind way of expressing himself. I kept saying, 'Boy, I wish he had some sons!' I guess I fell in love with his dad before I ever met Titus."

At age seven or eight, Merlin was also impressed with Nevin's "soft-spokenness and gentleness, and I knew he had to be a good man." It was at Merlin's home church in Au Gres, Michigan, that he had heard Nevin speak. Merlin was sitting near the front that day. "That image I have of him speaking from the pulpit is still as vivid in my mind as if it had happened yesterday."

Elmer, also from Au Gres, recalls his future father-in-law being in their home for a few hours in the mid 1940s at the close of the annual Conservative Mennonite Conference one summer, while waiting to be taken to the train in Flint. A young man of about 20, Elmer was impressed with how contemplative Nevin seemed. "I can still see him there, his eyes especially. You knew that he was thinking about something other than being in the Jantzi home. He struck me as a contemplative individual who would be processing while the rest of the world was going on."

Don has often teased Judy that she married him because she was really in love with his dad! Certainly the bond between Judy and her father-in-law was extraordinarily close and intuitive. Although Nevin had at first been bothered by the idea of his son marrying a Catholic, the reservations seemed to disappear completely once the Catholic was a person he knew and came to love and deeply respect. Judy and Nevin enjoyed many long conversations that were mutually nurturing and stimulating. Judy never knew Esther, but the connection with her father-in-law was one that would never be broken.

Paul and Don believe that the passionate rejection of authoritarian styles the children have adopted was one result of the parenting style of Nevin and Esther as well as Nevin's church leadership style. Several spouses of the Bender children have remarked, "Don't ever tell Benders' what to do. Request or suggest what they might do."

As the only daughter-in-law in the family for over six years, Ginny came to know Esther while most of the family was still at home. There was a special bond between Ginny and her mother-in-law. In a sense Esther became the mother Ginny had never known as a child. Communication between them was easy and relaxed. Having a grandson living near them was a special privilege, and both Esther and Nevin loved to have Paul Lynn come to see them. On one occasion Paul Lynn, less than two years old, started out walking along Route 36, and when Ginny caught up with him, he said, "I want to go see Grandma and Grandpa."

Ginny was often impressed by Esther's deep spirituality. To quote Ginny: "Hers was not a piety of words, but a faith that resulted in actions of love toward family and all the people in her world."

His first meeting with his future mother-in-law, Elmer will never forget. The timing of his arrival was uncertain because he had a long drive from Michigan and he turned up a little earlier than Esther expected. She was relaxing in her rocking chair when he arrived. Elmer describes the scene with relish: "She had just taken her afternoon bath and was in the living room, barefooted. Apparently there was no other door from the living room, and she had to come through the dining room where I was. I could see her skidding through the door, her hand over her mouth. It was a quick introduction!" A few minutes later she returned, properly dressed and poised, to graciously welcome her daughter Miriam's new and obviously serious boyfriend.

Miriam describes her mother thus: "She was very gentle; she just did what she had to do. She stood by Dad. She was quiet, unassuming and had a sense of humor. She was a good woman." Miriam adds that "she wasn't quick to show she was feeling sad. She didn't complain." No doubt, though, the sadness or anxiety crept through in ways other than words. She was subject to severe headaches, probably a kind of migraine; these seemed to lessen a great deal toward the end of her life. Different ones of the children remember what Lura refers to as "Mama's worried look." Mildred remembers well the difference in her own feelings and sense of well-being when her mother was happy and at ease, or when she seemed anxious and overburdened. Perhaps this anxiety was a part of the flip side of her total acceptance of people and her acceptance of her life as the wife of a minister and bishop who was much in demand. A great deal was expected of her in many big and also little, unnoticed ways.

Much more could be said about the gentle woman who was the center of the Benders' family life. Because of her husband's visibility and prominence as a church leader, in some ways she seemed to live in his shadow. People often tended to underestimate her, perhaps in part because she was very unassuming and downplayed herself. Even those closest to her tended to take her for granted at times. Yet there was in her a rock-like strength that obviously came out of her own deep sense of self, despite a tentativeness that those who knew her well sensed. This strength also came, quite simply, out of her dedicated relationship with God, not with many words spoken, but in the living reality of her daily life.

In a talk given at the Sisters' Meeting at the Conservative Mennonite Conference in the 1950s, Esther made clear her decision to be involved as a team with her husband and his ministry. She spoke of needing to consecrate her life again and again. This represented her conscious decision and commitment, a commitment she lived throughout her life with amazing love and integrity.

It was a family joke how easily Esther could fall asleep, not only at night, but also in church on Sunday morning or in the middle of telling a story to her children. Nevin, on the other hand, suffered from insomnia when he was under severe stress, and sometimes his restlessness would awaken Esther. Their children might hear the soft murmur of their parents' voices from their rooms in the middle of the night. But it was because Esther chose to be awake with her husband. Seldom was it because she was unable to sleep.

Of her father, Miriam said, "He had a gentle spirit although he was firm. He had tenacity. He reveled in doing small things for Mother. I recall once when Mother went out and got mud on her shoes that Dad cleaned them." Such thoughtful, chivalrous actions were totally congruent with Nevin's attitude toward his wife. He expected a lot of her, and he treated her royally. He treated his daughters with equal thoughtfulness and respect, and they were always proud to be accompanied by their father on any occasion.

Esther and Nevin could both be impractical and very creative in making one another happy. When Nevin was in the hospital for an ulcer operation in 1952, he found some of the hospital food more than he could stomach; he felt it made him sick. More than once, Esther, with a son or daughter driving, started the ten-mile trip to the hospital with a small kettle of boiling water. At exactly the right time, Esther would put eggs in the water, so that perfect soft-boiled eggs were ready when they reached the hospital. Her husband expressed his love and appreciation for this special treatment again and again. It was a story he loved to tell.

Esther and Nevin were never afraid to show their affection for one another, even when others were around. Lourene remembers this very well. "I was quite impressed with the affection Mother and Dad openly showed each other." Millard, the son-in-law who has been in the family the longest, describes the time he came up the walk and onto the porch. He reports, "Suddenly I became aware that Mother and Dad were embracing inside the screen door, so I hesitated, not quite sure what to do. And of course, Mother was slipping out, changing her position!" Even as little children, their daughters and sons enjoyed seeing their parents' affection. It made them feel deeply loved themselves and made their world feel warm and safe.

However, these nine Bender siblings were no longer children and it was up to them to continue to create their own world and to make it as safe as possible for their own children. There were engagements, marriages, the birth of children and emerging vocations. The birth of each new grandchild from 1948 to 1972 brought tremendous hope and joy to this growing extended family, bringing added strength and diversity.

In 1947 Lura was married to Millard Benner. They settled near Greenwood so were often home for Sunday dinner and cooperated in farming efforts including the harvesting of beans. Thus the marriage did not represent a complete separation from the family. Their first daughter, and Nevin and Esther's first grandchild, Dawn, was born near Greenwood in 1948, followed by four more girls, Dorothy, Hilda, Kathy, and Carol. Their son Steve was born while the family was living in Harrisonburg during Millard's years at Eastern Mennonite College (EMC, later EMU) as he prepared for high school teaching. Over seven years later, their youngest daughter Phyllis was born. A foster daughter, Lorraine Stutzman, joined their family along the way.

After Miriam married Elmer Jantzi in 1950 they moved to Elmer's home place in Au Gres, Michigan, where Elmer's mother lived with them for several years. Miriam's leaving was quite traumatic because she and her siblings realized that the family was now beginning to separate. John Nevin, the first grandson in the Bender clan was born in 1951. Their other four children, Joyce, Janet, Karen, and Philip were also born in Michigan and grew up on the Jantzi home place until the family moved to Ohio in the fall of 1969, where Elmer had begun teaching at the Rosedale Bible Institute several years earlier. Richly gifted in hospitality, Miriam and Elmer provided a "home away from home" through the years for various nieces and nephews and other students. Many friends and relatives found the welcome mat always out.

Paul and Ginny Riehl first settled near Greenwood after their marriage in 1952. Later they spent a year in Oregon and then returned to Greenwood. They bought land from Nevin and Esther and built a home just across the highway. They, too, were often home for Sunday dinners, and helped to plan different family events and celebrations—something for which Ginny, as well as Paul, had a special gift. Paul Lynn, second grandson in the Bender clan, was born in 1953. His sister Ann was born two-and-a- half years later, then twins Jean and Joan. They spent their childhood years living close to their Bender grandparents until those grandparents retired and moved to Mississippi. They then continued to stay close by often traveling the distance and spending time with their southern family.

Just before her marriage to Merlin Swartz in 1955, Hilda graduated as a registered nurse from Milford Memorial Hospital in Delaware. They spent the next year in Harrisonburg with Merlin in seminary and the next year in Goshen, Indiana, for Merlin to continue his studies. Several years later they left for Jordan, serving under Mennonite Central Committee (MCC), the arm of the Mennonite church which focuses on human, social, and economic needs of communities within the U.S. and around the world, to live and work with Palestinian refugees. Their oldest, Sondra, was born there. Daryl was born in Goshen where they spent the year after returning from the Middle East. After their move to Cambridge for further studies, Kenton arrived. It was between the births of their two sons that Wanda was chosen for adoption and joined their family.

Titus, with Mildred, left for Eastern Mennonite College (later University) in 1953, and was the first of the nine siblings to graduate from college in 1957. He continued the next year in the seminary and married Ann Yoder (also at EMC) in 1958. They moved to Meridian, Mississippi, after their marriage to start a voluntary service unit there under the Conservative Mennonite Conference. They wanted to create church/community with people in the area which happened slowly but surely. Their three children, Anita, Maria, and Mike were born in Mississippi. For two and a half years, Anita was the sole Mississippi grandchild to help ease the adjustment and sometimes loneliness of her Grandma and Grandpa Bender in their new life, after their move South in 1960. All their other grandchildren were a thousand miles away at that time.

Mildred, after starting college with Titus, stayed out for two years to teach at Greenwood Mennonite School (GMS). After returning to EMC and graduating in 1958, she again taught at GMS, then in Newfoundland as a volunteer with MCC. She moved to Mississippi in the early 1960s to join her parents in their work with the Choctaw Indian Tribe where she taught Choctaw youth on the Pearl River Reservation. This was after "home" itself had moved to Mississippi. Having a deepening interest in issues of justice and crosscultural living and education, she gave herself to the challenge of living, studying, and teaching in the South during the 1960s and in the Middle East, in Beirut Lebanon, in the 1970s.

Emma married Glenn Myers in 1961 after her graduation from EMC and a year of teaching in Ohio. They lived in Harrisonburg for the next year, with Emma teaching and Glenn finishing college. They then moved to Mississippi where they both taught school—Glenn in high school and Emma in elementary—and helped in the church community at Nanih Waiya, especially with the youth. Glenn later became the pastor there. They joined Nevin and Esther, and now Mildred, with Titus and Ann nearby in Meridian. Emma quit teaching when Mildred Lynne was born, feeling more than ready to devote herself to mothering and helping her husband and parents. Sheila was born shortly before her grandma died, and Beth arrived several years later.

Nevin James was married to Lourene Godshall in 1961, just after their graduation from EMC. Their next two years were spent in Harrisonburg, with Nevin in seminary while Lourene taught school. In 1963 they moved to Vermont to pastor a church in Bridgewater Corners, where their four children, Nevin III, Conrad, Marcia, and Angela joined the family. After their first three "home-made" children, they chose Angela for adoption. Her beautiful dark skin was quite a contrast to their three blonde children. Their experience with this adoption was so positive, that Nevin decided to take a four-year leave of absence from his work as church pastor to work with high-risk children in the area. He returned to the pastorate several years before his life-changing aneurysm.

Don moved to Georgia in 1966, after graduating from college (EMC) in 1964 and teaching a year in Virginia. He volunteered with MCC, teaching in Atlanta's inner-city schools. He met Judy Harak there as they worked and marched together in the peace and civil rights movements, and served in inner city Atlanta. They were married in 1969. Their daughter Anneka was born in 1970, almost twins with her cousin and later-to-become-best-friend, Beth. Chris, the youngest of the 32 grandchildren to bless the lives of Nevin and Esther (Esther lived long enough to know only 27 of her grandchildren) was adopted in 1972. He soon became bosom buddies with his grandpa whom he dearly loved and was privileged to enjoy for almost three years.

In 1965, with the nine children scattered in six different states and grandchildren now numbering 26, the desire for a planned family reunion began to be expressed, especially by

Nevin, the patriarch of this growing clan. Planning began in earnest, and in that same summer the family gathered for their first such reunion at the new Bethany Birches campground which Nevin and Lourene had been instrumental in creating. It was still in the rough. Families lived in tents and cooking was done over open fires and on individual campstoves.

The times of games and singing linger in our memories. With his guitar, Don led the children, then the rest of us, in the song:

> My daddy couldn't move a mountain
> Or pull down a big oak tree
> But my daddy became a mighty big man
> With a simple philosophy,
> Do what you do, do well....

But the mother of the "tribe" was not left out. The family will never forget the skit prepared and presented during an afternoon of entertainment. Don and Mildred put together both amusing and serious events from early days of the Bender family, using grandchildren to act out the roles. Esther frequently shook with laughter, tears streaming down her face as the happy and funny stories from their past came alive. Nevin had called the family together for this first (and last for Esther) family reunion. The vision of Nevin Jr. and Lourene helped create the setting for this important "homecoming" at Bethany Birches Camp for this first family reunion since the Bender clan had grown so large and become so scattered.

These reunions have continued ever since, meeting in alternate years and moving around the country, with different families hosting the event.

Six

Economic Life

Is there any more back?

—Question by Titus, son of Nevin and
Esther, as he saw food disappearing into the mouths
of nine Bender children with healthy appetites.

*N*EVIN AND ESTHER WERE MARRIED IN 1925, so through the early years their finances were adversely affected by the Great Depression. Also, Nevin's greatest gifts and keenest interests were in education and in his ministry. The first was paid poorly, and for the second he received no salary. He did often receive "Love Offerings" when he would go to other communities to preach. These were an important and essential contribution to the family's economic life. There were occasions when medical or other bills would be paid by members of the Greenwood congregation, although these actions depended on the good will of those who had the financial means. When Nevin's ministry took him away from home, Esther and the children had to run the farm themselves, sometimes along with hired help. The condition of the house and farm on occasion resulted in criticism for the Benders and particularly for Nevin.

One time that this criticism became focused was during the first church controversy, in the late 1930s. Those who were critical of his more progressive positions and inclusive leadership style also faulted him on the condition of his kitchen ceiling. This condition was cited as evidence that he was not a good provider. Ted Beachy, Nevin's brother-in-law with his great heart and practical skills, came to help repair the ceiling. When he left it was with a good-natured comment to the effect that now the critics would be silenced on that issue.

While finances were often difficult, Nevin always enjoyed unusually good credit. Millard recalls that Nevin would go to Delaware Production Credit to borrow money and would pick up a check the same day, based on his signature. Due to his reputation for honesty and responsibility, there was no need for a credit committee meeting.

GOING TO MARKET

Market was a venture which began around 1937. As Lura recalls those years, it was the market which made it possible for the family to survive the post-Depression years. They would load their Chevrolet panel truck each Saturday for the 75-mile trip to Wilmington, which took several hours. They would leave at about 4:00 o'clock in the morning and return about 4:00 in the afternoon. Often Nevin and Esther both went, with at least one of the older children and usually a little one. It was a treat for the lucky younger child and a help to the ones in charge at home. This varied through the years, as the older ones got their drivers licenses and could carry more responsibility, or when Nevin would be away in meetings. Paul sometimes went instead of his father.

Since they were usually up late the night before with preparations, Nevin was often tired for the trip. In the early days, when he was the only licensed driver, the children would sit beside him to help him keep awake and sometimes they would also steer a bit. On one occasion, with Miriam helping to steer, an officer saw the situation and charged Nevin with reckless driving. The children remember going fearfully with their father to the police station. Fortunately the offense only resulted in the payment of a fine of $13.50.

Preparation for market began on Thursdays when the eggs were picked up at various farms, referred to collectively as the egg route. Lura often ran this route after she got her license and recalls that they picked up as many as ten crates (300 dozen). Driving the egg route was a time-consuming task and on one occasion, Lura, who was then 16, was driving with Titus at night. They tried to save time by not stopping at stop signs and turning out the lights so they would not be detected by any patrolmen. (They had not learned this from their father!) With Titus doing the lights and Lura at the wheel, the coordination apparently went awry at one intersection, and they ended up in the ditch. Titus' leg and some of the eggs were the casualties, and Titus remembers having to walk on crutches. The crutches brought him lots of attention both at home and at school, and he admits using them a bit longer than necessary.

The eggs (which were gathered on Thursdays) were washed and graded for size on Fridays. Some of this grading was done by eye, but many eggs were weighed individually on a small scale to determine their classification. Also taken along to market were dressed chickens, turkeys (near the holidays), Swiss cheese, cream, butter, as well as sausage and other pork items. Many of the products were from the Bender farm, supplemented by those of nearby farms. The Swiss cheese, as much as one-fourth to one-half of a wheel (200 lbs), was bought from an Amish man in Dover.

Butter churning was a weekly task that could take significant time, depending on the temperature and the condition of the cream. It also was an excuse for a gathering of siblings, taking turns churning and usually being involved in a discussion, serious or otherwise. The finished butter had to be packaged; it was formed with a press and then wrapped in waxed paper.

Hilda remembers one week when her father seemed less than satisfied with the neatness of her wrapping. He told her that the previous week a customer had asked for one of the packages which was wrapped more nicely, his delicate way of encouraging her to improve her work.

The chickens and turkeys were largely from the Bender farm and were dressed on Fridays. The process of plucking feathers, was particularly tedious and time-consuming until a neighbor and uncle, Eli Swartzentruber, developed an electric plucker, a wheel with rubber flappers which speeded up the process somewhat. "Picking" the chickens became a community event as some of the Benders gathered at Uncle Milts, where a plucker was set up. Cousins helped as first the Bender chickens were plucked, then the Swartzentruber chickens, until all were finished. Even the little children helped with this task.

When the Benders arrived in Wilmington each Saturday morning, they set up their stands on Lincoln Street along with other farmers. This was in an Italian section, so the Benders received some cross-cultural experience and picked up some Italian words. Although prices were generally set, people often liked to bargain—or at least give it a try. Titus remembers one time that eggs, which had been selling for 35 cents a dozen, were lowered to 30 cents. A woman, assuming that the price was still 35 cents a dozen and driving for a bargain, offered Titus $1 for three dozen. He promptly accepted, until he heard his mother's, "Now Titus!"

Among the pleasant memories the children had of market in the summer were the lemon slushes—a kind of frozen lemonade, made in a freezer on the street. Also sold on the street were thick crusted pizzas which the children understood to be "gobble de gop" as the vendor pronounced the Italian term. During the winter the experience was somewhat different and not always so comfortable. The children recall the sense of community they experienced on Lincoln Street. When it was bitter cold, they were always welcome at a nearby furniture store, where they could warm up by putting their feet under the radiators. One woman would fry eggs for the children. She impressed Hilda by cooking them in deep oil.

On good sales days the children remember buying steak sandwiches or hot roast beef sandwiches with mashed potatoes for 40 cents at Steve's Restaurant, a place where they usually went near the end of the day to deliver eggs. Hilda remembers hearing from her brothers and sisters about exotic foods such as sodas and subs, until she had built up great expectations. When she finally had the opportunity to go to market and taste these new foods, she was sure that she had gone to heaven.

Their Italian customers did not have a custom of eating the gizzards, hearts, or livers of the chickens. This meant that those chicken parts were in bountiful supply for the Bender meals. Mildred remembers that on evenings of market days, Miriam would prepare a delicious giblet gravy (referred to as "hearts and livers") cooked with plenty of onions and served with mashed potatoes. Miriam recalls that this traditional meal also included dried corn. It was one of the family's favorite meals.

Titus remembers that there was a Goodwill store near their market. It was here that the family began its collection of Tom Swift and Rover Boys books. One not familiar with those series, could ask to see Titus' or Paul's current collections.

The Benders encountered some alcoholics from the street. When these men asked for money to buy food, Nevin sometimes took them to buy the food, so that the money would not be diverted to purchase alcohol. The family remembers Mr. Murphy, who would come to the stand intoxicated and would astonish the children by eating two or three raw eggs on the spot. He was remembered for the little tune he sang, "Chili, Chili Bean a Bean a Bean," in operatic style.

At the end of the day products were occasionally left over . When that happened they headed for Madison Street where Uncle Milt's and Uncle Eli's families were set up. Depending on how Milt's day was going, some of the products were left with them. On particularly slow days Nevin walked the streets, trying to sell the remainder of the products at reduced prices.

All in all, market day was not a day to be taken lightly. It was accomplished only through great teamwork and was, down to the smallest detail, a family project. Those who stayed home on Saturday—whoever's turn it happened to be—were responsible for the chores, thoroughly cleaning the house, and even doing some baking. Lura recalls that in setting her wedding day in 1947, she chose Tuesday evening to not conflict with market day or its preparation.

The profitability of market varied considerably. It began in 1937 during the Depression when prices were quite deflated. Lura remembers gross receipts of $100. At a later time Hilda remembers net receipts ranging from $75 to $100. Titus remembers one good day with income of $400. That was the time Nevin came home from market and could not find his wallet, which contained the receipts of the day and from which considerable money was owed. Nevin retraced his steps until his wonderful, awful discovery that his wallet had fallen into the outhouse. The money was recovered and laundered!

In 1948, toward the end of the marketing era, the panel truck stopped working and Milt, who had bought a new truck, lent his old one to the Benders. The Health Department was becoming involved and began to require that the products be sold from an enclosed booth. At this time the sales were dropping and on one trip, it was figured that the net income was about $10. The increased regulations and the decreased sales finally resulted in a decision to discontinue with the market.

LIMA BEANS

In 1945 the Benders bought a John Deere tractor known as the "H" model which pulled a two-bottom plow. Millard, who was doing alternative to military service in Powellsville, Maryland, was coming to Delaware at this time to visit Lura. He recalls that Eli Swartzentruber had bought a John Deere and this set the precedent for the Benders and others. Around this time, before discontinuing the marketing, the Bender family began to raise lima beans. At first they were in a group with Eli Swartzentruber, Ted Beachy, and perhaps some others. Paul remembers getting up in the wee hours of the morning, along with Earl Swartzentruber and Jay Embleton to start harvesting or "vining" at Eli's. At the end of the season they would get together to figure who had worked what hours and to settle the difference in cash. Several years later another group consisting of Ted, Nevin, and Millard formed. For a year or two Paul rented a farm in Lincoln and was a part of the group. The labor was handled more informally in this group, with everyone expected to do his part.

Initially the group had to haul their own beans to a company called Brakely. They bought a stake body truck for this purpose. Later the Benders and the group changed to the Draper Company in Milton, which picked up the beans at the farm. The truck was no longer needed for the farm and it became the first of a small fleet of trucks which comprised the Bender Poultry Company started by Paul in about 1948.

There were several fields on the Bender farm which had poor drainage and which were often wet, sometimes delaying the plowing. Paul and Titus recall working at night to catch up with delayed plowing. This night plowing was also needed because the delayed process had been further slowed down by the overgrown vetch. It was necessary for one person to ride on the plow to keep it from getting clogged while the other person drove.

Lima beans were a labor intensive crop, particularly during harvest. The bean viner, which was the focus of activity during harvest, was for many years located at the edge of the woods, not far from the house. Nevin usually arranged to be at home during harvest and was in charge of the viner. He kept it running smoothly and emptied the beans into boxes as they collected. Millard recalled that Nevin sometimes tried to do some small mechanical repairs and servicing while the viner was running. Once his hand caught in the machinery, but fortunately the resulting injury was not serious.

The viner was as large as a small house and had two cylinders. These cylinders were about three feet in diameter, twelve feet long and covered with a rubber cloth with small holes to allow beans to fall out. These outside cylinders rotated slowly and beaters inside rotated faster, a process which shelled the beans. The beans would then drop out of the cylinder through the small holes onto a canvas apron which bounced the beans to the bins in the front while carrying the dirt and leaves to the rear. The vines would move through the viner and out the back end, where they would be stacked. Later, after the vines had cured into silage, they were used as cattle feed.

The viner was powered by the engine of a steel-wheeled John Deere tractor of 1920s vintage with an immense fly wheel. Starting the engine by spinning this fly wheel each morning could be a challenge, and was usually a group effort with the men taking turns. Both the tractor and the viner were noisy, resulting in welcome silence when they were finally turned off at the end of the work day.

A full crew consisted of at least three at the viner and three in the field. Children were enlisted to pick up scatters—those beans the equipment missed in the field.

Timing was crucial in the bean harvest. Since the percentage green was critical to the price (one year 100 percent green was $180 per ton decreasing in price with each decrease in percent to 70 percent green. Since 70 percent and lower was $20 per ton, it was necessary to harvest at the time of optimum weight, while keeping the percentage in the very high 90s. An inspector came from the company to judge the percentage with a small scale and was watched carefully. Having the company provide the inspector could be compared to one team providing the umpire in a baseball game. Many discussions and some confrontations resulted from the inspector's judgment versus what was fair. Finally one day Titus ordered the inspector off the property. Since the Bender situation was not unique the state eventually hired inspectors to provide neutral judges. Although these state inspectors varied, they probably leaned slightly in favor of the farmers.

Since the percentage was so important and the ripening could be affected by the stage of the moon and the temperature, at times vining was done around the clock to maximize the best conditions. On rare occasions it was necessary to abandon part of a field when it was too white and the next fields were ready. Since the operation had to shut down at noon on Saturday and remain down until Monday morning, the weekend could be very problematic depending on the beans' stage of ripeness. Observing Sunday always took precedence over the needs of harvesttime.

The whole rhythm and work of the farm and of family life changed during the bean season, to maximize the results of this essential crop. During the days of intense harvesting, the girls took over the chores completely by milking and dealing with the milk, feeding the animals and cleaning out the stables. Emma remembers one evening when she milked all nine cows by hand herself. Perhaps her sisters were at outside jobs that evening or involved otherwise. There was a strong sense in the whole family that bean season called for a special working together, and everyone came through.

When the harvesting required rising as early as 4:00 a.m., or when working through the night was required, the entire family rallied around the harvesters with wonderful meals, lots of iced tea carried out to the fields and to the viner, and plenty of tender loving care for the exhausted men. The sisters became quite skilled in giving back massages. Don remembers the strong sense of emotional as well as physical support which was needed and freely given, from one person to another and to the family as a whole. The feeling of satisfaction that came with this exhausting work and the giving and receiving of support is difficult to describe. This was especially true when percentages were running high and the weight was good. There were times on particularly heavy weeks that the men would come in at noon on Saturday and, after a large lunch, would find the nearest floor space available and fall asleep.

In the mid 1950s developments in equipment somewhat simplified the bean harvest. Viners were smaller, more efficient, and were built on wheels so that they could be moved from field to field. Since the beans didn't need to be transported as far, they could be loaded more lightly and loosely, which made unloading the beans at the viner less demanding. Millard later designed a cart which did not require a person on board to stack while loading. Another position was eliminated by not needing to stack the vines, since the viner could be moved when the pile became too big. With this new set-up the required crew was cut almost in half. These developments were timely since they came as the available help at home was decreasing.

Although Millard and Lura lived five miles from the Bender farm, they worked cooperatively on the beans, as well as other projects. Millard, a skilled carpenter and mechanic, served as a father/older brother to Nevin Jr. and Don. This was especially true in their early teenage years after Paul had married and left home, Titus was in college, and Nevin was often away on preaching appointments.

POULTRY AND THE DAIRY

Each year the Benders raised a flock of 150-200 turkeys. These birds were kept fenced outside once they reached medium size. Their caretakers believed that turkeys deserved their bad reputation. When turkeys were moved as a flock from one location to another, one had to be careful that none escaped because if one turkey bolted, the entire flock would compulsively follow after. Some of them also wandered out of the pen and would look for places to perch around the house. They particularly liked shiny surfaces which made automobiles parked in the driveway fair game, to the chagrin of some car owners.

Turkeys were raised to mature around the winter holidays. They were then dressed and taken to market. When market was discontinued they were sold to companies that transported them to the city to be dressed. There were three chicken houses on the farm and chickens were also raised, but on an irregular basis. These chickens were also dressed for market or sold to poultry companies. For a brief time the Benders raised laying hens for egg production, but it was never a major income business.

Pigs were raised to be used for a meat supply for the family and, at times, for market. Milt's butcher shop was a vital link in this chain of raising pork as well as beef for the family. However, this also was never a significant money producer.

Nevin said on different occasions that it was the dairy herd which served as the dependable income for the family, and he always looked out for his cows as well as the rest of the animals. Early the herd consisted of less than a dozen producers who were milked by hand. Milking was a family affair with both boys and girls helping. The children learned to milk at a fairly young age and then became a part of the team. Mildred remembers her fascination with milking. At nine years, she begged to be taught how to make that milk come. With several good lessons she mastered the skill, but she had failed to look at the implications. On many a cold winter morning she wished she had never learned.

Getting up to do the chores, especially in the winter, before having breakfast and getting ready for school, was a task shared by sisters and brothers and probably not looked forward to by anyone. There were many mornings when it was difficult to get everyone out of bed to head for the barn and begin their day. Emma remembers the mornings the cows would switch their tails in her face and hair, and her feeling when she left for school an hour or so later that the smell of her hair definitely told the story of her morning's work.

The cows needed milking both morning and evening. There were also the tasks of throwing down the ensilage from the silo, hay from the mow, cleaning out the stables, bedding the cows down in the evenings, and of course, straining, cooling, and caring for the milk that was to be sold. The dairy took a lot of teamwork. Over the years, the herd was increased to about 20 milk cows. The interior of the barn, devoted to the dairy, was expanded in the early 1950s to accommodate a second row of stanchions on the north side of the barn. Milking machines were bought around this time also, after Lura, Miriam, and Paul were married and Titus and Hilda were away winters at school. After the purchase of the milking machines and with the family decreased in size for most of the year, Nevin Jr. and Don assumed the primary responsibility for the dairy. Probably no one was sorry to see these changes.

BENDER POULTRY COMPANY

In 1949 when Paul turned 20, he and his father explored ways of working together in some business venture that would provide income for both the family and Paul. Paul had worked for his cousin, John Yoder, catching chickens with a number of other young men. Out of this work, he had started going to the Philadelphia Poultry Market with cull chickens left behind when the catchers were finished. Chickens weak, crippled, and not suitable for the dressing plant could be bought for little. Frequently the Philadelphia market supported a demand that made even a load of 10 to 25 coops of cull chickens worthwhile.

Through these Philadelphia contacts, certain dealers encouraged Paul to buy a truck that would hold 150 chicken coops and to buy healthy chickens for one of these dealers on Front Street named Izzi Polin. Nevin and Paul bought the truck with the understanding that it would be a shared venture. There were ups and downs in this business with sometimes moderate to good income, but there were also losses. The dealer promised one price for chickens, but then usually cut the margin just enough to keep it from being as profitable as it should have been.

Paul did not have the experience or the training and Nevin was not closely enough involved to assess adequately the long-term profitability of the business. They both thought the business was making money but gradually realized expenses were exceeding income. When this trend became apparent and it was clear that indebtedness had accumulated more than they had realized, both Nevin and Paul attempted to correct the downward spiral of the business. They had partly succeeded when one of the dealers went bankrupt and the others no longer provided profitable markets. Without an adequate cash flow the indebtedness caught up with them and they were forced to face the deficit. In 1952 they closed the poultry business.

Since Nevin had the farm as collateral, he attempted to get money from the bank. When he had some difficulty doing this, he appealed to several members of the church. Perhaps they did not fully understand that the business was no longer in operation and that repayment would come from farm income. At any rate, they agreed to help, but with the stipulation that they manage the family business. This was a severe blow to the pride of the Bender family and seemed to indicate a basic lack of trust which the family was unwilling to accept. The children remembered that through the years their father had taken risks for a number of persons in the church—persons for whom Nevin's cosignature opened fresh possibilities.

Not all would have been considered good business risks, although with Nevin's encouragement and trust in them, they usually came through. The family decided they would find another way to save the family farm. A close and longtime friend of Nevin's from Pennsylvania provided a loan and, through significant sacrifices on the part of the whole family, the debt was repaid and the family honor was saved.

During this time Nevin developed a bleeding stomach ulcer, possibly related to the stress. From the night that Nevin was rushed to the hospital in an ambulance until after his surgery the family lived with both hope and fear. Nevin's life hung in the balance as he faced serious surgery, no one knowing what might be found beyond the bleeding stomach ulcer. Additionally, the family's financial future was in a precarious position. This was especially heavy for Nevin as he tried to gain strength for the ordeal ahead. Esther was worried, too, but mostly for him. Alone in his hospital room the night before surgery, struggling to commit his family and the future to God, Nevin came to that "peace beyond understanding." He was held by divine love in a personal mystical way that was not new to him but which was especially profound that night. He knew deep in his soul that all would be well. He did not know how.

After he wrote a letter to his family in case he would not live through surgery, he slept soundly. He never spoke much of that night but shared it simply with his family. The relief for the family and for him was immense when he came through surgery successfully. In the days ahead, it became clear that all was well.

Nevin recovered from his surgery and the family gradually recovered from the economic crisis. Without any request from the family, a number of people from the congregation paid Nevin's hospital bill which was a significant one. For the family, this was a healing gesture.

After this hospital experience, Nevin and Esther borrowed a trailer and took a two-week vacation on the Delaware seacoast. They both thoroughly enjoyed relaxing in this peaceful atmosphere. They enjoyed daily fish for meals and even invited their children to the trailer for a fish fry. They were healed both in body and spirit after the difficult time they had been through together.

HOUSEWORK

While farming was the primary income producer, operating the house was a crucial part of the economic system. The housework—cleaning, washing, ironing, and cooking—as well as many other tasks— tended to be the work of the women and girls, though the men and boys helped at times. They certainly were not above such work. There was also the garden which provided fresh vegetables for the summer and for canning and freezing for the winter. Fruits such as apples, peaches, and berries were picked at nearby orchards and were also canned or frozen.

While the gardening and food preservation did not result in income, it helped tremendously on the other side of the ledger by keeping the family expenses for food to a minimum. Many hundreds of quarts of fruits and vegetables such as peaches, tomatoes, and applesauce were canned and frozen each summer and fall. This frequently became a project for the entire family. At butchering time, scores of quarts of beef cut up in chunks were also canned. The canned beef eaten with potatoes was a favorite.

WORK OUTSIDE THE HOME

From the time that 14-year-old Lura took a job at Hatfield's in Greenwood for $4.00 a week, "working out" was an important way that the family income was expanded. The girls, especially, were counted on for this. Sometimes it would be a two-week stint doing "baby cases," as they were called, which meant caring for a new baby and the mother, often along with other children in the family. Mildred and Emma remember taking a number of jobs like this. These were demanding jobs because a lot was expected of the "hired girl."

"The thing that was the hardest for me was being alone with the husband and children for a day or two before the wife and baby came home from the hospital," Emma recalls. "I usually cared for the baby during the time I was there, and found this responsibility rather overwhelming. I discovered that as a young Mennonite, it was assumed I was trustworthy, responsible, and a good cook, which frankly scared me, but I tried my best to live up to it, even if I had to fake the cooking a little!"

Sometimes the young women worked for an extended period of time when a mother was ill. This involved running the house and often involving practical nursing as well. Or the job might be as housekeeper, babysitter, and cook. Lura, who worked for the Adams family in Bridgeville before she married, passed the job on to Hilda. Similarly, Hilda, who worked for the Bowden family in Greenwood for a few months before entering nurses' training, passed that job on to Mildred. It is probably true that each of the girls remembers at least one job that she dreaded returning to on a Sunday night. Part of the problem was that each of the sisters would much rather have been at home working just as hard, but with people they loved being around. There were, of course, jobs that were quite pleasant as well.

Miriam taught school for one year, soon after high school, but decided it was not work she wanted to continue. Later she, Lura, and Hilda were fortunate to get jobs as nurses' aides in the Milford Hospital for quite a period of time. While not high-paying work, it was interesting and provided good experience. A sewing factory, first in Greenwood and later in Milford, provided income for most of the girls at some point. For both the sons and daughters in the family, money earned was turned over to the family until they became 21. This economic necessity was taken for granted. Again, there was the sense of working together for the sake of the family and, together, bringing in the needed income. (The exception was Lura, who married at 20.)

A job for two provided steady income for awhile during the difficult financial time following the failure of the chicken business. Instead of going ahead with their senior year at Lancaster Mennonite School (LMS), Emma and Mildred gave 24-hour care to the two elderly and wealthy Elfreth sisters in Milford. The steady income of $85.00 a week from fall of 1952 to fall of 1953, helped to tide the family over. In many ways, it was an ideal arrangement, with one sister working at night, getting some sleep, and often going home the next day to help with the work there while the other one took care of the cottage and "Aunt Sue and Aunt Lillie" during the day. This was one of many jobs that their Aunt Savannah found for them over the years.

Although Mildred was disappointed to delay her senior year at LMS, she soon began to talk with her parents about entering college the next fall instead of graduating from high school at age 20. Emma, however, wanted to get her high school diploma, so when she needed to stay out a second year she was determined to take her high school equivalency exams. This was not without regret. She remembers, "It was difficult to give up the special experiences that go along with a senior year, and I'm sure I did my share of complaining. I remember Mother, in an understanding and yet matter-of-fact way, telling me that experiences like this made a person strong, and it would be the making of me. I remember telling her, 'Well, I don't want to be made any more than I am. I'm made enough already!' I always felt she understood my frustration, but wasn't going to coddle me."

In fact, her mother was very encouraging as Emma continued the job a second year and began to prepare for her exams. Mildred left for Eastern Mennonite College that fall, entering on the basis of her GED scores. Titus went to EMC the same year to prepare for seminary. With the help of her mother, who even went with her to Newark to take her tests, Emma finally earned her diploma. She started college a year later, while Mildred stayed out to teach at Greenwood Mennonite School, but now bringing in a salary less than when she worked for the Elfreth sisters.

The sacrifices required to deal with this difficult time related to finances were shared by others in the family, as well. Nevin Jr. and Don attended the local high school to avoid the expenses of LMS, as well as to carry on the work of the farm.

Looking ahead to college helped them put up with attending public school their last two years.

The sale of the dairy herd in 1959, and a few years later of the farm equipment, enabled the family to pay off most of its debts. Later, the sale of the farm itself to Millard and Lura, enabled Nevin and Esther to finish paying off all their debts and to leave a modest distribution in their estate for their children, as well as a number of gifts to churches and church organizations.

Seven

EDUCATION

The more I learn, the more there is to learn.
—Nevin's frequent comment as new
informationchallenged answers earlier considered final.

NEVIN AND ESTHER'S FORMAL EDUCATION was somewhat limited in their youth. Esther, as noted earlier, attended eight grades in Juniata County. She was a quick learner and in the Bender family was the spelling resource. Her reliable answers meant that the dictionary rarely needed to be consulted. Nevin had attended "normal school," which was necessary for getting teacher certification. This was the equivalent of college level courses.

Nevin taught school for several years in Maryland before he was ordained as a minister. Later, when the Greenwood Mennonite School (GMS) was formed in 1929, Nevin became the first teacher. He later returned as principal and teacher in 1954-1956 at the special request of the school board. He also served as janitor and bus driver during that time. These duties were in addition to pastoral responsibilities and serving on the Executive Committee of the Conservative Mennonite Conference. He would get substitute teachers when he needed to be out of town to attend committee duties.

More important than Nevin and Esther's formal education was the attitude they brought to learning. They were open to new people, information, and ideas. This quality grew as they matured, including openness to the new ideas of their children as they returned from college with new experiences and insights. They listened and considered ways of looking at society to which they had not been previously exposed. Religious and social ideas in particular, which had been passed to them unchallenged for generations, were held up to scrutiny. From their parents' openness, the Bender children learned to listen to their own children and to be challenged by their new ideas and the new experiences they faced. Many of that next generation were not raised in the protected Mennonite environment of their parents. As some of them faced difficult challenges, their parents were made to stretch and by that stretching to become better educated.

When Nevin and Esther moved to Mississippi in the 1960s, they learned to respect the culture and social customs of the Choctaw Indians. Both white and African-American people were also a part of quite separate societies which existed in Philadelphia, Mississippi, and they learned from all of them.

Nevin's visit to Beirut, Lebanon, is covered more extensively later in this book but it is important to note that the attitude of open-mindedness and inquiry, which was evident in Beirut, was the attitude he developed and taught his children from an early age. Particularly in his last decade as a leader in Greenwood, he was open to those who were challenging the accepted practices of the church and this openness provided a fertile bed for education. This attitude provided Nevin and Esther's children the space to pursue learning both formally and informally.

For the beginning of their formal education, the Bender children all attended Greenwood Mennonite School (GMS), which was founded in spring 1928. Initially the Mennonite children of the Greenwood community attended the public school. After World War I, Delaware passed a law that students were required to salute the flag and recite the Pledge of Allegiance each morning. Some Mennonite students did not salute or recite the Pledge, and gradually the number increased after discussions in the church regarding the meaning of the Pledge. Specifically, the issue was whether or not the Pledge indicated the willingness to join the military and participate in war.

For about three years the refusal of Mennonite children to salute the flag was ignored. However, when some non-Mennonite children also began to refuse, the principal at Greenwood, Miss Gibson, asked the state superintendent of schools what she should do. She was advised to enforce the law. Several men, including Nevin, discussed the issue with board of education members, but their request for exemption was not granted.

In the newspaper *Every Evening News,* Nevin was reported to have called the flag an emblem of war and the report included other distortions, as well. Nevin responded with a letter to the editor, correcting the paper on his point of view. His letter begins by generously saying that "the article may be due either to misunderstanding or to the correspondent having been misinformed." He stated that Mennonites did not regard the flag as an emblem of war and that they respected the flag. Rather, he said, their opposition to saluting the flag was "primarily because in the Pledge is made a promise, which to be true to the promise, in the event of war would to us be a violation of such Scriptures as 'the weapons of our warfare are not carnal'—2 Corinhtians 10:14; 'Love your enemies'—Matthew 5:44; 'But I say unto you resist not evil'—Matthew 5:39."

Nevin's children remember his often recounting his conversation with the state superintendent of schools, H. V. Holloway. Nevin had asked him if the Pledge meant, in his view, that a person was agreeing to defend his country by participating in war, and Mr. Holloway indicated that if it didn't mean that, it didn't mean anything. It was this understanding of the

Pledge that served as the basis for the refusal of the Mennonite children to recite it.

The children continued to go to school, but when they persisted in their refusal to recite the Pledge, they were suspended. Miss Gibson wanted the children to come back and argued that the Pledge was recited without meaning by many students and could be recited by the Mennonite youth without them giving it importance. The Mennonites responded that they did not want to make meaningless pledges. When they would not agree to reconsider, the children were expelled. GMS was founded a month later under Nevin's active leadership. GMS has the distinction of being the first Mennonite school in the United States. Many other schools founded by Mennonite churches or groups followed during the next decades.

GMS began with Nevin as the first teacher, meeting in the church auditorium and using discarded books from the county public school system at Georgetown. The following year (1928-29) the school moved to the church basement with Nevin again as teacher. They continued to meet in the church for two more years with another teacher, Irene Zook, and in 1932 built a school on land donated by Nevin's father, Feldy. This first elementary school facility was known as the "Brown School" and served as the primary school for all the Bender children. This building was just across the field from the Bender home, an easy walk (or sometimes a mad dash) from their house.

In 1947 when a new church building was constructed, the old church building was moved to land owned by Milt and Savannah Swartzentruber. Savannah was Nevin's sister. Beginning in 1948 this building was used for grades seven to ten. The building was separated in 1950 with a partition down the middle made of large sliding panels so that it could be opened into one room for opening exercises as well as public meetings. Grades five and six were moved to that building. Now grades five to eight were on one side and grades nine to eleven were on the other, the eleventh grade having just been added that year. The eleventh grade was dropped in 1953. Grades one through four continued to meet at the "Brown School."

When a new GMS building was built in 1958 in a new location, the former school lots were returned to those who had donated them. The Brown School was sold and moved and the lot was returned to the Bender farm. The land remains a part of the farm owned by Millard and Lura at the writing of this book.

In the Brown School there were initially eight grades in one room taught by one teacher. Teachers were paid very low wages and often had only a high school education. Yet dedication on the part of both teachers and students helped to compensate for these limitations. Students, who later went to other schools, often excelled.

Lura completed all eight grades at GMS and then spent a year doing housework for a Hatfield family. After one year she attended Greenwood High, the public school, the Pledge no longer being required. In 1942 Lura as a sophomore and Miriam as a freshman went to Eastern Mennonite School (EMS) in Harrisonburg, Virginia. Lura graduated from there in 1945.

In 1943 when Miriam was ready for tenth grade and Paul was ready for ninth, GMS was expanded to include those grades. Eight students in two grades met in the basement of the school called "Cozy Corners." They became known as the "Victory Eight" and sang as an octet. They even toured to sing at nearby Mennonite churches. All of the students were first cousins taught by Esther Swartzentruber, also their first cousin.

After attending GMS for the available grades, the final years of high school for the five oldest were taken at Lancaster Mennonite School in Pennsylvania (LMS) or EMS, in Virginia. Miriam attended EMS for the final two years and Paul graduated from LMS after attending one year at EMS. Hilda and Titus both graduated from LMS, after attending for two years. Mildred and Emma attended GMS for the 11 years which were temporarily available at that time and then Mildred was accepted into college by taking the GED Exam. Emma took state tests on four specific subjects to finish her high school requirements and get her diploma. After ten years at GMS, Nevin and Don both attended public school at Greenwood High for their final two years

Class sizes varied considerably when the Bender children were attending GMS. Nevin Jr.'s class had only three students during most of the years and was the smallest. Classes more typically had five to eight students. Since different grades were combined in the same room the number of students in one room was usually between 30 and 40. The total enrollment ranged from around 55 in early 1940 to around 85 in the mid 1950s when the youngest children finished.

Life in these multi-grade one- or two-room schools was unusual compared to today's education. It was unusual for that time as well, although not unknown, as other rural parts of the country sometimes had such schools. At Greenwood the teacher would call one grade at a time to the front of the room for a particular subject while the other classes worked on their assignments. The class in the front could be distracting, but the plus side was that faster learners could benefit from listening in on the older classes as they were reciting.

Games were played at recess. Softball, a favorite choice in the older grades, was usually coed. Prisoners' base was also popular. In this game a player was empowered to tag and imprison a player from the opposing team by leaving base last. Prisoners could then be freed by being tagged by one's teammate before that teammate was tagged by the imprisoning team.

In the spring, the younger children entertained themselves for long periods of time catching tadpoles in the newly formed ponds in the low lying area near the Brown School. "Handy over" was also an elementary grade game in which groups got on separate sides of the school building and threw a ball over the roof. If a receiving team member caught the ball, that player could run around the building and if she threw the ball and hit someone, the person hit joined her team. The strategy in running around the building was to keep secret the identity of the empowered person with the ball! The teams were on the honor system as to whether or not the ball had actually been caught.

While support for elementary and high school education was strong at the Greenwood Mennonite church, support for higher education was mixed. Nevin and Esther were unusual in their full support for higher education. Since a significant number of people in the church had recently come from the Amish, some of them were quite fearful of higher education and its potential for eroding the traditions of the people. There was a particular aversion to attending non-Mennonite colleges where it was feared that students might lose their faith.

However, the Greenwood church was more progressive on higher education than some of the others in the Conservative Mennonite Conference, due in part to Nevin's advocacy. Some churches of the conference did not allow higher education. The Casselman Church in Grantsville, Maryland, was the congregation from which the founders of the Greenwood Church had come. Those who attended college from Casselman were expelled from the church, so some young people from that congregation transferred their membership to Greenwood to attend college. These included Paul Peachey and some of his siblings, who were second cousins of the Bender children.

Nevin and Esther were not fearful of exposure to broader education and supported their children's exploration of new ideas. Clearly Nevin and Esther were also open to and influenced by those ideas. The Bender children were encouraged and even'—particularly the younger ones—expected to attend college. There was no difference in the educational expectations for the sons and daughters and it was with surprise that the children later encountered friends whose parents did discriminate—who only expected their sons to attend college, since their daughters would "just end up getting married anyway."

When the three older Bender children completed high school, higher education didn't seem a viable option. Few of the Greenwood community were going and money was scarce. Besides, there were more immediate and practical concerns. Later after they were married and had small families, some of them made the decision to go to college at a time in their lives when such a decision presented a significant challenge and required sacrifice. Millard, Paul, and Ginny each made such a decision.

Beginning with Hilda, the rest of the Bender children went on to post high school education before marriage and not long after completing their high school or its equivalency. Hilda completed her nursing degree just three months after her marriage to Merlin Swartz and later finished her college degree, while living in Beirut. The next five attended Eastern Mennonite College (EMC) in Harrisonburg, Virginia for their undergraduate education. Three of these met their future spouses at EMC. Over half of the siblings and their spouses went on for post graduate degrees in theology related studies, counseling, education, science, and social work.

But the degrees themselves were not important. Each received what they needed to do the work they chose to do. More importantly they carried a spirit of exploration and adventure as well as openness to new ideas, a spirit they learned from their parents. For some this took the form of international travel and work. Hilda and Merlin lived in Jordan, later in Beirut, Lebanon, and then returned much later to Syria for a year of research. They traveled throughout the Middle East and Europe.

Millie, enrolled in post-graduate work, and Nevin also lived in Beirut while Hilda and Merlin were there and traveled in other parts of the Middle East and also through Europe. Merlin's education and scholarship in Islamic studies influenced the expanded thinking of Nevin as well as many others of the Bender family.

Some achieved on-the-job education in diverse areas of the United States. Nevin and Lourene oversaw the purchase and development of a camp in Vermont, which continues successfully to the present. In Mississippi, Titus and Ann, along with Mildred, Emma, Glenn, Nevin, and Esther started Pine Lake Fellowship Camp, which also continues successfully today. None of these had experience in such efforts but with creativity and self education in the skills they needed they were successful in these endeavors. These Mississippi folks also received a cross-cultural experience in the Choctaw community. Titus in particular was a leader in the cauldron of racial ferment that was Mississippi in the 1960s.

Don in Atlanta lived four blocks from Ebenezer Baptist Church, where he often went to hear Dr. King preach before King's assassination. He and Judy, whom he later married, expanded their horizons by their involvement in the civil rights and peace movements. Later, Don learned on the job as he worked to revitalize several in-town neighborhood business districts as a real estate redeveloper.

Paul and Ginny spent time in Oregon and in Kansas City experiencing very different social settings. Returning near where they grew up, they invited African-Americans and people of other backgrounds to their home. This expanded their horizons; they toured the world from home. Paul's clarity and courage in speaking and acting for racial justice influenced the commitment his younger siblings made to this effort. Expanded understanding was inevitable for those who took a clear position on racial issues in Lower Delaware, which only became desegregated at around the same time as the deep South.

Elmer educated himself through extensive reading and the development of an impressive library in biblical studies and psychology. Lura, also an avid reader, didn't let the lack of a formal degree limit her education. Miriam learned much through hosting many people, including international guests.

Millard expanded his horizons not only by his degrees in science but also as he served as a bridge builder in a sometimes divided Greenwood Mennonite community.

Most importantly, as education and experiences have influenced Bender siblings in different directions of thinking, the spirit that allows all to continue their educational growth is the commitment to hear and respect each other even when the other's ideas are different.

Every one of the Bender family and their spouses have at one time or another been teachers, whether in graduate school, college, elementary school, high school, elder care, or theology related schools. Several of the Bender family taught at the Greenwood Mennonite School. Miriam, soon after high school, taught for one year in 1947-48. Mildred taught with her father from 1954-56 after one year of college and taught again after graduating, from 1958-60. Emma taught part of one year in 1956-57, and Millard was later to teach and serve as principal from 1959-63, which was after the last Bender children had graduated. Lura was often called on for substitute teaching.

The year after Esther died, Nevin, accompanied by Mildred, went to Beirut to live with Merlin and Hilda and their family. While there he spent much time in healing reflection as he walked the shores of the Mediterranean. He also took courses at the Near East School of Theology (NEST), an ecumenical Protestant seminary which trained ministers for work in that region as well as Africa and Asia and was racially, culturally, and religiously mixed. Nevin thrived in this atmosphere as he studied ideas which would have been considered less than orthodox in his earlier years. Merlin commented, "I was struck with his eagerness to learn about things he hadn't had time to pursue before."

Clearly Nevin and Esther's attitude of inquiry and openness to new ideas and influenced the entire Bender family. Their children have pursued the education needed for their chosen fields and opened themselves to new cultures and new ideas. The next generation, Nevin and Esther's grandchildren, have continued this tradition, and it continues as well into the next generation— their great-grandchildren. Their legacy is one of remaining open to new ideas and experiencing learning as a lifetime process.

Eight

CHURCH LIFE

All you preach is love, love, love.

—Comment by a somewhat
frustrated member of an audience when Nevin preached.

A DISCUSSION OF THE CHURCH AT GREENWOOD is critical to understanding the Bender family, because the church with all its facets was central in their life together. Nevin served as a minister in the church beginning in 1918, seven years before his marriage to Esther, and was ordained as a bishop in 1933. He resigned from both positions in 1960. It was in the ministry that he excelled and on which he focused his life. The economics of the family suffered from this focus, since it was an unpaid position. Occasionally, this economic difficulty became an issue to some church members because they did not consider him to be providing properly for his family. Church life was also central because most activities—not only religious, but also educational, recreational, social, and even economic—happened within the church community.

As the leader of the church, the bishop was also the most visible public leader of the community. Being a minister, and more particularly a bishop, was regarded as the highest position a man could be asked to fill, though it was not considered appropriate to seek such a position openly. The Mennonite church at this time also had what they referred to as a plural ministry. Since the ministry was nonprofessional and unpaid, it was shared among several men. The different ideas and leadership styles of the ministers was often at the heart of congregational conflict.

FIRST LEADERSHIP CONTROVERSY

The first major church controversy involving Nevin lasted from 1935-1940. One critical issue was who would have the right to preach and another was Nevin's leadership style. Levi Bontrager, who had been ordained as an Amish minister, moved to Greenwood in 1933 and in 1934 was accepted as a minister in the church. He was a more conservative man and his positions on questions of traditional dress contrasted sharply with Nevin's. They also disagreed over leadership style. Were the ministers the authority of the church—Levi's position—or were they to lead and seek the consensus of the congregation? Nevin's approach was the latter.

Also involved in this controversy was Noah Swartzentruber (brother to three of Nevin's brothers-in-law). Noah had been ordained as a deacon in the mission at Flint, Michigan, where he had preaching privileges. He decided to leave the city in late 1934 and moved to Greenwood with his family. He was accepted as a deacon at Greenwood, but was not extended preaching privileges. The position of the Conservative Conference, at this time, was mixed on the issue of whether deacons should preach. Noah expected to be able to preach and was supported by more conservative men, who generally opposed Nevin's leadership.

Noah and Levi brought the various matters to a head and the conference intervened. As a result, Noah was prohibited from preaching, Levi lost his preaching privileges, and Nevin was asked to discontinue his bishop responsibilities from November 1938 to April 1940, but he did continue as a minister.

Nevin Jr. was born in the middle of the controversy (July 1938) and Don several days after Nevin resumed his responsibilities (April 1940).

Lura remembers long discussions after church during which she lingered near her father listening. The tone of those opposing her father seemed quite harsh. These impressions were deeply imbedded in Lura, a child of eight or nine years at the onset of the controversy.

NEVIN'S MINISTRY

Nevin's home congregation was Greenwood, a part of the Conservative Amish Mennonite Conference. While the word "Amish" was later dropped from the name, the conference was generally a blend of Mennonite and Amish ideas. For many leaders, education beyond high school was feared rather than valued. Some of the early correspondence to Nevin reveals marginal educational standards among some ministers. Many new members of the Conservative Conference had recently converted from the Amish Church, where education beyond the eight grades at parochial schools was much discouraged. Nevin, though also of recent Amish descent, was thus a bit unusual with the value he placed on higher education. He was self-taught beyond his formal training and maintained a spirit of inquiry and learning until his death.

Preaching styles differed widely in the conference and in the Mennonite church generally. Many of those who were used widely for evangelistic meetings were very emotional preachers, and focused on the consequences of not living by the standards of the church. That style of preaching usually resulted in higher numbers of people responding to the invitational hymns during the course of the meetings and, for many, those numbers equaled success. Nevin by contrast had a very quiet but eloquent manner of speaking, and was used widely for special meetings, including evangelistic meetings, in both the Conservative Conference and the wider Mennonite church. His sermons were well organized and his outline notes quite clear and logical.

Nevin's themes varied, and he was known for the many biblical passages he had committed to memory. One primary topic for him was love. Nevin emphasized the need for love and understanding and believed that any problem could be worked out, if people would listen carefully and try to understand each other. A member of a congregation where he once preached came up and said with some frustration, "All you preach is love, love, love!" Nevin interpreted this as an unintended affirmation.

Nevin's sermon notes from as far back as 1945 show an emphasis that is remarkable for those times, when so much attention focused on the negatives of sin and its consequences. He always emphasized the importance of family relationships. Notes from that era on a sermon entitled "The Home" contains as point 1, "Having esteem and showing respect that is due," with the subpoint, "Parents teach much by example." Point 3 was "Considering each other's highest good in the marriage relationship." Another sermon on the home began with the first point, "The characteristics of thoughtfulness."

Nevin tried to take a "redemptive attitude," as he put it, toward those who were harsh with him. One member, who wrote a letter to Nevin in 1949, said first that he thought the articles of discipline read at a previous "Council Meeting," should be burned. Later in his letter he said, "I appreciate the way you visited me when I was in sin and it had much to do to make me want to come back." This sentiment indicates Nevin's desire never to write someone off. Given enough time and love, he expected everyone to find his or her way. A familiar phrase, at the conclusion of many of his prayers indicates this inclusiveness. He prayed that when we are finished here on earth that God would receive us "without the loss of one." Increasingly, this became a central theme of his life.

Nevin served on the Executive Committee of the Conservative Mennonite Conference from 1944 until 1957. There was a decision in which he was involved in 1956 which led to the second major conflict or "church trouble" at Greenwood. In his capacity as an Executive Committee member, he was called into other churches to help resolve differences when they had difficulty resolving the issues themselves. These difficulties usually centered on leadership conflict and conflicts regarding distinctive dress. This emphasis on distinctive dress was no doubt influenced by the arrival of so many new members to the Conservative Conference from the Amish tradition.

The original separation of the Mennonite and Amish churches in Europe had been over the issue of whether or not those who left the church should be placed under the ban—shunned or socially ostracized. The Amish believed in the ban. Thus, a family member who left the church was not allowed to eat at the same table as the Amish members of the family. A communication to Nevin during his tenure on the Executive Committee wonders whether they should "place . . . into the ban" some folks who were not conforming or whether they should be "patient with them a little longer." The committee was encouraged to go to the problem church to help find a solution.

Lura recalls that the church and even the Bender family initially practiced a form of the ban. A man who stayed with the Bender family was a church member and was also an alcoholic. When he reverted to alcohol, against the church discipline, he was served at a small table next to the family table. He was included in the table conversation and not treated unkindly. Under Nevin's leadership, the church later discontinued this practice, apparently without any serious objection.

While the practice of shunning for meals was discontinued, those not practicing the rules of the church were not allowed to take communion. Even on that issue, as indicated by sermon notes, Nevin was careful, urging that the church not "use communion as a whip." This was an obvious reference to those who wanted to hold back from communion those who were not following the church rules. Those who didn't take communion were at best second class members and therefore in imminent danger of losing their "salvation." The ministers who denied communion in this way, to a degree held the "keys to the kingdom," much like their counterparts in the sixteenth-century Catholic Church. It was against that authority that the Anabaptists (early Mennonites) rebelled, believing rather in the "priesthood of believers."

Nevin was much in demand as a speaker, not only in the Conservative Mennonite Conference, but even in other Mennonite conferences and other denominations. His children were often surprised at the number of places, far from home, where they discovered people who had known and looked up to Nevin because of his positive and loving manner. Young people particularly responded to him because his warmth toward young people stood in contrast to the more rigid and critical attitudes they sometimes experienced from many other ministers.

Nevin was gone from his family for as long as six weeks at a time, although this was seldom. A two-week period away from home was not unusual. He later believed he would have been wiser to decline some of the opportunities and spend more time with his family. In those early years in the Mennonite church, it was considered inappropriate to refuse any call to preach, so invitations were usually accepted unless there was a schedule conflict.

Nevin's many absences from the family left Esther to carry much of the responsibility at home, which she did with grace and a good spirit. In retrospect, one is impressed with the critical role she filled with such a quiet ease that it was almost taken for granted. She was a competent partner who made Nevin's more public contribution possible. For example, as noted earlier, summer of 1948 was a crisis time for the family. While Nevin was gone for six weeks of meetings in Canada, Paul overturned a tractor on his groin which could easily have been fatal; 10 year-old Nevin Jr. burned his hand badly narrowly escaping electrocution while standing in water in the basement trying to unplug a sump pump. Also during this time, Mildred came down with rheumatic fever. Esther assured Nevin by phone that she could handle it all!

Those who describe Esther simply as a silent, supportive companion, did not know her well, much to their loss. Supportive? Certainly. Silent? No. She could be quiet, just as she could be outgoing. When it came to difficulties related to church leadership, Esther was far from neutral, or simply a passive onlooker. She supported Nevin completely. There was little they did not talk over together and she felt free to disagree with him and introduce a different perspective. She believed in Nevin implicitly, and she saw much more deeply into issues, attitudes, and motivations than some gave her credit for.

On one occasion a member of the church came to the Bender home to critique Nevin's leadership. Through the study walls, where they were talking, Esther heard sharp tones and words of relentless criticism. It seemed clear to Esther that the member was posing in a supportive role by putting the harsh criticism in terms of "But Nevin, people are talking." When the church member emerged from the study he greeted Esther warmly, "And how are you, Esther?" Esther's reply was cryptic and honest, and her usual warmth was absent. "I'm not very good," was the response she allowed to hang between them. Daughter Hilda was a bit surprised and also proud of her mother's honesty and loyalty. When they were alone, her mother finished the conversation with another honest and for her, vehement statement. "If they can't be nice to Papa, they don't need to be nice to me."

MISSION WORK

One of the primary reasons the Feldy Bender family moved to Delaware was to establish a mission church and to reach out into the community. That emphasis was central to the Greenwood church life.

After the Greenwood church formed a mission board in 1942, a period of organized mission activity began. The distribution of *The Way*, a monthly evangelistic publication, began shortly after the formation of the board. This tract was distributed door to door by young people, one Sunday afternoon a month in the small, nearby city of Milford. Activities such as cottage meetings and jail and hospital visitation began later. A musical quartet and a speaker were the usual fare and were a regular Sunday afternoon activity of many young people, including the Bender children. The cottage meetings were held in private homes where people were confined to bed. At the hospitals the quartet would sing a couple of songs from each wing of each floor of the hospital while the leader went to visit with the patients.

In 1946 a mission sunday school was begun in Wilmington and in 1948 Melville Nafziger, accompanied by his wife Esther, went from Greenwood to serve as pastor. In the early 1950s churches were started near Milford (Laws Mennonite Church) and Dover (Central Mennonite Church). Laws, since it was only about ten miles from Greenwood, provided an opportunity for people who wanted a smaller, more intimate fellowship. Central Congregation was located near an Amish community to accommodate those who were making their first step away from the Amish traditions.

In 1950 churches were started by the Conservative Conference Mission Board, using Greenwood people as leaders in Kentucky, and in Gladys and Schuyler Virginia.

Many of Nevin and Esther's children later became involved in what was described at that time as mission work. Their son Titus and his wife Ann went to Meridian, Mississippi, to found a church in 1957, and their daughter Hilda and her husband Merlin went to Jordan to work with a Mennonite Central Committee (MCC) refugee program. The same year Nevin Jr. and his wife Lourene went to Vermont to take a pastorate in 1962. Nevin and Esther, followed in a couple of years by their daughters Mildred and Emma and Emma's husband Glenn, went to Mississippi in 1960, to work among the Choctaw Nation of Native Americans. Millard and their oldest daughter, Lura at Tressler, near Greenwood, and Elmer and their second daughter Miriam in Au Gres, Michigan, ministered in their local churches, with outreach into the community. Their oldest son Paul and his wife Ginny went to Kansas City to take a pastorate in 1968. Their son Don served in Atlanta's inner city for two years in the mid-1960s also with MCC, working and living with African-American youth. Not all were comfortable with the label "missionary" as they came to value the contributions of other cultures and religions.

CHURCH MEETING SITES

Church meetings were central to community life at Greenwood. When they first arrived in 1914, the families met in homes for worship and Sunday school. Later they gathered in a public school house, but had to move from there during World War I, because of community opposition to their pacifist position. They then met in a barn and other homes until the first church was built in 1920. The first church building was a white frame structure 30 feet by 40 feet. Twenty-seven years later it was packed to overflowing and a new church was built. This was a brick one completed in 1947, which was more than double the size of the first church building and which is still in use at the writing of this book.

SUNDAY SCHOOL AND WORSHIP SERVICES

There were many religious and social gatherings through the week but the focal point was Sunday school and worship time on Sunday morning. A cappella singing was an important part of the service. There was a song leader for the Sunday school hour and another for the worship service. The Sunday school began with appropriate comments on the lesson of the day by the superintendent before everyone divided up into their separate classes. Teachers were appointed for the lower grades while the youth and adult classes elected their own. Not all ministers were talented speakers and the morning worship service could seem long, especially for young children. The Sunday school began at 9:30 a.m. and the end of the morning worship service came at around 11:30 to 12:00.

Everyone was also expected to attend Sunday evening services. That event usually consisted of several topics taken from the *Program Builder* put out by Mennonite Publishing House. These three or four topics were assigned to people by a program committee, which also selected the moderator and song leader. The service usually lasted about one and one-half hours but people often stayed around after church to visit or to debate issues.

The young people usually gathered outside after the Sunday evening service to discuss their own issues. The boys had their group on one side of the entry and the girls on the other. It was at this time that boys often asked the girls for dates, with the more timid ones waiting until the crowd had thinned a bit, as it was obvious to all present what was happening when a boy crossed to the group of girls. A refusal could be embarrassing. The more organized boys would call before the service to make arrangements and to avoid the challenge of asking in front of an audience.

PRAYER MEETINGS

Prayer meetings were held on Wednesday evenings and attendance was about 25 percent of the Sunday morning group. After a single presentation or talk, usually by a lay person, the balance of the meeting was devoted to prayer requests and then praying together with all who wished volunteering a prayer. Almost all prayers in church services and prayer meetings, except closing benedictions, were done kneeling on the floor with elbows on the bench seats, facing the rear of the church.

EVANGELISTIC MEETINGS

Evangelistic meetings happened about twice a year, usually just before communion. They encompassed two weekends and the week in between. For nine consecutive nights the congregation gathered to hear the visiting evangelist preach. Each meeting was preceded by a short prayer service attended by the most dedicated, in a small room behind the pulpit. The evangelists' styles varied considerably and some were quite dramatic.

At the end of each service invitational hymns were sung while the evangelist urged the members of the audience to consider if they were right with God. Those who did not feel that they were right with God, were asked to raise their hands or stand, and after the service to come forward to receive counseling. Raising one's hand at an evangelistic service was also the usual method for people to show they wanted to join the church, usually between the ages of eight and twelve. It was also a time for people who felt they had fallen away, to repent. Some members of the Bender family remember more vividly than fondly, raising their hands during the course of most revival series, just to be sure, because the consequences of not being right with God were painted quite vividly.

As each series neared its end, the emotion often became so intense that several family members who were too young to act themselves, recall urging their mother to raise her hand. It seemed important that someone act to avoid the awful consequences being pictured. Esther always assured her children that she felt she was right with God.

Nevin Jr. particularly remembers his uneasiness and even fear during some revival meetings. Sensitive, and not one to talk easily about his feelings, he struggled with a fear that he needed to respond in some way to repeated invitations at some of these meetings. Yet he could not bring himself to raise his hand or put himself through the steps "required." He was greatly relieved when his father approached him and wondered if he wanted to join the "instruction class" in preparation for baptism. His "yes" helped him feel he had escaped the dire consequences focused upon by visiting evangelists.

It may not be unrelated that Nevin Jr. also struggled with severe nightmares over an extended period of time as a child. His siblings remember their father holding him and trying to wake him as he cried out in terror. He finally broke free of these frightening dreams.

Perhaps it was some of these early experiences related to revival meetings that caused Nevin Jr. to turn from an approach of fear, becoming a giving and compassionate pastor a number of years later, with a message much more like his father's than "scary" evangelists.

COMMUNION AND FOOTWASHING

The evangelistic meetings were usually followed a week later by "counsel meeting," at which time each member was asked to consider whether they were prepared to "take communion." To participate was a solemn responsibility, for to take part "unworthily" was, in the words of St. Paul in the Bible, to "eat and drink damnation unto oneself." Those who felt themselves prepared stood to indicate that they were at peace with God and each other. Nevin usually followed with personal counseling for those who had not stood or who in other ways had indicated their uncertainty about their spiritual health. The communion service followed the Sunday after counsel meeting.

Held twice a year, communion was a serious and important event. The service included a sermon followed by eating of the bread and drinking of the wine (grape juice). Then came foot washing in which everyone paired off, same gender only, to take turns washing each others' feet. Foot washing was practiced to obey Jesus' command that his disciples should follow his example at the Last Supper. While many denominations observed communion or the mass, only the Mennonites and a few other small groups practiced foot washing by the entire congregation. (To some denominations this practice, no doubt, seemed rather inconvenient and, perhaps, even somewhat embarrassing.) Mennonites taught that they should practice "all things," observed foot washing, as they believed Jesus had instructed them to do.

QUARTERLY MEETINGS

Quarterly meetings were sometimes called all-day meetings. There would be one or two visiting speakers to address a particular theme, beginning with a Saturday evening meeting. The regular Sunday morning service was followed by a break for people to go home for the big Sunday dinner. Services resumed again at 2:00 p.m. There would be another break around 4:00 p.m., for people to go home to do their farm chores and eat supper, and the evening meeting would resume at 7:00 or 7:30. As the title suggests, these special meetings happened about four times a year, and children, especially ministers' children, were expected to attend all of them.

If this schedule seems a bit demanding for children and teenagers, one is reminded that the belief was that the road to heaven was narrow and the entry very restricted. This provided the necessary motivation to do all one could, in light of the alternatives.

YOUTH ACTIVITIES

Activities for youth in the Greenwood church were numerous and provided an opportunity for social interaction. There was an activity for most nights of the week which weren't already taken up with special church meetings. Almost all recreational, social, educational, and religious activities took place under the auspices of the church. Even the school was operated by the church, so the church permeated nearly every aspect of life.

The literary society was a youth organization which met once a month and provided a time for singing, special music, poetry recitation, and even some drama. Adults were sometimes invited as special guests. The Bender children remember the night Nevin and Esther sang "Precious Memories." Several programs consisted of debates on such topics as "Resolved That the Women's Place Is in the Home" and "Resolved That Schools Should Be Racially Integrated." Prolonged and vigorous informal debate often followed the formal event.

This was also an early opportunity for leadership experience since officers changed every six months. Formal membership began at age 16 and attendance was taken at each meeting. A business meeting came at the end and had to do with various issues about which there was often vigorous debate. Roberts Rules of Order were followed, more or less carefully depending on the president and parliamentarian. The final input of the evening was from the critic, giving his or her opinion of the program and pointing out opportunities for improvement.

The chorus was an important part of youth life. Chorus practice was held every week, usually Tuesday nights, and church programs were given during special seasons. There were also occasional trips to nearby churches in the Greenwood area and to Mennonite churches on the Delmarva Peninsula. Many members of the Bender family, including Paul, Titus, Nevin Jr., and Millard served as directors of the chorus during the 1950s.

A missionary project was another activity, which consisted of the raising of a crop, with the proceeds going to a "mission station." The young people would plant, cultivate, and harvest the crop which was usually about an acre, and send the proceeds to the missionary project of their choice, decided on by a vote.

CHURCH LEADERSHIP

In Greenwood as in many parts of the (Old) Mennonite Church of the 1920s-1950s, the ministers were not professionally trained. At most they usually had a high school education, and received no income for their work. Ministers were chosen from the congregation by the use of the lot, which has been described earlier. There were usually two ministers in the first 25 years at Greenwood and from then until Nevin's resignation in 1960, there were usually three in the Greenwood congregation. Ministers, who served the nearby churches at Laws and Central were a part of the same ministers group and would preach at times at Greenwood.

The question of ordaining women at Greenwood did not even surface as an issue at this time. St. Paul's view of the role of women as expressed in his letter to the Corinthians in the Bible was definitive for many Mennonites. Paul asked women to cover their heads when they prayed, to show that they submitted to men as men submitted to God. It would have been considered a violation of the biblical order to ordain women. Women did teach Sunday school classes for children or other women, and could participate in the Sunday evening presentations referred to as "topics" and in leading singing. They were not elected as choristers, Sunday school superintendents, or for other congregational roles through 1960. The youth group leadership, however, did not have gender limitations.

Nevin was ordained in 1918 and the two older ministers in the congregation soon moved away, leaving Nevin as the sole minister. Nevin's brother-in-law, Eli Swartzentruber, was ordained in 1921 and the two served together in the ministry for many years, generally in harmony until the final controversy in 1956-1960. The first minor controversy regarding the wearing of buttons on coats in 1923-24, happened while Nevin was single, and was previously discussed.

Until 1933, the Greenwood congregation was served by Bishop John L. Mast, who lived over 200 miles away. Some people felt there should be a local bishop, but as on most matters in Greenwood, there were differing opinions about how this should be done. Some wanted to ordain a third minister, no doubt to broaden the choices, since the bishop would be chosen from among the ministers. Feldy Bender, though ailing, went around to the various members and secured their approval to ordain a bishop, though it was given reluctantly in at least one case. Nevin and Eli were in the lot and Nevin was ordained.

Alvin Mast was ordained as a third minister for Greenwood in 1946 and was chosen as bishop of Laws church in 1959. He assumed the bishop duties of Greenwood when Nevin resigned in 1960. Alvin was a low-keyed, likeable man and usually avoided taking controversial positions. Other ordained ministers were: Melville Nafziger (1953), Mark Swartzentruber (1953), Daniel Yoder (1955), Amos Bontrager (1957), Owen Guengerich (1959), and Eli Bontrager (1959). All of these ministers were cousins or married to cousins of the Bender family. Melville was ordained to serve in Wilmington.

When Laws began, Alvin was asked to serve as their pastor and Mark was then ordained to serve in Greenwood. Serving with two older men, his father and uncle, he appeared to be in line to become bishop. During his first three years of ministry he was very supportive of Nevin. Though he had limited exposure outside of Greenwood, he was a fairly gifted speaker and had a strong following due in part to his conservative convictions. He believed that the traditional plain clothes should be required of all church office holders. When Nevin, as a member of the Conference Executive Committee, supported the position of the congregation in Alden, New York, that plain clothes would not be required for office holders, Mark was concerned that this would happen in Greenwood also and began actively to oppose Nevin's positions.

On April 28, 1957, Amos Bontrager was ordained and served as assistant pastor at Central Church in Dover, before moving in early 1958 to Wilmington, to serve as pastor in the Mennonite mission church. Amos was married to Lois, the daughter of Eli and Amelia Swartzentruber. Ministerial relationships were difficult when he entered the ministry and served at Dover and he initially tried to stay neutral. The lines had been drawn, however, and he carefully took a less rigid position, more in line with Nevin's views. He was only in the Greenwood area for less than a year after his ordination, and left well before Nevin's resignation in 1960.

On June 14, 1959, Owen Guengerich was ordained in a service packed with especially high drama. Ministerial relationships were strained and the new minister would possibly be one of two ministers from whom the new bishop would be chosen. The congregation saw its direction hanging in the balance.

The choices were clear among the four candidates. Millard Benner and Titus Bender were the son-in-law and son of Nevin Bender. Both were college educated and Titus also had seminary training. Both favored a consensus style leadership and were considered more progressive on the issues the congregation faced. Owen Guengerich and Earl Swartzentruber were the son-in-law and son of Eli Swartzentruber. Both were considered more conservative. Millard Benner had been invited to be the pastor of the nearby Tressler Mennonite Church but delayed his acceptance until after the selection of the minister at Greenwood. Titus Bender was in Meridian, Mississippi, and asked that the congregation decide whether or not he should be in the lot in absentia, considering that he was obligated to Meridian for several more months.

This set the stage for the drama which Don remembers viewing from the vantage point of the balcony, because every seat in the main auditorium was taken. The vote to include Titus in the lot was substantially more than the majority needed. The evening climaxed with Owen Guengerich being selected by lot. Millard, shortly thereafter, accepted the pastorate of Tressler. Later in 1959, Eli Bontrager was chosen for the ministry in the Laws congregation.

LAY LEADERSHIP

The two men who started the Greenwood Church, Val Bender and Will Tressler, were laymen and lay leadership continued to be important in the church. With ministers not having formal training, an active decision to enter the ministry was less likely. Also the fact that they were not paid enhanced the importance of lay leadership. Those chosen to be in the lot for the ministry were usually already effective lay leaders. Thus, for those who felt called to the ministry, there was motivation to develop as an effective lay leader.

The Sunday school superintendents were the most visible officers. They were the "masters of ceremony" for the Sunday school hour, which preceded the morning worship service each Sunday morning. Many people were used as Sunday school teachers, as noted earlier. The adult through the youth classes elected their own teachers annually, while the younger class teachers were appointed by the superintendents.

Four choristers (head song leaders) were elected annually by the congregation: two for the worship service and two to share the Sunday school service. The music for each service, usually four hymns each, was chosen by the chorister. In some evening services, people from the audience were invited to lead songs of their choice.

SECOND MAJOR CONTROVERSY

On May 13, 1956, Nevin, as a member of the Executive Committee of the Conservative Conference went to Alden, New York, to help that congregation decide what position to take regarding plain dress. Based on the counsel of the congregation, the ministers recommended that the plain coat and cape be encouraged but not required for holding church offices. That decision raised fear on the part of some of the ministers in Greenwood that it would only be a matter of time until the same decision would be made in their congregation.

Nevin returned to Greenwood, and the annual school picnic followed in early June. Don remembers well the conversation which began in the afternoon of the school picnic between Nevin and Mark Swartzentruber. At the end of the day, Don and Nevin Jr. waited in the car for over an hour and then finally went home to do the chores. They returned and again waited until long after dark on that late spring night, as Nevin and Mark stood talking in front of the school house—the original church building—by a gold fishpond fashioned out of an old bath tub, buried in the ground. Finally, that initial discussion ended late at night but many more hard discussions followed.

The issues at Greenwood became focused on whether or not men who wore the lapel instead of the plain coat and women, who didn't wear the cape, should be able to hold office. A related issue was whether or not people should be expelled from membership for owning television. The more profound underlying issue continued to be whether the ministers should make decisions about these matters for the congregation or whether the congregation should have a voice in the decision. In the minds of many, the heart of the issue in the struggle of this congregation was whether the primary influence would be Amish, where the authority of leadership was recognized, or Anabaptist, with its concept of the priesthood of believers.

By 1958 there was an impasse at Greenwood. Nevin's notes reflect his frustration with the situation. He felt that some of his coworkers were insisting that he use coercion to enforce the wearing of the plain coat and cape, which he felt he could not do. They apparently had no suggestions to break the impasse, other than to insist that Nevin support their position or resign. In one note he indicated that information which had been conveyed to the conference leaders by his coworkers had been accepted as fact, with no opportunity for discussion. Two members of the Executive Committee asked him to resign based on this information without the benefit of hearing the facts from his perspective. He responded to them, "I desire to face all the accusations made against me before unbiased brethren."

In a page entitled, "Offers I Have Made," Nevin lists nine offers ways to resolve the problem, ranging from letting the congregation decide, to bringing in different people to help resolve the differences. Point number ten was simply a question: "How many offers have my coworkers made?" In a page entitled "Ministers' Meeting," Nevin characterizes the positions of his coworkers regarding plain clothes. As he understood most of their positions, they believed that the plain coat and cape should be the standard held up by the ministers and that anyone who could not conform should find another church.

A final attempt was made to solve the impasse in 1958. After two of the Greenwood ministers had been to Kentucky and talked to Alvin Swartz and David Showalter of the Executive Committee, Andrew Jantzi sent a letter dated April 30, 1958, speaking for the Executive Committee. It stated:

We are agreed on the following points:

1. That Greenwood has several problems.

2. The discipline problem (plain coat, tie, cape dress, T.V.).

3. Using members in office that do not wear plain coat and sisters that do not wear the cape dress.

4. The question of ordaining a bishop.

Bro. Alvin, Bro. David and I have agreed on the following steps we feel should be taken.

1. We feel the Executive Committee should not enter into the Greenwood problem yet. . . .

2. That Bro. Nevin take up the problem and questions with his congregation as soon as convenient. . . .

3. We strongly urge you to give every consideration to your congregation and let them express themselves regarding the issues involved.

Based on this letter, Nevin handed a questionnaire out on Sunday morning, July 20, 1958, and the voice of the congregation on the issues was as follows: "Do you feel the wearing of the plain coat and the wearing of the cape should be enforced?" The response was 75 percent, no. "Do you believe that television should be made a test of fellowship?" The response was 68 percent, no. "Do you approve of our general policy in discipline?" The response was 75 percent, yes. To the question "Do you favor ordaining a bishop in the near future?" the response was a bare majority of 53 percent, yes. Don remembers that he was one of those 53 percent who wanted his father to be finished with the controversy in Greenwood and who voted, yes.

The response was apparently a surprise to the Executive Committee and to the other Greenwood ministers. The Executive Committee which just over three months before had urged Nevin to consult with his congregation, in a new letter dated August 11, 1958, written by David Showalter, stated: "Because the questionnaire used Sunday, July 20, and reported on July 27, was not the work of the whole ministry, we recommend that the questionnaire and its results be dropped from the picture for this time and decisions made through the leadership of the entire ministry."

After some long ministers' meetings, Nevin decided that it was time to give up his responsibilities and recommended in October 1959 that Alvin Mast, who was about to be ordained the bishop of Laws, also be accepted as bishop of the Greenwood congregation. The vote of the congregation was unclear. About one-half of the congregation voted and of those, about 65 percent favored the recommendation. On November 22, Alvin was ordained bishop of Laws, but the ordination of bishop at Greenwood was postponed.

Nevin and Esther decided to go to Meridian, Mississippi, where their son and daughter-in-law, Titus and Ann, were living. They went for a six-week "second honeymoon" to reflect on their next appropriate step. There was one last "gasp" of anger from several persons in the Greenwood congregation. While they were in Meridian a petition was circulated, requesting Nevin to resign as bishop immediately. The effort ceased almost as soon as it started for lack of support.

From Meridian, Nevin wrote to Erie Renno and Alvin Swartz. He reported the results of the vote and the recommendations of the ministers that "1. We share the result of the vote with the congregation. 2. A decision was difficult at this time in light of the vote. 3. More time for prayer and a clear leading of the Lord is needed. 4. Bro. Alvin Mast is available, and 5. We look forward to counseling with the congregation in the spring." On Feb. 17, he wrote that he felt the light vote and the congregational differences made it advisable to go slowly and that there was a need for "the congregation to reach God's decision together." He wrote that he intended to make a recommendation to the congregation in the spring and in essence, that if they felt the need for help from the Executive Committee, they would ask. The Executive Committee responded that they recommended that Erie Renno be asked to return and take the counsel of the entire congregation.

In the spring Nevin returned to Greenwood and presented his recommendation to the congregation with the following message:

> My heart thrills to the greatness of God's love as I come to you, my brothers and sisters in Christ, to talk over a matter that I trust you've been praying about. You will remember that in December, I made the recommendation to you that I should hand over my bishop responsibilities here at Greenwood to Bro. Alvin Mast. The time is here now to take up the matter again with you. We as ministers have asked Bro Erie Renno to come in to help us. . . .
>
> God has been very good to us. I count it a sacred and a joyous privilege to have been able by God's Grace to serve you and minister to you these past 42 years. I have made mistakes. No one knows that better than my Heavenly Father and myself. But He knows too the peace and joy I've experienced as I've sensed His leading and tried by His Grace to follow it. I sense that you as brothers and sisters generally speaking have a deep respect for and that you have shown a very warm attitude

toward your bishop. I do desire to thank you sincerely for this and may the Lord richly bless you for it, but I feel that the time has come to hand my work here to a younger man.

So again may I recommend to you that Bro. Alvin Mast be accepted as your bishop. Handing over my responsibilities to him does not mean that with it goes my concern. I love the church as deeply as ever and I will certainly continue to pray for you as a church and help in any way I can.

I make this recommendation willingly and joyfully and desire to ask you to accept it.

We know that Christ is the true builder of His Church.

Let each of us allow Him to live His life in us so completely that He can use us in His building.

Most Lovingly,

Your Brother in Christ, Nevin Bender.

Erie Renno came to take the counsel of the congregation through individual contacts. The vote was favorable and on May 1, 1960, Alvin Mast was installed as bishop. In this way the saga at Greenwood ended and the third part of this story began the next day when John Garber wrote a letter inviting Nevin and Esther to Mississippi to work with the Choctaw band of Native Americans.

PART THREE

WITNESS IN MISSISSIPPI

Nine

A MAJOR MOVE

There is an open door.
—Invitation from Pastor John Garber to Nevin
and Esther to move to a Choctaw community in Mississippi.

TO THE OUTSIDER, NEVIN AND ESTHER'S move to Mississippi, after retiring from over 40 vigorous years of leadership at the Brick Church in Greenwood, might have seemed preposterous. But let's attempt to get inside the thinking—and the hearts—of this couple on a morning in early May, 1960, to understand their courageous and unusual decision. . . .

Nevin was sitting in his study, reflecting on the events of the previous weekend and months. Alvin Mast had been installed as bishop two days earlier. With the relinquishing of leadership responsibilities, he and Esther were free to move in some new directions. What would be next for them? he wondered, as he looked out into the woods he loved.

The last months had been difficult, and the coming of spring had coincided with their return from Mississippi. He and Esther had spent six relaxing and healing weeks in Meridian, near Titus and Ann and the lively VS (Voluntary Service) unit they had begun two years earlier. Don had gone with them. Their small apartment on Highland Avenue had become a real honeymoon suite, and the

South had been for them a warm and hospitable place, as they attempted to rest and get clearer perspective and discernment on the situation at Greenwood concerning church leadership. They both needed to prepare for the next step; it was a time of beginning a transition internally.

Nevin kept in close communication with friends and family back home during those six weeks, as well as with the Executive Committee who had been involved in the process. The time away provided the distance he needed to help bring greater clarity about the direction he wanted to move with the congregation and, in fact, had already begun before taking this break. As no clear, fresh leadership had emerged in the last several years, Nevin felt that it was time to move forward and encourage the congregation to accept Alvin Mast as their bishop for this next period of time.

The petition that had been initiated by several men and circulated almost as soon as he and Esther had left for Mississippi, seemingly in an attempt to circumvent the ongoing process and force Nevin's hand, had received less than ten signatures. So, although this action had been painful for him and Esther, as well as the family and others, it was clear that the congregation as a whole was behind Nevin's plan for moving to new leadership.

They both, at ages 68 and 62, had far too much energy and vision to simply sit and "be retired." He also wondered if his presence might make it difficult for the next bishop, whose task would not be easy at best, given all that had happened the last several years around the issue of leadership and change.

He was remembering this morning that a highlight of their time in Mississippi had been their contact with the Native Americans in the Neshoba and Noxubee County area—the Choctaw Tribe. He had felt strangely drawn to this people whose ancestors had refused to take "The Long Walk," also known as "The Trail of Tears," over a hundred years before, when the Choctaw and Cherokee Nations had been forced to migrate to Oklahoma. Many thousands died on the way. Those who refused to leave Mississippi had gone underground, living in caves and, as a people became invisible. While their descendants still attempted to cling to their own culture, it had been eroding mercilessly through the years. With sharecropping now a way of life for many of them, they lived under the control of a "boss man," who often took advantage of their limited English and illiteracy.

In the contacts that Nevin and Esther had had with them during those six weeks, these native folk had been remarkably open and welcoming to this older couple from the North. The visits with the Weavers, a family who had recently moved to Noxubee County from Alabama to live and work among the Choctaws, had stimulated much reflection and interest. They had also spoken to John Garber, who was the pastor from Ohio giving oversight to this new venture with Native Americans in Mississippi. John and Nevin had ministered together occasionally through the years, and had deep respect for one another. This feeling of kinship with Native Americans was not new to Nevin. The possibility of sharing the gospel with this native people living on the edges of society, and perhaps together work to build a community of faith, had hovered around the edges of their thinking during their visit there.

Nevin looked up and saw Esther standing in the doorway with a letter in her hand. It was from John Garber and was addressed to both of them. Her smile as she handed it to him was one he never forgot—but often referred to later; he felt her love and support keenly in that smile. A few lines riveted their attention as they read the letter and particularly what John had to say about the work among the Choctaw people:

> "I do think there is an 'open door and effectual' there. I have visions of great possibilities there in several different avenues of witness and service.... If the Lord should lead you and whoever of your family and (or) friends to cast your lot with us and work together for the cause of Christ in Mississippi, we heartily and warmly invite you to do so. I should be glad to hear from you in the near future."

The timing of the invitation seemed truly providential. Only three days before, on May 1, Alvin had been installed as bishop, freeing Nevin of his leadership responsibilities; on May 2, John had written this letter which they now held in their hands....

The days of May passed quickly as Nevin and Esther explored the possibility of a move to Mississippi. A decision began to emerge as they talked it over with their children and their closest friends. Sometimes it really seemed not so much like a decision as simply a discovery and a knowing of where their path was leading. They prayed much and looked hard at the tremendous implications. It did look big, particularly to Esther; she did not try to hide that reality, even amid her support and courage. With all that they had built through the years, it was indeed bittersweet to think of leaving if even for awhile and beginning again. But when they finally reached a decision, it was one they both shared. Their family, as well as others whose counsel they had come to value through the years, supported them in this decision.

It was a busy summer; there was much to deal with, even as they savored the last days of what was surely the ending of an era. Don, their youngest, had remained in Mississippi and he came back in time to prepare to leave for his first year of college. Nevin James, planning to be married the next summer, spent this one at home, doing the farming before returning to EMC for his senior year. Emma, at home after graduating in May, was preparing to move to Ohio to begin her teaching career. And Mildred, who had been teaching in the Mennonite school the last two years and living at home, was getting ready to leave in the fall for a two-year teaching assignment with MCC in Newfoundland.

Lura and Millard with their family of six would move to the home place, while continuing to farm their own land five miles away, giving them time to decide what to do about the major repairs needed on their own house. The decision seemed to be good for everyone. Don would probably return to Greenwood in the summers to farm the land that had been planted in lima beans these last years, providing a cash crop, and perhaps Nevin and Esther would return to help, as well.

As September came, with the four youngest leaving to pursue their new work and their education, a heavy load fell to the two families who lived nearby. Many decisions, big and little, had to be made. Ginny, who had found in her mother-in-law a much longed for confidante and friend, gave particular help in this time. Paul was also right there; they lived just across the road on the land they had bought from their parents, in the home that Paul had built.

Lura and Millard, as they were doing their own packing and sorting, also gave time and emotional support. Lura and Ginny helped Esther sort through many things, deciding what to take with them and what to store or give away. These two couples, oldest daughter and oldest son, with their spouses and families, all lived in the Greenwood area. The growing children had spent a lot of time with Grandma and Grandpa. They all felt the impending separation.

In early November, Nevin needed to spend a week in Ohio for meetings, a commitment he had made earlier. He left Esther on November 4, and spent the night in Pennsylvania. As he was traveling the next morning, he evidently stopped for breakfast and decided he had to write to her immediately. His letter to her that morning is a precious piece of correspondence that reveals the tenor of this time. He began writing on Saturday at 8:16 a.m. from Allentown:

> Dearest Esther, my bosom companion, my darling, my heir with me of the grace of life,
>
> I left Bro. Jake Glick's this morning at about 5:25. I have traveled 119 miles. It is raining slightly, it is cloudy, but my heart is filled with joy.
>
> The Lord has filled my heart anew with His Holy Spirit and I am moving toward Ohio with confidence and trust. I am resting in Him.

When I left I noticed a certain loneliness in your face, but I know the Lord is with you. As I think back I can hardly see how you could bear to carry the load at home with the children while they were growing up, but you have always been such a self-sacrificing companion. I carry with me the most pleasant memories of you

Mother, don't let the things of the past worry you. The Lord is going to take care of the future. We are resting together in Him. The joy I have this morning can come only after experiencing suffering. May the Lord be very near to you as you lean upon His everlasting arms.

Continue to pray that the Lord may continue to fill me with His Holy Spirit and endue me with power for the work ahead.

May the Lord fill you with His Holy Spirit as you wait upon Him. I know He will bless you and the children as we together follow Him.

Most Lovingly, Mother, you are dear to me.
Father

Several days later he wrote again. He spoke of seeing a film about Africa and the great change that was occurring and how great the need was. He wrote: "Mother, I feel that we have made the wisest decision possible to seek to do our bit among the Indians in Miss.—I am praying that the Lord will show us the way He wants us to take."

November most of the family came together to celebrate Esther and Nevin's thirty-fifth wedding anniversary just passed. Amid the festivities, as they shared memories and joked and cried and laughed, the bonds as a family grew even stronger. The stormy times they had weathered in these last years had deepened their loyalty and love. They knew they could count on one another.

An excerpt from a letter Esther wrote that same weekend to Mildred in Newfoundland, who had missed the celebration, reads:

It will seem very quiet when they all leave but I do have Papa and that means everything. No, not everything. (Christ is that.) But we do appreciate and need each other more all the time, it seems. Thirty-five years doesn't seem long as we look back. The pleasant things far outweigh the unpleasant ones. I am so glad we didn't stop when our first children were born because our younger children mean as much to us as they do. May the Lord bless you day by day.

Most lovingly, Mother

There were farewell get-togethers with family and friends, shared dinners, then a farewell evening with the congregation. The gift of a set of beautiful Samsonite luggage from the congregation became a treasured and much-used gift through the years, in their many trips between North and South. Amid the farewells, there was much remembering with gratitude, as well as looking ahead with hope. It was both wonderful and difficult. They were leaving, physically, this community that had been home for them for their entire life together. It was especially painful to leave some of Nevin's sisters and their families, who had both given to them and received from them extraordinary support through the years and were keenly feeling the loss.

Uncle Ted came up one day to help, and his wry sense of humor and gentle presence helped them to keep perspective. Finally, on a cold morning in early December, Nevin and Esther said their good-byes and headed south in their Volkswagen. They stopped for the night and then headed on down to Meridian to Titus and Ann's. Paul and Ginny followed in a day or two, driving the truck loaded with their belongings. The thousand-mile trip between Delaware and Mississippi is one that they traveled many times in the future. But on that December morning, both hope and a sense of the unknown must have been strong within them, and also within their loved ones whom they were leaving.

As they drove into Titus and Ann's place in Meridian two days later and were royally welcomed, they experienced a sense of homecoming, of returning. And a grandchild, two-month-old Anita Eirene, was there to greet them, too.

Eager to settle into their new home, they drove the 50 miles north the day after their truck arrived, to a little sharecropper's cabin perched on a red clay bank in the rolling fields near Noxapater. The directions had been sent by John Detweiler, who had found and rented this place for them at $25.00 a month. He had also sent a copy of the floor plan of the four-room dwelling, indicating doors and windows, and the general setting. It had two double windows in the living room and a screened-in porch; Nevin with his vivid imagination pictured this little house in his mind. He could even see curtains at the windows and the homey touches that Esther was so good at giving!

The little caravan, including the truck with their belongings, as well as Titus and Ann and even Ann's parents who were visiting from Ohio, turned off the main route onto a gravel road. There was another turn and a narrower road. And then, with a final turn they saw it—a box-like, tin-roofed, once-painted—white sharecroppers' cabin. A steep, red bank which showed signs of much erosion, dipped down from the small yard overgrown with weeds to meet the gravel road. They turned up the short, steep driveway.

They were not quite prepared for the reality they faced as they walked inside. The place had obviously not been lived in for some time—not by humans—and had recently been used for storing grain. Large holes in the ceilings and walls revealed the presence of other creatures. It took only minutes to make a tour of the house—four tiny rooms swept clean in preparation for their coming. The whole house could almost have fit into their farmhouse living room in Greenwood. They found the outhouse back among the weeds, near a fence. And then they went to the neighbors, to get water to prime the outdoor pump so they could do some cleaning and begin to move in some furniture.

Everybody pitched in and helped. Later in the evening, as they hooked up the refrigerator and moved in the last box, Nevin put a cushion on the floor and did what he had always loved to do—sometimes in a playful mood, and sometimes to lighten a somber mood when the situation was grim—he stood on his head! Everyone laughed and clapped; Esther's face relaxed and the worry lines softened. She knew they would make it.

Paul and Ginny stayed for several days to help them settle in, and when they left, the little home was well into its transformation. Wide, heavy wallpaper worked wonders, in covering the rat holes (after they stuffed them) and the dingy walls, bringing a touch of color and beauty. With tables, a washstand and boxes, they made cupboard and counter space in the kitchen. The two sets of double windows in the living room looked inviting as curtains and blinds were put up. It was beginning to feel like home.

This was, in fact, to become a home they loved. During their first year there, Esther wrote a letter to Mildred after they returned from a trip north: "We really were glad to get back to our little nest again. We like our home very much." And several years later, after they had moved to Nanih Waiya (with some genuine regret on Esther's part) she wrote in her journal about taking some guests to places in the area that were significant to her and Nevin: "We went back to see our little house."

The transformation of this little house into a genuine home, filled with warmth and hospitality, received a marvelous boost at Christmastime two weeks later. Family began to arrive; Miriam and Elmer with their five children from Michigan with baby Philip only 18 months old, Don from EMC and Emma and Glenn who would become engaged during that vacation. And of course, Titus and Ann and Anita were there for Christmas day. Sleeping seven adults and five children in the small space worked amazingly well. Wall-to-wall people in the living room on mattresses with plenty of covers, Don remembers as one of the delightful experiences of the vacation. Talking, visiting till late, they would lie down to sleep, and when the sun awakened them, they could simply sit up in bed and continue the conversation! The screened-in porch, now covered with plastic for the winter, provided an extra bedroom.

Nevin, always a lover of these family times, took special delight in helping Esther stuff the turkey and make things work in their makeshift kitchen. Free of former responsibilities, he had more time for this now. Their dining table, which had been crafted by an Amish man from Lancaster County and had served them well in their big house in Delaware, was stretched from one end of the kitchen/dining room to the other. What a feast they had! Later they called briefly on their new neighbors, who had already fallen in love with "Brother and Sister Bender," and introduce their children to them.

Nevin and Esther went with their family one day to the Choctaw Burial Mound at Nanih Waiya (meaning Great Spirit, and also known and revered in legend as the birthplace of the Choctaw Nation). This place, sacred to the Choctaws, was one they would take many of their guests to visit during the coming years. They also drove to Meridian one day where Titus and Ann hosted them all. Their sons and daughters remember being deeply moved, both by the courage of their parents and the quality of life they were already beginning to find and create in Mississippi.

As the New Year of 1961 dawned Nevin and Esther began to settle into their new life and the work they had come to do. They began to have intentional and regular contact with the Mennonite families in Noxubee County. David and Ida Weaver with their six children, and another family, Rudy and Mahala Detweiler with five children, Mahala's sister Barbara and daughter Lorie, all welcomed them warmly, grateful for the maturity and richness of experience which Esther and Nevin brought. John and Ruth Detweiler, who were to help the Benders in the Noxapater area, were very supportive, as they came over each week. Their two little boys quickly adopted

"Grandpa and Grandma Bender." Weekly prayer meetings on Wednesday nights provided a time of sharing and fellowship in this group. Both Nevin and Esther looked forward to the 25-mile drive across the back roads and through the cotton fields of Mississippi to gather with these new friends.

They started visiting Choctaw families around Noxapater and soon began inviting families into their home to share a meal. Though the language was a barrier at times, the young people who were in school particularly enjoyed practicing their English with Nevin and Esther. Sometimes communication broke down, and there was nervous laughter or an awkward silence, but it never lasted long. There was much laughter with Nevin's attempts to learn Choctaw words. He became adept with greetings, and gradually added a few other words to his Choctaw vocabulary. But it was not with words that the deepest communication took place; the spirit of loving presence and acceptance reached where words could not.

Before long, they began a time of worship in their home each Sunday—singing, telling gospel stories, and usually sharing some simple food afterward, often sandwiches and cookies. Esther, instead of baking cookies for her grandchildren, was now baking them for Choctaw Indian youngsters who loved them as much as the grandchildren had! These were children who knew a great deal about working in the cotton fields, if they were old enough, or taking care of the littlest brothers and sisters while parents picked. The Choctaw families seemed to feel right at home, coming from their own sharecroppers' cabins into this one.

Sunday afternoons often found them heading fifty miles to Meridian to be with family. Times with Ann and Titus were a rich and essential part of their new life. Anita, the only one of their eighteen grandchildren within a thousand miles, was a sheer delight. They enjoyed the energetic volunteers who were part of the voluntary service unit that shared the household with Titus and Ann, as they worked in hospitals and did a variety of VS assignments. Esther and Nevin were always welcomed as part of the family when they came.

One of the results of the new life they were creating was deeper dependence on each other. Doing the laundry was a shared venture, since they had no hot water and Esther did not drive. Together they drove the five miles to the laundromat at Noxapter; that became its own social occasion. Esther learned to know other women who came regularly to wash. This warm and gentle Mennonite woman in her plain garb won the hearts of everyone she talked to—and there were few around her that she did not talk to! Nevin was often amazed at the conversations she would be involved in, when he came back from the bank or some other business.

They carried their drinking water from the neighbors, Guy and Jewell Johnson, a middle-aged couple who were also their landlords. Going the half-mile to fill their gallon jugs every day or two provided another occasion for visiting and forging new friendships. They were often back and forth with their next door-neighbors, Jesse and Ruth Hartness, as well as the Parkers who lived on the hill.

Part of a weekday was usually set aside for writing to their nine children. They sometimes made carbon copies but often wrote individually, sharing the task. It was a privilege and a responsibility they took seriously and in which they partnered as long as they both lived; Nevin continued this after Esther's death. A letter written by Nevin to four of their children on July 17, 1962, gives a poignant glimpse of their life together.

> It's a real pleasure to sit down and have a chat with you again. I'll let you have a little peep into our home for a bit. It is now 3:30 a.m. I had a very good sleep until about 1:30; then it seemed to come to an end. So I thought I'd write and study. Mother got up and is now preparing several cups of Ovaltine. We have learned to like that real well, so I'll be writing and sipping Ovaltine.

The letters they wrote were quite different, even when they had decided what news they wanted to be sure to communicate—and sometimes they'd even make a simple outline, to make sure they would not miss anything. Esther jokes about their difference in style in one of her letters to Merlin's, Mildred, and Nevin's in summer 1962.

> Papa and I both decided to write in this letter. Neither one of us have an outline, well now, maybe Papa does .... I am writing as it comes to me and he likely will too. It may be we will be repeating but I'm sure mine will be jumbled up and his is systematic. I'm glad we are not alike in that. If we both were like myself, system would indeed be lacking!

It was exactly this freedom to write as it came to her, with plenty of details and interesting tidbits of news, that made her letters so delightful and she knew that her children loved them. In fact, she was one of the most interesting letter writers her children have ever encountered. Both she and Nevin made sure that their children received news of each other, since not many letters went back and forth between some of the siblings.

A letter from her father written to Mildred in Newfoundland earlier that same summer reveals a sweetness that was often present. He writes,

> Mother wanted to write to you this week but she has been quite busy cleaning house and getting ready to go traveling again, so I am writing this letter to you. Mother has even called on me to help clean in some of the corners, as for instance the pantry. Well, you know I just love to do little things for my sweetheart.

He goes on to write a very newsy letter of five pages, written on both sides!

The letters that Nevin and Esther received in return, from their children as well as from other relatives and friends, helped to ease the loneliness that they struggled with at times. They both missed their community back in Greenwood, particularly some of the close relationships.

The bonds with people in the North made trips back of special importance to both of them. The annual church conference and ministers' fellowship, as well as preaching and speaking engagements, weddings and other family occasions, were made a priority in their new life, and they always looked forward to these trips. A modest, comfortable guesthouse in Marion, Virginia, which they discovered on an early trip, became a favorite stopping place. Their hosts there learned to know them and welcomed them in a personal way when they stopped.

These trips often included a visit with Esther's 90-year-old father and her sisters and brother in Pennsylvania, as well as time in the Greenwood community. There they caught up with Nevin's sisters and their families as well as their own children and grandchildren plus their many friends. Nevin's rich bass voice ringing out during the singing on a Sunday morning was always an announcement of their presence in the congregation, even before he'd get up to preach, which he was often invited to do.

Many people also traveled to see them. Few weeks went by that they did not have guests in their home. Besides family and other relatives, there were church leaders from the General Mission Board and from various Mennonite conferences, as well as friends from the Mennonite churches in the Gulf States—and from all over. Their guest book with its beautiful olive wood cover, a gift from the Middle East given to them by Hilda and Merlin, reveals the names of people of great diversity and from many places. Many of them returned more than once. Prominent among the names in the guestbook are those of their new Choctaw friends.

With the desire to build genuine relationships and understanding, Nevin soon found an opportunity to meet the tribal leaders. He also developed relationships with personnel from the Indian Agency, under the Bureau of Indian Affairs. Superintendent Rennie J. Smith, who later hired Mildred as a teacher at Choctaw Central High, found in Nevin a knowledgeable and compassionate advocate for the Choctaw people. A strong mutual respect grew between the Benders and Harold Keyes, director of social services with the agency, who carried the interests of the Choctaws in an unusual way.

In summer 1961 they went north for two family weddings. Nevin James and Lourene married in Pennsylvania in June, and Emma and Glenn planned an August wedding in Delaware. Nevin and Esther arranged to spend several months in Greenwood to help prepare for their youngest daughter's wedding and to help Don with the farming. Living in the house Millard and Lura had vacated, with the youngest of their children, they farmed and made preparation to receive the family "home" for the wedding.

They gathered in Delaware from Massachusetts, Michigan, Mississippi, Newfoundland, and Virginia—the nine children, seven spouses, and eighteen grandchildren—and celebrated with Emma and Glenn and with their parents. With the family becoming more scattered, their times together were increasingly important for all of them, and particularly for the patriarch and matriarch who were a source of great cohesion and strength for this "clan." And then again they scattered. This coming together and scattering far, while still keeping close connections, was—and still is—something of a metaphor for the Bender family.

Back home again in Mississippi, Nevin and Esther felt their roots deepening there as summer moved into fall, then gave way to the rainy Mississippi winter. As their relationship with the Choctaw people grew, both in depth and in broadening friendships, it became increasingly clear that their Sunday fellowship was outgrowing their little home in Noxapater. They were learning to know a number of families in the Nanih Waiya area, some having moved from near Noxapater. Nanih Waiya, about 15 miles distant, held a special appeal because of its sacred origins and significance for the Choctaw people. As they looked ahead, they began to wonder if they should begin to focus their work in that area. Should they find a house and move there? Was it time to begin to plan the building of a chapel as a place for worship and other gatherings, perhaps near Nanih Waiya rather than Noxapater?

As they discussed these questions together with their Choctaw friends and with coworkers, with John Garber and especially with their family, and as they prayed together, they sensed a rightness in actively exploring these possibilities and a readiness within themselves to act on them. The decision would mean a deepening commitment for them, it was true. Yet, they felt more than ever that they had been called and that God was with them; it seemed their new work had only begun. With this sense of settling in more deeply, the next couple years were a time of expansion and of moving ahead.

Land was bought—bartered in fact—about a mile from the Nanih Waiya Burial Mound, and the deed was signed in June. The Choctaw family, Will and Emma Thompson, who owned the one-acre plot, exchanged it for extensive carpenter work to be done on their house which was badly in need of repair and just across the road. In the fall of 1962, Mildred, just home from Newfoundland, came to assist her parents in their work. She traveled down with two older couples, her Uncle Milt and Aunt Savannah Swartzentruber and Milt's brother Dan and his wife Dora. The men were coming to do some of the repair work on the Thompson house.

Mildred remembers vividly the trip down with these two couples in their 60s as well as the energy the men, with Nevin, brought to do the carpenter work needed and the love all of them shared with the Thompson family with their four little children. Compassion and a delightful sense of humor permeated the work and the many interactions that week.

In December that year, 1962, Esther began to keep a journal. She had done this occasionally through the years, usually for a very short stint, but this time she continued until the last weeks of her life. One can't help but wonder if she sensed in her deeply intuitive way, that these were significant times and that they would, in fact, be helping to weave their own personal history into the much larger struggle for justice among minorities during the 1960s. Perhaps. At any rate, her journal, filling four notebooks during the next five years and kept so faithfully, has proved to be one of the most treasured and loving gifts she could have left her family.

Just after Christmas and before the New Year, the chapel was begun, with a load of carpenters arriving from the Marlboro congregation in Ohio, a community that would give in an almost unlimited way of their time and skills in the coming years as the chapel would need to be rebuilt, again and again. Don, home on vacation from EMC, was a part of that beginning. The next week, another load arrived. Always, of course, this meant a lot of cooking for the women—Esther and Mildred, as well as others who came to help. They usually took a hearty, hot lunch the fifteen miles to the chapel site.

Esther wrote, after some volunteer builders had left, "Very nice congenial group. So much pleasure doing for them." And it's clear she meant it. Then there were smaller groups, sometimes one or two offering a specialized skill for a day or more, from Meridian, Macon, and other places—both men and women—young people as well as seasoned carpenters. On February 10, 1963, the chapel, built with great love and dedication, was ready for its first worship service.

In May the Benders moved from their little home near Noxapater to one which was somewhat larger, very near the new chapel, and just down the road from an infamous bootlegger. (Neshoba was supposedly a dry county at that time.)

In June, Emma and Glenn arrived, fresh from EMC. They taught in Meridian for a year while looking for teaching jobs closer to Nanih Waiya. They were choosing Mississippi as their home so they could also give their support in helping to build the faith community that was emerging among the Choctaw people. They spent much of their time in Nanih Waiya during the summer and then continued to come up for the weekends after their school started in August. In August, Mildred was hired to teach at Choctaw Central High on the Pearl River Reservation. She was well-received, despite being an "outsider."

The next year Glenn did indeed secure a teaching job "closer home"—at Neshoba County High—so they moved to Philadelphia in the summer, shortly before their first child, Mildred Lynne, was born.

In general, things seemed to be going forward smoothly. The "settling in" for Nevin and Esther was becoming still deeper, with more of the family around them. This biracial church was growing, both in the numbers of people being drawn into its community, and in maturity, not only in the Choctaw members but in the white members as well. There had been a number of baptisms since Nevin and Esther first arrived, some boss men were losing control of some of "their" Choctaw women, and people's lives were changing; that was evident. (This caused tension with some of the "boss men" who were feeling threatened with changes. The Choctaw women were refusing to be such easy targets for the desires of the white men.)

An active youth group was attracting many young people, some of them also students at Choctaw Central. Summer Bible schools were busy times, but also energizing, because the Spirit was strong, and some of the Choctaw adults and youth were assuming responsibility in teaching and in a variety of ways. And always, connections with the church at Mashulaville and Fellowship Mennonite Church, where Titus and Ann continued to pastor, were a source of mutual nurture and support.

In her journal, Esther records in her concise but detailed way many little happenings of interest in this time—trips taken, family get-togethers, babies born, guests welcomed, illnesses, sometimes quite serious—of family members and others. She writes of Choctaw family happenings, a race-relations conference in Atlanta, and a trip north taking three of the Choctaw teenage girls along and times with her sisters and brother in Pennsylvania. A telling notation on November 22, 1963, stands out, "This p.m. at two o'clock when we tuned in for the news we got the sad news that President Kennedy was assassinated in Dallas, Texas. We could hardly work anymore."

Changes were coming, not only in the country, but especially in the state. And this little church community at Nanih Waiya was about to enter into some turbulent times.

Ten

FACING VIOLENCE

The Lord has given grace.

—Esther's comment in her diary upon the destruction
of the meeting place of the Nanih Waiya Mennonite Church.

From 1964 to 1967 the Nanih Waiya Mennonite Church was thrust into the limelight of the civil rights movement in central Mississippi. Three times in 1964 and 1966 their chapel was destroyed with dynamite. These were years of pain and triumph for that congregation and for the Bender family. Two questions beg to be asked: "Why did it happen?" and "How did the family respond?" Nevin was pastor of the church. He and Esther, their daughter Mildred and their son-in-law and daughter Glenn and Emma Myers, with their children, were giving themselves in living out their faith alongside their Choctaw sisters and brothers. These family members are living proof that tragedy can be a stepping stone to triumph.

Why was the building destroyed three times? To understand the violence toward the Nanih Waiya Church we need to understand what was happening in the deep South, especially in Mississippi. Segregation was being challenged in the courts and in the streets. In summer of 1964, between 500 and 1,000 students came to Mississippi to help mobilize within the

African-American community for voter registration, adult education, and a variety of activities to apply political pressure for Mississippi to change its accepted ways of segregation. It was called "Mississippi Freedom Summer." Many white Mississippians felt invaded. The Ku Klux Klan was gaining momentum. African-American church buildings across the state were going up in flames, especially those that raised questions about the violence and isolation they faced. Eventually about 70 church buildings were destroyed.

Michael and Rita Schwerner had preceded the Mississippi-bound students by five or six months to help pave the way. Just as students were beginning to arrive in June 1964, James Chaney, "Mickey" Schwerner, and Andrew Goodman were murdered by members of the Klan. For weeks their bodies could not be found. (This event has been the basis for at least two movies, "Mississippi Burning" and "Murder in Mississippi.")

Mickey Schwerner was a friend of Nevin and Esther's son Titus. Dr. Vincent Harding, a friend of the Bender family, had helped train the students who were coming for "Freedom Summer." He felt a great deal of responsibility for Schwerner, Chaney, and Goodman, as well as the additional students who were on their way to Mississippi. Hearing that the automobile used by the murdered civil rights workers had been burned and abandoned about three miles from the Bender home and the Nanih Waiya Choctaw community, Vincent called Titus and Nevin to ask for any possible leads as to whether Mickey and his friends were alive, or if dead, where their bodies might be hidden.

The Bender family wanted to give their support in any way they could. The family also felt the urgent need of support from Vincent in these days of vulnerability. Titus called Vincent and his wife, Rosemarie, a number of times. Vincent later told Titus he believed that these calls may have been intercepted by the Klan, leading to the dynamiting of the Nanih Waiya Mennonite Church building three months later.

Vincent and Rosemarie Harding played an important role in helping the Bender family understand the events of these years. They provided historical perspective on the surrounding violence. They came to visit and to affirm the family. Without them it is difficult to see how the Benders could have successfully found their way through these crises in Mississippi during the mid-1960s.

the following chronology may help explain why the Nanih Waiya Mennonite Church was destroyed. Three times the building was dynamited, and three times it was rebuilt and a stronger church community rose from the ashes:

- *June 1964:* James Chaney, Mickey Schwerner, and Andrew Goodman were murdered while visiting the site of an African-American church building that had been burned in the Philadelphia, Mississippi, area.
- *September 19, 1964:* Nanih Waiya chapel was destroyed by dynamite the first time.
- *February 19, 1966:* Nanih Waiya chapel was destroyed by dynamite a second time.
- *Summer 1966:* Security lights at the Nanih Waiya chapel building were shot out.
- *Summer 1966:* The house of Glen Myers (now the pastor of the Nanih Waiya church) and Emma was shot into with a high powered rifle while they were away.
- *December 23, 1966:* Nanih Waiya chapel was destroyed by dynamite a third time.
- *February 1966:* Nanih Waiya chapel was completed a third time.

Violence toward Choctaw people was only one side of the story. Despite the bashful, yet trusting smiles of Choctaw children, there was evidence of hardship in daily life. Some parents revealed great courage as they struggled with jobs that did not provide enough income for their families to eat adequately. Some parents caved in under the load by turning to alcoholism.

Choctaw Central High School was a place where Choctaw children and youth struggled to remember who they were. Nanih Waiya Mennonite Church was a place where people were accepted as they were. After the first dynamiting occurred early in the morning on September 19, 1964, Esther tells of the bombing in the following journal entry.

> This morning at seven o'clock two men came for Papa to go along to the church. They did not tell us anything but we were, at once, apprehensive. When he got there he saw our church was gone, had been "blown up." We had heard the explosion but thought it was something a distance from here. . . . It was a total loss. Who could have done it and why we do not know. The Lord alone knows, and we humbly bow to our all-wise God. The Lord has given grace.

Titus remembers Sheriff Rainey and his deputy, Cecil Price, as they "investigated" the destruction of the chapel that day. They were laughing, seeming to him to be enjoying the scene. These same officials were later implicated in the murder of the three civil rights workers several months earlier. Nevin, who was at the scene, refused to be disheartened by their attitude. Plans were made to rebuild the chapel promptly to avoid any doubts in the minds of both Choctaw and white community people about the family's intention to stay.

Three days later clean-up of the destroyed building began with friends from the Mennonite Church at Macon, Mississippi, helping. Others came from Jackson and Camp Landon, Mississippi; Des Allemands, Louisiana; Blountstown, Florida, and people from as far away as Hartville, Ohio, to show they were standing with the congregation. By October 11, twenty-three days after the destruction, the congregation met in the partly finished building. Fifty-nine people were there celebrating the reality that love and hope are stronger than violence.

It became clear that local Choctaws whose lives the Nanih Waiya Church had touched were not going to lose heart. It also was clear that Mennonite congregations from near and far were standing with them. But this was not enough to satisfy Nevin and Esther and their family. They saw themselves as part of the whole community—Choctaw, white, and African-American. It was important to them that local Choctaws and the congregation be understood and supported.

Daughters Mildred and Emma remember Esther's ability to relate to local Choctaw women and local white persons with equal skill and enthusiasm. They remember the friendships she nurtured at the local laundromat. Esther, who had spent most of her energy caring for and standing by her nine children, impressed them with her ease in making new friends from different cultures. Nevin spent a lot of time explaining to the local community the family's reason for being in Mississippi, believing most people would be supportive if they knew the truth. He went to Sheriff Rainey on several occasions to try to help him understand the honest intentions of the Nanih Waiya Church. He and the Sheriff developed a measure of trust between them.

During this time Mildred also found herself bridging the "two worlds." At Choctaw Central, where she was teaching, she had convinced the senior class that, among other things, they could begin and continue a yearbook. From some fellow faculty members, who were primarily white, she frequently faced probing questions and even suspicion. But students were quick to recognize her concern for their empowerment.

While there was some increased understanding of the congregation by local white residents, visible support was longer in coming. Many white neighbors feared what their white friends would think. Since progress was being made, it came as a surprise when the chapel was dynamited the second time during the night of February 19, 1966.

Esther wrote:

> Plans changed very suddenly when our church was again destroyed about 10 o'clock tonight. We heard the blast and had fears but did not know. We dressed to go up to

see but some of the Choctaw people came driving in, and told us what had happened. We were so shocked because we had no idea this would happen, again. The Lord is again showing himself strong in our behalf.

Two days later Jerry Miller flew down. He was pastor of the church in Marlboro, Ohio, with which Nanih Waiya had a special relationship. Two days later Choctaw and white people of the congregation, Jerry Miller, and persons from the Mennonite Church at Macon, Mississippi helped begin the cleanup. One week after the dynamiting about forty people joined in the effort. This time Mennonite Disaster Service (MDS) helped rebuild.

There was also a significant breakthrough in terms of local white involvement. Pastor Doug Herring, a local Methodist minister, worked hard to get white community people to stand with the church by helping rebuild. He met with some of his friends who were members of the Fellowship of Christian Athletes. That group decided not to get involved because they saw it as "too political." But Doug Herring came and stood with the congregation. Again Nevin went back to Sheriff Rainey to help him understand the goals of the church.

Efforts to relate to both Choctaw and white neighbors continued. A number were increasingly supportive, but dissenters were also stepping up their pressure. During summer 1966 the security lights at the chapel were shot out. Glenn and Emma's home was shot into with a high-powered rifle while they were away one night. The Sheriff's department came and saw "no evidence." When Glenn took to the sheriff a bullet he found at the scene he was told, "We can't tell anything from that." Clearly they were embarrassed. At least one person in the community, the one who dynamited the church building, was finding the deeply involved approach of the Nanih Waiya Church unacceptable and was striking out at the congregation.

Then nine months later, the night of December 23, 1966, it happened again. Esther wrote in her journal, "Tonight our chapel was again destroyed. What a shock! Thirty Choctaw youth had just finished caroling when it happened." Mildred and Glenn who were with them remember the tears of the Choctaw youth as one of them, Dean Hickman, echoed their sense of being violated. "They've bombed our church again," he lamented. Mildred remembers that something was different this time. It seemed the congregation and the family sensed that this was a last gasp of hatred.

In this third rebuilding of their chapel the local Choctaw members were centrally involved, which is clear in the following quotations from *Mission Service Newsletter,* the periodical of the Conservative Mennonite Mission Board (April/May, 1967).

> After the members got together and decided to rebuild the chapel, I felt pleased with it. It gave a great joy in helping rebuild the chapel. It gave the feeling because I could say that I go to the chapel that I helped build. They had also come to realize that a bombed building does not mean a destroyed church. —*Hayward Bell, an eighteen-year-old MYFer*
>
> The thing I am most happy about is that the building was destroyed, not the church itself, because the building could be rebuilt again. —*Mary Zella Gibson, a fifteen-year-old MYFer*
>
> I felt fine when the church went back up. We just went back and built the church again. I still keep praying and going back to the church again. The last bombing, I just about quit. But I just went again, and still had courage. We can't hate because we're all Christians. We can't seem to find out who did it, but some day he'll find himself out. —*A young mother of six children*
>
> A long time ago the old people used to say that one of these days, there would be bad trouble. And so they think it is this, especially the old Choctaw people. We don't know who the persons are that are doing this, but we love them whoever they are. —*Dean Hickman, another eighteen-year old MYFer*

This time a number of white people from the community finally came forward to own the problem and try to stop the violence toward their Choctaw neighbors. Pete DeWeese, a trusted local businessman took leadership. The local newspaper, the *Neshoba County Democrat,* told the story with some candor. An effort by Mr. DeWeese to raise money for the rebuilding resulted in limited financial help, but the increased local ownership of the problem made significant difference.

This was not the only time that Mr. Deweese stood by the Bender family when race-related difficulties befell them. A couple months after the third bombing, Nevin's and Esther's son-in-law, Glenn Myers, was fired in spring of the 1966-67 academic year, from Neshoba Central High School. This was the first year of token desegregation there. Glenn had been straightforward on several occasions about mistreatment of African-American students, including purposely tripping them in the hallway. With the support of Mr. Deweese, Glenn was hired by the nearby city high school, Philadelphia High, within a matter of months. Their acceptance of Glenn was clear as he was named "Star Teacher" of that school several years later.

The white community's response to the third dynamiting contrasted with the refusal of the FBI to accept responsibility for solving the crime. Titus remembers sitting in the FBI van, talking to several of them at the scene of the third dynamiting. He had grown weary of the standard inquiries about how Nevin and Esther were doing, without mentioning the violation being felt by the Choctaw people. With some skepticism he asked them if they were prepared to seriously try to discover who had done it this time. Defensively, one of them asked, "Was it a civil rights building?" When Titus responded that both he and the FBI agent knew it was a church building, the agent's reply was curt. "Then we cannot do anything about it."

Titus told the FBI agents in the van he was considering contacting *Life Magazine* to create public pressure. But as usual, the foresight of Nevin and Esther led the Bender family to focus upon trying to communicate with the local white community again.

Several months later one of the same FBI agents told Titus, "Tell your parents not to worry. Local neighbors have seen to it that there will not be another dynamiting." In retrospect it seems clear that the initial dynamiting involved the Klan. And likely the second and third dynamitings were the work of a local man who resented the extent to which the Nanih Waiya Church was involved in all aspects of the lives of the Choctaw people, possibly as it related to the oppressive way he was treating Choctaw women.

Even though the intensity of the focus on Mississippi in the civil rights struggle created a climate in which anger was seething, why was the Nanih Waiya chapel the target for violence three times? Likely this was because treating Choctaws as brothers and sisters was "off limits" for many in the community. Few non-Indian people from the community objected to churches telling Choctaw people how to change their ways. But at that time too few were willing to treat them as brothers and sisters.

To Nevin and Esther and their extended family at Nanih Waiya, telling Choctaw people about faith without being part of their everyday lives was dishonest. They invited them into their homes for dinner, were concerned about jobs where pay was too low to feed their families, were angry when Choctaw women were treated as property by a few men in the community, and were disturbed when a church camp near Macon refused to make their facility available when the Choctaw youth of the church needed it. To some white people in the community this deep involvement in the lives of Choctaws seemed like "meddling."

What difference did it make when Nevin and Esther and the family around them refused to "write off" the local white community?

As noted earlier, after the second dynamiting, in addition to the vigorous support of local Choctaws and a host of Mennonites, local white pastor, Doug Herring, provided vigorous initiative in standing with Nanih Waiya Mennonite Church. He tried vigorously to mobilize community white people from Philadelphia to show support by helping to rebuild the chapel. However, his efforts met with limited success. Some person(s) even showed increasing anger by shooting out a security light at the chapel and by firing a high powered rifle through Glenn and Emma's bedroom one night while they were away.

After the third dynamiting, in addition to widespread Mennonite support and increasing support of local Choctaws, several examples of increased responsibility occurred in the white community.

Mr. DeWeese tried hard to mobilize the community in a fund raising effort to put the weight of community support behind the church. He spoke out in the local paper, placing his prestige on the line to stop the violence against the Choctaw congregation.

The local paper, the *Neshoba County Democrat,* told the story of the dynamiting in a candid manner.

> Neighbors warned the person who dynamited the chapel the third time (and probably the second time) that if he persisted in his violence he would pay the consequences!
>
> In reaching out the hand of friendship to white neighbors, Nevin and Esther did not waver in their identification as a brother and sister to their Choctaw friends. One evidence of the trust they earned came when the tribal council voted Nevin an honorary member of the Mississippi Band of the Choctaw Tribe after his death. Clearly they were able to "get into the shoes" of their Choctaw friends.
>
> Vincent Harding, a longtime friend of the family, has commended the Bender family for their refusal to limit their association to just one part of the community in a place and time of alienation. They were involved in

the emerging relationships among Mennonite churches of Mississippi and neighboring Louisiana. In the mid-1960s there was a great deal of diversity among these congregations, and even within some congregations. Three ethnic races were represented. Predominantly white congregations were in the majority. Two congregations were predominantly Choctaw, one pastored by Nevin Bender and one by David Weaver. The VS unit at Camp Landon, near Gulfport, was primarily focused within the African-American community.

Titus described efforts to work with the diversity among the Mississippi, Louisiana, and Alabama Mennonite churches in the 1960s. He wrote:

> A number of us spent a great deal of time in African-American, Choctaw and white communities. Theologically our congregations were diverse. Some were heavily influenced by Fundamentalism. Others had a vision of transporting the ways and leadership of some specific ethnic Mennonite community, intact, to a new state. Others struggled with some ambivalence, to take seriously the cultures among which we had come to live—Choctaw, African-American, and white—without losing the authenticity of our faith. Some of us believed we should confront racism openly; others believed that would be "meddling in politics." We also had barriers of age within congregations. For example, the annual Youth Rally was planned and primarily led by middle-aged and older adults. It was urgent that we "get into each others' shoes." Some came to believe that if we could have a camping program in which all of the churches could come to have a common sense of ownership it would help us work seriously at some of these problems.

This diversity created a challenge when churches working with Native Americans requested to use a camp owned by a "born again Christian" man near Mashulahville, Mississippi, and were turned down. He admitted that ethically they should be able to use it, but he feared the possible response from his neighbors. Titus and the Nanih Waiya Mennonite Church considered created their own camp. He describes the developments as follows:

> Eight persons/families bought a seventy-acre parcel of land with a seven-acre lake and a partly completed house. We paid $7,500, with over half of the money coming from Nevin and Esther Bender. The rest of the money was contributed by Mildred Bender, Titus and Ann Bender, Glenn and Emma Myers, and Ann Zimmerly (who was working with the Native American congregation at Mashulahville), all of whom borrowed to contribute.
>
> In summer 1966 a few of us conducted an informal weekend camp under makeshift plastic tents. Rain destroyed our tents on Sunday and we had to call off the remainder of the outdoor aspects of the camp. But the youth were so enthusiastic that they carried their sense of excitement back to their home churches.
>
> We had an organizational meeting in January 1967 and organized a board with eighteen participating persons, six participating churches, and two participating VS units. We named it Pine Lake Fellowship Camp under the ownership and direction of the churches and VS units in Mississippi and Louisiana. Many of the dreams of the camp have been realized through the years since 1966.

A footnote to this story is the origin of the Bender House at the camp. Nevin used a memorial fund in memory of his wife Esther who died in 1967, and added money for a $1,000 gift to have a building constructed in front of the lake. The camp board decided to name it the Bender House. When Nevin died in 1975 he left $1,000 to the camp. Glenn and Emma asked if it could go to pay off the Bender House The family added a plaque for Nevin to be placed by the one for Esther.

One incident illustrates the irony and effectiveness of the determination of Nevin and Esther to continue the struggle for reconciliation, while keeping their principles. Several years after Esther had died and Nevin had moved from Philadelphia, a close family friend, Larry Miller from Mashulahville, Mississippi, was traveling through Kentucky with his family and a number of Choctaw youth from the Mashulahville area. He stopped for gasoline.

To his surprise, out came a husky man who saw the Choctaw youth in Miller's van and wanted to talk about Mississippi, where he had previously lived. During the conversation this stranger asked about Nevin and Esther Bender. Larry, somewhat apprehensive about the man's seemingly deep interest, was in a hurry to leave as the stranger kept talking. Upon his return home, Larry looked at pictures in the daily newspapers from the time of the murder of the three civil rights workers in 1964. He confirmed that the "stranger" who had been inquiring about the Benders was none other than Sheriff Rainey who, years before, had been linked to those murders and had conducted the initial "investigations" of the dynamitings at Nanih Waiya Mennonite Church. To at least some extent, Nevin and Esther had "gotten through."

Eleven

ESTHER'S PASSING

O for a faith that will not shrink.
—Hymn by William
Hiley Bathurst, led by Nevin at Esther's funeral.

IT WAS A CHAPTER FINISHED, BUT THE BOMBINGS and the rebuilding, though the ongoing work of creating deeper understanding among races in Mississippi would never be finished. The chapel, rebuilt for the third time and this time destined to stand, was dedicated in a simple service on February 5, 1967. That evening Esther wrote: ". . . tired, but happy for our chapel once more, and the people who are standing by so nobly. Our prayer still is for His protecting care to be over both the building and the church. His name be praised for everything."

It was also a new chapter for Esther and Nevin. They turned their attention to building their own little home, which they had begun to plan some months earlier. They had bought a lot in a quiet, wooded area on the outskirts of Philadelphia, about fifteen miles from the Nanih Waiya Church. The plans to build their own home in Mississippi had not been lightly conceived. It raised some important questions, particularly for Esther, concerning the implications of owning a home in Mississippi. The sense of family and "settling in" had become increasingly strong for Esther and Nevin, with three of their children now living in Mississippi, five grandchildren nearby, and their youngest son in Atlanta.

Their roots were reaching more deeply into the red clay soil of the South. While this gave them an increasing sense of being at home, it also caused some uncertainty about the future. What if they wanted to return to Delaware when they'd "retire" again? Would owning a house here hold them back? Esther wondered where she could best live without Nevin if something should happen to him. Mildred remembers her mother voicing these fears and their talking together about different possibilities. It seemed to help just to look these wonderings and insecurities in the face, to give them words, and realize that their deepening roots in the South need not limit future choices. So the plans to build went forward.

Again, their good friends from Ohio came with their generous hearts and excellent skills, and the shell of the house was put up with much of the dry walling completed within a week in late February, 1967. The contractor was Jerry Miller who, with his wife Sarah and family, had moved to Mississippi from Ohio to work with the Bender family alongside the Choctaw people. Jerry, along with six carpenters, worked hard, and the weather, often rainy in the winter, was cooperative.

Sheila Kay was born to Emma and Glenn that same week, amid all of the activity. The last weeks of Emma's pregnancy had been especially difficult for her, trying to deal with the trauma of the third bombing and the ensuing demands. She recalls her mother's strength and support at this time. One day in particular, amid a week of cooking for the carpenters, Emma had a doctor's appointment. Feeling close to the edge, both physically and emotionally, she was grateful when her mother and Mildred urged her to take the day for herself. They assured her they could keep little Mildred and handle the cooking. But sitting alone in the Steak House in Philadelphia, tears of exhaustion and discouragement threatened to take over this time of reprieve, and she did not linger long. She remembers feeling amazed at her mother's strength and encouragement, when she felt she should be the one to be strong for her 68-year-old mother.

When the carpenters left at the end of the week, Jerry continued to work on the house in Northwood, with family members and friends helping as volunteers, doing painting and other jobs as they were able. There was no time out from the other responsibilities of life, as the house took shape. Esther's journal for the next seven weeks until their move into their new home reveals a wide variety of activities and events, including a marriage, a funeral, and a baptism.

During this time, Don called to say that he and his fiancée had broken their engagement. He flew home a few days later to spend a long weekend. Esther's love and concern for her youngest child are evident in her journal. Don remembers how totally he experienced this care from both his mother and dad and the rest of the family who were around that weekend.

The stress of the last year was taking its toll on both Esther and Nevin, but perhaps especially on Esther. Mildred recalls a conversation in which her mother spoke of being very weary and seemed concerned about her health, wanting so much to stay well. "Papa needs me," she said. Especially because of occasional chest pains, the family insisted she see a doctor. She was relieved when, after a thorough examination including an electrocardiogram, the doctor diagnosed stress and stomach problems, and gave her medication for her nerves and her stomach. When the medication brought her relief, both she and the family felt that her problem had been addressed.

After some busy days packing in early April, the move to the new house was finally completed on April 17, though there was still finishing work to be done. That evening Esther wrote in her journal, "We think we will be very happy in our new home." Three days later she and Nevin left on a two-week trip north for some speaking engagements in Ontario, Canada, and time with Esther's family in Pennsylvania before her sisters, Mary and Gladys, prepared for a sale later in the summer. They left Mildred, with Emma and Glenn's help, to continue to settle into the new house.

On this trip Esther had her first plane ride and decided this was not her preferred mode of travel. After their time in Ontario, which included preaching, visiting with longtime friends, and sharing about their work in Mississippi, they spent several days with Esther's brother and sisters in Pennsylvania. It turned out to be a real family reunion and a particularly poignant time. Only once had they all been together since their father's death twenty months before. Grandpa Lauver had "gone home" at age 94 in September, 1965. Esther wrote on Monday: "We spent the day together. Had a very nice time.... We looked through some of Papa's and Mamma's things. Memories indeed!"

When Nevin and Lourene, who were visiting in the Souderton area with their young sons, came to take them to the train two days later, Nevin and Esther were ready. It had been a good trip; still, they were glad to get home. Their whole Mississippi family was there to meet them at the train station when they arrived. They were especially glad to have time to settle more deeply into their new home and prepare for a family summer. And a family summer it was.

Paul and Ginny with their four children came in June to spend a month in Mississippi. They helped at Pine Lake Camp in Meridian, camped at the Gulf, and spent time with their Mississippi family, especially Nevin and Esther. Lura and Millard, traveling in a van with their seven children, came to spend a few days in July, as part of a three-week camping trip west. Hilda and Merlin, preparing to sail for the Middle East again for a three-year term in Beirut, Lebanon, arranged their time to overlap briefly with Lura and Millard's family, arriving with their four children in mid-July for a week. Don also came for occasional weekends, as was his habit. The overlapping of several of the visits gave the brothers and sisters time together, and it also gave the little children a chance to learn to know their cousins better. Nothing delighted Nevin and Esther more than to have the family together and enjoying one another. Nevin remarked on such occasions how wonderful it was to "be together like this." The setting in Northwood was peaceful and felt almost like country. They were learning to know their new neighbors, who must sometimes have wondered about the many comings and goings of the Bender's extended family and Choctaw friends.

There were particular moments that stand out in that summer. An evening with Millard and Lura's family up at Starkville with the Myers for a barbecue (Glenn was finishing his Master's Degree at Mississippi State) ended in a late night music festival. "We sang almost all of the way home," Esther wrote. Hilda recalls the day they went to Meridian, as she and her mother got into the back of the van. Esther seemed happy, almost bouncy, as she settled into the seat and seemed to be having such a good time. One afternoon they went into a nearby department store to buy small presents for the children—some games and activities that would help to occupy them on their six-day journey across the Atlantic. Esther explained to the checkout clerk that part of her family was leaving for the Middle East. The woman seemed truly interested as Esther explained the reason for her purchases. There was warmth in the exchange, and once again, one of Esther's children saw how simply and unassumingly she related to everyone she met, and how warmly people responded.

On the last day of the family visits, with Hilda and Merlin planning to leave the next morning, Esther wrote, "We ate dinner at the Colonial House. Merlin's had us as guests. The children did very well and we had an enjoyable time. This evening Glenn's came for supper and Titus' came after supper. . . . We had a lively evening. Somewhat a lonely feeling goes with all this—the girls not expecting to see each other for a long time."

Then, on Friday, July 28, Esther wrote after the last of the family had left and Mildred was away for a two-week workshop in Georgia, "I washed. . . . also did some cleaning. . . . Seems very quiet. This has been such a wonderful month of July with so many of the children coming to see us. Paul's, Millard's, Don, and Merlin's."

A sense of completeness, thinking over the summer, was felt, not only by Esther and Nevin, but also by those who had shared those days with them. It was indeed satisfying for their children to see Esther and Nevin settled in their new home, the church growing, and the chapel standing firm in the pine grove at Nanih Waiya. Glenn and Emma along with Mildred were carrying more responsibility for the church. Glenn had been ordained in 1966, giving Nevin more freedom from church responsibilities.

The timing seemed perfect for a trip north, an extended vacation/honeymoon which they had been planning for many months. It was a trip that would take them to New York to see Merlin and Hilda off for the Middle East, and from New York City, to continue their journey in the white VW station wagon they were buying from Merlin and Hilda. The trip was growing in the planning, and their children encouraged them to take as much time as they wanted. It was to be the first trip they had taken in several years where they would be traveling alone in their own car. (The old Rambler had ceased to be travel-worthy a couple years before.) The children remember how much their parents were looking forward to this trip. Nevin and Esther promised to be careful and also to take their time and not travel long days.

The family agrees that one of the many things that their parents did well was to "honeymoon"! Nevin expressed his romantic side more overtly than Esther did, but it was flowering in both of them in some fresh ways at this stage of their life together. Their two-week honeymoon to Niagara Falls had not been typical in 1925, especially in Mennonite circles. The six-week honeymoon to Mississippi in 1960 as they reconsidered their directions was another interlude from life as usual. And now, into their seventh year in Mississippi after three especially demanding and violent but grace-filled years, the extended trip they were planning was well deserved and greatly anticipated.

Emma and Mildred remember the closeness they felt in helping their mother prepare for this trip. They made her three new dresses (one, a soft, brown and white floral print that Nevin had given her for her birthday and which she especially liked). Mildred cut and sewed at the machine, Emma did the hand sewing, and Esther brought coffee, cooked and made herself available to be fitted at a moment's notice. They enjoyed these relaxed yet busy days as they talked and teased and got a lot accomplished. Sometimes Glenn kept the little girls. Esther made a promise to Emma during those days: when they returned from their trip, she would keep Mildred and Sheila some weekend, so Emma and Glenn could get away to relax.

On Sunday, August 13, eighty persons met to worship at Nanih Waiya, five were baptized, and two others were welcomed as new members. Esther and Nevin said good-bye to their Choctaw friends, aware that it would probably be six to eight weeks until they would see them again. They could not know that this was Esther's final good-bye to these Choctaw sisters and brothers with whom she and Nevin had shared life so deeply. Early Monday morning they left on their trip, going with friends from Macon to the annual Conservative Mennonite Conference in Ohio.

Admittedly, for some people there would be no honeymoon quality in going to conferences. But for Nevin and Esther, it was much more than meetings and speakers. They had friends in this scattered community that came together once a year. Many of these they had known for more than forty years. Nevin had helped new and struggling church communities in numerous areas. Many people had been guests, both expected and unexpected, in the Bender home through the years, in

Delaware and more recently in Mississippi. At conference they experienced the fruits of their labor of love over many decades and the love and respect people had for them.

After the conference they went "home" to Delaware to visit with family and friends. Nevin preached in the congregation he had pastored for so many years. This was the last time Esther visited the community in which she and Nevin raised their family. Ginny vividly remembers that during this visit she and Esther went through the cedar chest which contained clothes that the children had outgrown and other things related to Paul and Ginny's wedding. Ginny will never forget the fun she, Esther and the children had together as they laughed and reminisced.

From here Nevin and Esther went to Mennonite General Conference in Souderton, Pennsylvania. The Sunday after the conference, they went to three different churches in the area where they had been asked to speak about their life and work in Mississippi.

On August 28, it was time to say good-bye to Hilda and Merlin and their children as they sailed for London, then on to Beirut. Nevin and Lourene with their two little boys drove Esther and Nevin to New York Harbor. Lura and Paul with their families also came to join in the farewell. It was not easy to say good-bye, especially for Hilda and her mother. Lourene remembers Esther saying more than once at the pier, "I don't know why it's so hard to see them go." A sentence in Esther's journal states simply: "Quite an ordeal to again see Merlin's leave...."

Nevin and Esther left New York City in their station wagon with their sons helping them drive out of the city. And then, clearly enjoying the independence and freedom of having their own car to continue their trip, they said good-bye to their children, and headed for Laurelville Mennonite Camp in Western Pennsylvania for their first Senior Citizens' Retreat.

Esther's journal during the next month sketchily records their travels and the "still points" revealing a time of connecting with friends and family, sharing their work, and traveling with the total freedom to rest or eat whenever they wanted to. They spent time with each of their children and their families not living in the South, with Nevin's sisters in Greenwood, and with all of Esther's family in Pennsylvania at the time of the Lauver family estate sale on September 23. Different ones who saw them at the sale later recalled how thoroughly Esther seemed to enjoy this reunion with many cousins and childhood friends as well as family. Lura remembers someone whom Esther had not seen in many years coming up to Esther, and exclaiming, "Well, you must be Esther Lauver!" She saw her mother laugh heartily as she caught herself for the moment forgetting the years and briefly being a Lauver again.

Several days after the sale they continued westward, taking time for visits with friends in Ohio, then on to Michigan to be with Miriam and Elmer and their family. One of Miriam's memories is of Esther's organization and enjoyment in washing and ironing their clothes for the last leg of their journey, and in pressing Nevin's suit in preparation for his talk at a Mennonite women's conference in Kansas. This care for her husband's appearance through the years is a memory that all of Esther's daughters share. "Pressing Papa's suit" and carefully folding his white shirts was a regular and loving ritual before any of his trips.

They had a good visit with Nevin's brother Earl and his family in Indiana. They also stopped with friends in Iowa as they continued their trip both west and southward, toward Kansas and their last speaking commitment. Next would be Mississippi and HOME.

Meanwhile, their southern family was counting the days, particularly Emma, Glenn, and Mildred who were eager to have their parents see what had been done on their new house while they were traveling. Yet when Esther called from Kansas after the conference, her daughters encouraged them to take the weekend in Hutchinson, with the church where Nevin had served as bishop for many years. These folks warmly invited them to spend the weekend, and they wanted Nevin to preach on Sunday morning. Their children at home in Mississippi felt this might be easier for their parents than arriving home on a weekend with all of its church responsibilities. It was a warm, happy conversation. Esther seemed to be in good spirits and was looking forward to getting home. Emma remembers that none of the three wanted to stop talking, although they would see each other within several days. Nevin got on the phone briefly, but it was mainly Esther's conversation. They decided to wait until Monday to start home, then take two days.

On that Monday, October 9, Ann received a phone call from Nevin in the early afternoon. He was calling from Oklahoma. It was a call that would change forever the lives of the Bender family. Esther had died of a heart attack. Nevin himself needs to speak here. These words were written as part of a personal letter of reflection to his children two months later for Christmas.

> As I look back to that memorable morning October 9, 1967, unconsciously I said, "Oh my, this day looks big to me." Mother answered with her usual thoughtfulness of me, "Well, maybe we would better not start today and just rest." I answered, "Oh no, I feel strong enough to undertake the journey." But I did not know what lay ahead.
>
> We had a good breakfast in the home of David Miller and his wife and grown sons. After breakfast we had a very enjoyable period of family worship and not wanting to hurry, we left around 8:00 o'clock or a bit later. We drove to the home of John Helmuth's where we loaded our bags of apples, and after saying good-bye we started home around 9:00 o'clock. We drove casually, talking about the joy and the blessings we had experienced and then, since Mrs. Allen Erb had given us an invitation to visit them, we decided to drive to Hesston

and spend perhaps ten or fifteen minutes with them. We were there for thirty minutes and then started for home at 11:35 a.m.

During the next three and one half hours, Mother took her flight, suddenly, silently, leaving my side, without my knowing it and went to be with the Lord. She had spoken several times during this period of time of not feeling so well, and we stopped a number of times. Finally before crossing into Oklahoma we sat in the car and wondered, "Should we seek to find a doctor?" But Mother suggested "moving on." We had planned to stop early and secure a motel to enjoy a good night of rest. About ten minutes later Mother said, "My pain is all gone; I feel good now," and then added, "Let us both pray that it won't come back again." This we did silently as we drove on. About five minutes later I noticed Mother's head slowly move back to the top of the seat back. This took place because Mother had gone to occupy "a building of God, a house not made with hands, eternal in the heavens" . . .

It was a wonderful Triumph for Mother.

Daddy.

It took time for the full import of Esther's passing to sink into Nevin's consciousness. Numb with the shock, he put a call through to Titus and Ann in Meridian. When he spoke to Ann, he wondered if he could bring "Mother" on home from Oklahoma to Mississippi in the car. It seemed he felt that in this way she would be with him another day and night. Ann gently helped him decide to call a funeral home.

When Titus arrived in Meridian from Jackson an hour later, he made plans to fly immediately to Oklahoma City to meet his father. He and Ann met Emma and Glenn and Mildred at the airport to continue to make the calls to the rest of the family and to be together in their shock and grief, until Titus' plane would take off. But the overwhelming need in everyone's mind was to get to their father as quickly as possible. When Titus met him at the airport a couple hours later, Nevin appeared numb but ready to begin the lonely trip to Philadelphia, Mississippi. While Nevin had been waiting for his son, the undertaker, almost like a father, had helped him to put Esther's body on the plane and had stayed with him at the Oklahoma City airport until Titus arrived.

When Nevin and Titus turned into the driveway of the home in Northwood late Tuesday evening, their southern family was waiting. Nevin walked into the new home that he and Esther had moved into less than six months before. In that moment, grief broke through the shock that had mercifully been protecting Nevin. He broke down, and through heart-wrenching sobs cried, "I wanted to bring Mother home with me."

The next morning, following a night of little sleep and much struggling, he found a place of grace and quiet within that would provide an anchor, a faith amid grief, in the days ahead.

A memorial service was held in the chapel at Nanih Waiya, before taking Esther's body back to Greenwood for the funeral and burial there. It provided a chance for the southern half of their family to share with their Choctaw friends and the many other friends and neighbors who had come to love Esther—to share both their grief and their gratitude for the gift of her life. One young Choctaw mother said at the service, "She was like a mother to us." Different ones said simply, "We'll miss her."

The whole family was together for the funeral in Greenwood, except Merlin and their four children. . A cablegram had been sent immediately to Hilda in Lebanon. The family all went together to pay for Hilda's flight home, Merlin making the arrangements for her in Beirut. The family was together in Paul and Ginny's home when the cable arrived, saying she was flying into Dulles Airport the next day. Nevin's response was so like him: "Then we can all be together." The community at Greenwood helped to make this possible. They held the Bender family in their hearts during those days, providing meals, giving them time alone, being ready to help in any way at a moment's notice—and sharing their own profound sense of loss.

During the funeral a memorable moment stood out for all the family and friends gathered to say good-bye to this gentle, unusual woman, to celebrate her life and grieve her leaving. Nevin stood up to speak to his and Esther's friends and family. He wanted to share with them about their last weeks and hours together. Before he began to speak, he asked them to sing with him. Nevin's deep voice, rich in both sorrow and confidence, led the congregation in singing all four verses of the hymn, "Oh, for a Faith That Will Not Shrink." Some of the lines were especially poignant. Faith reached out to comfort and strengthen those who joined Nevin in singing—and many voices broke in the singing. Faith sustained Nevin again and again in the coming months and gave him the courage to go on.

The hardest days were ahead for the whole family, but especially for Nevin, learning to live without the companion who had shared forty-two of his seventy-five years. The return to Mississippi that cold October night was anguishingly bleak as they drove in two cars from Atlanta after the plane trip from Greenwood. When they arrived in Philadelphia, they decided to stop and buy oysters and eat supper together before Titus and Ann drove on to Meridian. Walking into the dark emptiness of the new house that had had so little time to become home, Esther's absence was palpable. They all tried their best to be present to each other, especially to their father.

It was decided that Emma and Glenn would move in with Nevin and Mildred temporarily, to help ease the loneliness for Nevin. The two little girls, Mildred, four, and Sheila, eight months, helped to bring a lot of activity and affection to their grandpa. Within a few weeks, Nevin knew that it was time to come to terms with days alone, when Mildred would be teaching. Going out to visit with his Choctaw friends was often a part of his day. They had known and loved Esther, too.

Later that fall, a violent and devastating event happened that shook Nevin profoundly and caused him to go ever more deeply into the faith that had been holding him. Soon after she and her family moved back to Nanih Waiya, Emma was raped in her home while Glenn was at school and her little girls were with her. The drunken Choctaw man was not someone the family knew. The Choctaw community was very angry and felt betrayed that this should happen to Emma, who was like one of their own.

Nevin anguished over this violence that had been done to his youngest daughter, who was in certain ways like her mother. He did his best to offer strong support and love to her and Glenn, he went to visit the man in jail, he spoke openly and compassionately with the Choctaw people, and he struggled to understand and to come to terms with the question that had no answer—why?

For Emma it was a terrible violation and a wound that would take much time to heal. Glenn's total and loving support was key, as well as that of family and friends and the whole community. This experience, and her profound courage and openness in finding healing, gave her compassion and authority in the years to come with other women, white and Choctaw, who themselves experienced the trauma of rape or other violence.

Six of the nine children were able to be home for Christmas that year. Miriam and Elmer, as well as Lourene and Nevin with their families, joined their father and southern siblings. Various members recall how freely both tears and laughter flowed. A special project, a memory scrapbook for their father, was a therapeutic and moving gift that everyone contributed to, with pages even arriving from far away Lebanon. It was a surprise for Nevin when they gave it to him on Christmas Eve. All of the children and grandchildren had contributed, and it was a gift that he treasured and read often.

Nevin's gift to each of his children was also one of self-giving. With copies of his and Esther's wedding picture, as well as a photograph of them sitting together on the porch of their new home, which they had enjoyed for only four short months, Nevin wrote a reflection of his last hours with Esther and then a very personal and individual "love letter" to each child, expressing his appreciation and care. These gifts of self to each other allowed the grieving and healing to merge. The Christmas letter that they wrote together to send to the hundreds who were standing by them was another part of the healing.

As the months passed, Nevin began to think again about the possibility of going to see Hilda and Merlin in the Middle East, an idea they had discussed together before they had said good-bye in August. He still had a desire to take that trip for both Esther and himself. Since Mildred had an interest in doing graduate study abroad, the idea gradually developed for them to go together and possibly spend an academic year in Beirut. They began to explore options with Hilda and Merlin, who then became the prime movers of this venture and planned and worked in practical ways to make it possible. Nevin and Mildred began to talk seriously with the rest of the family, especially Emma and Glenn, whom such a choice would most affect, and gradually plans began to take shape.

Some of Nevin's grieving perhaps was put on hold, as they began to take the steps needed to turn possibility into reality. The grieving and healing would find plenty of space and time to continue beside the Mediterranean and in the land where Jesus had walked. In August, 1968, Nevin and Mildred said their good-byes and headed, first west to see Paul and Ginny in their new home and pastoral assignment in Kansas City, then north for some visits with family and friends there. Glenn and Emma would be living in the new home in Northwood for the next year. In September, they boarded their Lufthansa flight and were on their way to the Middle East.

Part Four

SOJOURN AND RETURN TO GREENWOOD

Twelve

YEAR IN BEIRUT

O Healing River,
Send Down Your Waters

—Anonymous Hymn

THE YEAR 1967 WAS ONE OF SPECIAL SIGNIFICANCE in the life of Nevin and his family. Merlin and Hilda and their four children had spent a good part of that summer preparing to go to Beirut, Lebanon, for three years where Merlin would be teaching at the American University of Beirut and the Near East School of Theology. The decision to spend three years in the Middle East had been a difficult one for them as well as for Nevin and Esther, though their strong belief in the value of serving others made it easier for them to accept the decision that Merlin and Hilda had made and even to share in the excitement.

As the larger family discussed the move to Beirut, Nevin shared his longing to some day visit the Holy Land. There was talk of how nice it would be if he and Esther could go to Beirut while Merlin and Hilda were there and use this opportunity to make the dream come true. Esther had a fear of flying, but otherwise thought this was something she would like to do. Hilda believes that if Esther had lived she would have been on the plane that eventually brought Nevin and Mildred to Beirut, and she remembers that it was easier to leave them knowing that they might be able to join them later. But she also remembers that it was especially difficult to say good-bye to Esther as the family boarded the ship for Beirut. In hindsight, she thinks there was some sense of foreboding—unconscious at the time. Hilda remembers how difficult it was for Esther to see them go. As they were saying good-bye and young Kenton was crying, Esther, who was laughing through her tears, said to Nevin, "Give them a dollar to buy something for Kenny!"

Little did Hilda suspect that she would be recrossing the ocean in October, only several months after their arrival in Beirut, to join the family at Esther's funeral. Hilda now comments, "If I had known this, I don't think I could have gotten on that ship."

At Esther's funeral Hilda does not remember talking to her father about coming to Beirut—the loss was too acute for that. But as the months passed and letters came and went, they began to talk again about Nevin's wish to visit the Middle East and how that might be possible. It was the family's belief that Esther would have very much wanted Nevin to be able to go for both of them. There was also a sense that it could be a healing experience for Nevin at a very difficult time in his life, and this is indeed what it proved to be.

At that time Mildred was living in Mississippi, and she began to talk about possibly coming to the Middle East with Nevin to spend the time in study at the University of Beirut. Nevin and Mildred first talked about renting an apartment in Beirut, but as Merlin and Hilda considered the expense involved and their own adequate living quarters, they suggested that Nevin and Mildred live with them and share food expenses. As Merlin and Hilda's family discussed this idea, it became obvious that their apartment could easily be arranged so that Mildred and Nevin could each have their own room and a bathroom between them. There was another bathroom at the other end of the apartment which was sufficient for the rest of the family. Hilda remembers how excited the children were at the prospect of Grandpa and Aunt Millie coming to live with them and the fun of preparing the rooms for their arrival.

The day Nevin and Mildred flew into Beirut in September, 1968, was especially exciting. The children could hardly contain themselves and insisted on going along to the airport to welcome them to Beirut. The meeting itself was a poignant one. Amid the excitement there were memories of Esther and the wish that she, too, would be arriving with Nevin and Mildred. Nevin's and Mildred's response when they were shown their rooms was especially heartwarming to Merlin and Hilda and the children. Nevin expressed how relaxed he would be there, and how pleased he was to be able to have his own desk for study and writing. Hilda says, "I can still see the expression of excitement on his face as he entered that small, very simple room. Whatever time and effort went into the preparation for Dad's and Millie's arrival was rewarded many times over by their delight and appreciation."

Almost daily Nevin walked along the Mediterranean Sea, sometimes with Daryl, sometimes with other family members, and sometimes by himself. A well-protected walkway skirted the waterfront, but at other places one could reach the rocky ledges that overlooked the water. Nevin loved to sit on the rocks and meditate as the powerful waves dashed against the rocky coast. He found a favorite rock jutting into the sea, and spent many hours there when the weather permitted.

Sometimes he chose to walk along the waterfront and mingle with the people who had gathered to enjoy the scenery and the fresh breezes that came in off the Mediterranean Sea. A number of expensive apartment buildings and hotels catered to an international clientele. But the majority of people who frequented the waterfront were working-class people, and many of them appeared to be rather poor. "All of us noticed the look of peacefulness on his face when he returned from these walks"

Hilda comments. "I truly believe that the sea—the 'heartbeat of God' to borrow Don's phrase—carried away with it Dad's grief and gave in return an acceptance, a tranquility, a renewal of his zest for life that would have been more difficult without that experience. He and Daryl had many wonderful conversations during these walks along the sea. Daryl still talks about how much those occasions meant to him." Nevin shared his love of the sea with all of the children. The apartment in Beirut had a small veranda on the front side, and Wanda remembers Grandpa being with them on the veranda and helping them climb up so they could see the Mediterranean Sea.

Meals together as an extended family of eight were special times. Since Nevin and Mildred contributed generously to the food budget, the family was able to buy things that previously would have been difficult to afford. Because Mildred and Hilda planned the meals together and shared the cooking, meal preparation was not difficult. Once a week they ate fish prepared southern style and often had oven-baked chicken on Sundays, plus many other family favorites.

It seemed that the children ate everything in those days—having eight people seemed to make the food more special and mealtimes more fun. They fixed bean soup for Nevin regularly, since this was a favorite of his, and Hilda remembers eating lunch alone with him when the children were all in school and Merlin and Mildred were at the University. Fresh oyster stew was even a greater favorite. Since these were not available in Beirut at that time she bought canned oysters for oyster stew, but after a few meals of these, he gently told her that they just weren't the same as fresh oysters and she shouldn't go to any special trouble to buy them.

There were long discussions at the table following the Sunday dinner. These were often between Nevin and Merlin. Hilda became anxious as they discussed controversial subjects and suggested to Merlin that he didn't need to discuss all of these things with Nevin. But Nevin insisted that he did not want to be protected and that "if I'm wrong I want to know it." Mutual respect, always present, grew between Merlin and Nevin as a result of these honest discussions. Merlin admired his openness and his intellectual honesty. More than once he remarked to Hilda: "If I can be as open and receptive to new ideas as Dad is when I'm his age, I will be grateful."

Nevin's proximity to the Near East School of Theology helped him decide that his stay in Beirut was an ideal time to experience more of academic life. He considered whether he should audit courses or take them for credit. He decided reluctantly to audit them, but with the understanding that he would take the exams. His hearing was a bit of a problem and made understanding the lectures a little difficult at times, especially when the professor's native language was not English, but he took notes faithfully and bought some of the recommended books.

He was frequently exposed to different ideas, some of which gave him some concern, but again he insisted that he wanted to learn as much as he could from others. He was asked to participate in the life of the school, and was invited a number of times to speak during the chapel service. (One of the talks he gave at the Near East School of Theology is included in this book in its original form in the Appendix.) Professors and fellow students all respected and loved him. When Nevin left Beirut in 1969 they gave him a beautiful Iranian vase.

The family shared many good times at the Cite Sportive, a large Olympic-size outdoor swimming pool with high diving boards, located at the edge of Beirut. On many hot summer days, especially on weekends, the family packed a picnic lunch and spent hours swimming, diving, eating, sunning, and talking. Nevin loved to dive from the highest boards, and several photos show him doing just that. The children loved to show off their diving skills to Grandpa and Aunt Millie.

On other weekends they sometimes planned day trips to various places in Lebanon that Merlin and Hilda wanted Nevin and Mildred to see with them. As a result they saw much more than they would have otherwise seen by themselves. Again picnic lunches were a regular part of those excursions.

Nevin's intense interest in history, and particularly biblical history, made many of these trips especially exciting for him. Merlin remembers driving to the Cedars of Lebanon, going by way of and stopping at Byblos, which contains Phoenician ruins and excavations of a large burial site dating back to at least 1000 BC. The road to the Cedars goes through gorgeous mountains overlooking villages and terraced gardens nestled below. A Sunday cookout among the Cedars of Lebanon filled Nevin with ecstasy.

Merlin also remembers a visit to Nahr al-Kebl (Dog River), about thirty miles north of Beirut where there is a large rock formation bearing ancient inscriptions by Ramses I, a pharaoh who reigned before the time of Moses. He remembers Nevin remarking that he was actually seeing something that was there during Moses' time. Another Sunday trip was made to the Jeita Caverns north of Beirut where Nevin was thrilled by the rich colors and the intricate rock formations. A trip to Tyre and Sidon, cities visited by Jesus near the end of his life, was especially meaningful to Nevin. In Tyre he also saw ancient Greek and Roman ruins and an active seaport used by fishermen employing the old-world style of fishing. Nevin was excited and pleased at these glimpses into the past.

During the time that Nevin and Mildred were living in Beirut, they were very thoughtful of the needs of Merlin, Hilda, and their children. Hilda was taking several courses at the Beirut College for Women, Merlin as busy with teaching, and Mildred was studying at the American University of Beirut. Nevin did everything possible to help with the household chores and contributed immensely to the life of the family, as did Mildred. Hilda remembers: "In the morning I wasn't a very bright and shining person, while Dad almost always awakened with a smile on his face and a spring in his step I was not always able to match his morning enthusiasm, but he was very understanding of the demands on my time, my moods, and the responsibility of caring for four growing children."

The trip Nevin, Mildred, and Hilda took to Egypt is a particularly vivid memory, and a very special experience for them. Merlin helped them plan the trip and stayed at home with the four children so that Nevin could travel with his two daughters. They were gone about a week. (Nevin's account of that trip is included in the Appendix without editing.) They flew to Cairo accompanied by an American friend, Shirley Harcourt and her son, who decided they would like to join Nevin, Mildred, and Hilda on the trip to Egypt. Since Shirley had lived in the Middle East for some time she was frequently helpful.

When they arrived in Cairo, Nevin decided that getting his dollars changed into Egyptian pounds was the first order of business. Shortly after their arrival in Cairo from the airport, a man came up to him and said he could give him a good exchange rate on his dollars if Nevin would go with him. In his excitement and with his trusting nature he went with this man, whom he had never met, down the side streets, to purchase Egyptian pounds on what turned out to be the black market (which of course he was unaware of). When Mildred and Hilda discovered his absence, they began looking for him. And as the minutes passed, they became increasingly concerned.

"Sheer panic best describes our feelings as time passed with no sign of Dad," Hilda remembers. "After perhaps twenty minutes Dad suddenly reappeared, all smiles, because he was so pleased with his purchase of Egyptian pounds. We admonished him about the risks of going off in a foreign city with a strange man, especially since he didn't know a word of Arabic, and of the need to let us know what his plans were. *Irrepressible* is the word that keeps coming to me as I write about Dad's stay in the Middle East. He made experiences and excursions such fun by being able to enjoy them so fully, but also sometimes a little nerve-racking."

While Nevin, Mildred, and Hilda were in Egypt they spent time in Cairo at the Egyptian National Museum and went out to the Pyramids and saw the accompanying music and narration, *Sound and Light*. Hilda remembers how thrilling it was to sit with Nevin and Mildred in front of the Pyramids and the Sphinx at night as the lighting revealed them in all their majesty and beauty, and as the music and narrators carried them back in time thousands of years. During that visit they also flew to Luxor and Aswan in the south of Egypt and saw the Aswan Dam, Ancient Egyptian Karnak, the Nile River and much more.

Sadly, during this trip the Israelis bombed the Beirut airport. On their return to Beirut, Nevin, Mildred, and Hilda were greeted at the airport by the hulks of burned-out airplanes and a bomb-scarred tarmac, a harsh reminder of the continued Arab-Israeli conflict.

Nevin was always troubled by the poverty that he saw in the course of his travels in various parts of the Middle East. In his frequent walks and trips by *service* (a Middle Eastern style taxi) in Beirut, as well as in travels outside the city and in other countries, he would see beggars on the street asking for *bakshish* or gifts of money. It was impossible for him to walk by them without responding, yet knowing that the little help he could give would not make much of a difference for them. In Lebanon, as in Mississippi among the Indians, he responded with love and gave of himself in addition to the *bakshish*. But there were times when the need overwhelmed him.

One of the more frightening experiences in Beirut was when Nevin developed problems with his heart and needed to be taken to the local hospital with chest pain. This was very worrisome to the family located in Beirut, since they had lost Esther less than a year before and were so far away from the rest of their loved ones. It was a great comfort, though, for Mildred, Merlin, and Hilda to be able to share together in this. They knew how difficult it would be for the rest of the family if anything were to happen to Nevin in Beirut, and, most importantly,. how much they all needed and loved him. Fortunately, with medication and rest he improved. Then came the hard part—to keep this vital, irrepressible man from overdoing things and assuming he was immortal!

They worried every time he went to the Near East School of Theology and returned late, and when he first went for walks by himself along the Mediterranean, going further than they and the doctor thought he should. Daryl went along quite often, but Nevin enjoyed having some time alone, too. They worked out an agreement that he would plan on a certain length of time for his walks, and he tried to be careful to return on time. He derived such pleasure from pushing himself to the limit, then telling them all what he had done, but sometimes it didn't amuse them. Nevin was a thoughtful person and he tried hard to do what would make all of them comfortable, but it may have been a damper on his spirit at times. Despite this he had a wonderful year in the Middle East.

Christmas in Beirut in 1968 was a memorable one for the family—putting up the tree, buying gifts for each other, and making the necessary preparations. Sondra remembers the Christmas plays she, Daryl, Wanda, and Kenton planned and gave for Nevin, Mildred, Merlin, and Hilda. They were always an enthusiastic audience. Students from the Near East School of Theology sometimes joined the family for Christmas dinner. Nevin always enjoyed having students in for meals or special occasions, entering into the conversations eagerly. He especially enjoyed the African students who were well represented in the student body of the School of Theology. They came frequently to the house.

During the year in the Middle East Nevin and Mildred were able to travel to Palestine and fulfill Nevin's dream of visiting the Holy Land. This trip and its significance for him is described by him in an article found among his writings (included in the Documents section, back of book). In Beirut, as everywhere Nevin ever lived, he had the gift of making friends. On his walks to the Mediterranean he occasionally met someone on the street and initiated a conversation. Sometimes the other person didn't even speak English, but it took more than that to stop Nevin from trying to communicate. Several times he was invited into stranger's homes for tea. The universal language of love worked especially well for him. Merlin and Hilda's apartment was next door to the Beirut College for Women, which had a beautiful campus. Nevin often walked over there and enjoyed the peacefulness of that place. He initiated conversations with some of the secretaries and soon became a familiar face. Fortunately, in that part of the world he was appreciated for his warmth, experience, and wisdom, and was not seen as someone disturbing their routine.

Thinking back over Nevin's year in the Middle East, Hilda comments, "One of the things that is clear about Dad's life is his total consistency, as well as his amazing flexibility in adapting to different circumstances, people, and cultures. The inner core of values which made him who he was transcended differences and guided his life and actions wherever he found himself. Mother possessed these same qualities of consistency of values, of flexibility and openness to people. These qualities best describe their essence. I am so grateful that they passed these values on to their children."

Thirteen

TRANSITIONS

The times, they are a changin'.
—Song by Bob Dylan

TRIP THROUGH EUROPE

The sojourn in the Middle East was over. It was time for Nevin to return home to Mississippi to pick up the threads of his life there. In June 1969, Nevin and Mildred said good-bye to Hilda, Merlin, and their children and left Beirut and this family that had provided a loving and nurturing home. Nevin had experienced such deep healing, acceptance, and stimulation, that he felt complete and ready to return. Mildred would travel back with him, then return to Beirut in the fall to complete her graduate studies.

They spent three weeks traveling touring Europe, a trip that Merlin had carefully helped to plan and arrange, to the countries and places that Nevin particularly wanted to visit. These weeks proved to be rich beyond all expectations. He kept a careful record of the places he and his daughter visited and the experiences they shared, and recorded meticulously every one of the many pictures he took. He brought the same zest to this new experience as he had to his travels in the Middle East.

In Nevin's travels, he repeatedly experienced a sense of the vastness and the rich history of the world. Then, in little unexpected events, he realized just how small and interconnected this world was. There was the moment at St. Peters in Rome, when Nevin heard a familiar voice, "Well, if it isn't Brother Bender!" as Myron Augsburger, president of Eastern Mennonite College, reached out to shake his hand.

Each city and country they visited was rich in its own way. Their itinerary included Athens, with a cruise to several of the Greek Islands. In Rome they saw not only St. Peter's Basilica and the Sistine Chapel but also the catacombs where the early Christians hid and met to follow "The Way" and where some were also buried. The drawing of a fish on the wall at a crypt indicated that a follower of Jesus was buried there.

Switzerland was a country dear to Nevin, so rich in Anabaptist history and breathtaking natural beauty. In Zurich, especially, he delighted in walking the streets with Mildred, studying the maps, and finding the markers that indicated the significant places and events in that history. Nevin was visibly moved as he stood by the Limot River, where among other martyrs, Felix Mantz was drowned when he refused to recant his faith. To go from that experience up into the Alps by train, called for allowing oneself simply and fully to experience the moment. This was the only way to hold these amazing contrasts that stirred such deep emotions. For Nevin and Mildred the sight of the Matterhorn, the famous towering peak among the Alps, was truly unforgettable.

They took a day to visit Luxemburg where relatives were serving as missionaries. And, of course, they visited the Netherlands. They saw the area where Menno Simons lived and the spot where a simple memorial has been built to this priest turned radical Anabaptist.

It was in Germany, however, in a little village called Langendorf that they stepped back in time and seemed to touch in a very personal way something deep and nameless. They were looking for the town where Nevin's great-grandfather, Daniel Bender, had last lived. After careful searching (there were at least three Langendorfs in Germany) going by plane to Frankfurt, then by train, and finally by a little-used bus, they arrived in a small village called Wohra, and found a *pensione* where they spent the night. It was hard to sleep that night, in part because of their excitement at being so close to what they might discover about the Daniel Bender family, and also because their rooms turned out to be directly above a much-used bar!

In the morning they walked the mile and a half to the village. It took time, and the best of Nevin's Pennsylvania Dutch and Mildred's limited German, to reach the right place and find the right book with the help of the pastor, where the name was recorded: Daniel Bender. It was the record of his death. The only word to describe the look on her father's face is "ecstatic." It was 1830. The Benders were living in Langendorf. A courageous woman was preparing to leave for America with her sons after burying her husband whose name was written in the book recording his death. Nevin felt that their pilgrimage was successful. They had found the place that had been home to the Bender family before Wilhelm, Nevin's grandfather and Daniel's son, had emigrated while his father was still living. Daniel Bender had not lived long enough to follow with the rest of the family.

What more could one ask? Nevin was filled with gratitude as he and his daughter boarded the plane to fly home. With that fullness came its counterpart—the loss he felt as he thought of the community in Greenwood, and remembered his oldest and youngest sisters would not be there to welcome him. Savilla had seemed not to know Nevin when he told her good-bye. Mentally, she had left many months before and her death was not unexpected. But Pauline, his youngest sister and only 59, was extraordinarily close to him. The news of her death in February had been a severe blow, even though she had been struggling with a serious illness for several years. He still remembered her smile when she had told him good-bye. She gave him a big hug, then put a hand on each arm and looked up at her big brother as she said, "Nevin, I'm glad you're going! Have a wonderful year." Her daughter Grace feels that her mother knew that this was their final good-bye. Now Nevin was on his way home and Pauline would not be there. He was also keenly aware of returning to the life that he and Esther had shared, where there would be reminders of that life at every turn. At the same time, he had family waiting for him, and he was looking forward to getting home.

RETURN TO THE STATES

When Nevin and Mildred arrived back in the States from Beirut, his children became aware that his outlook had broadened. The experience of relating to people of Muslim faith as well as being exposed to different perspectives from people of Christian faith at the Near East School of Theology had resulted in more openness. Issues did not seem as clear-cut as they had when he was a young minister or even as clear as they had seemed before his visit to Beirut.

Although Mississippi was home for him, Nevin primarily lived with Emma and Glenn and their three girls for the next two years. He also went for long visits with his children in other states during that time. One of his first visits was with Paul and Ginny's family in Kansas City. Paul noted that their communication was much easier than it had ever been and that Nevin was more open to exploring new ways of looking at issues. He was very affirming of what they were doing in Kansas City. He was also as adventuresome as ever even though he was in his late 70s. Paul remembers Nevin riding a giant slide, seven lanes wide and very high, which was waxed and very fast. It was intimidating to people half his age. He enjoyed his grandchildren as much as they enjoyed him. Even though he missed Esther very much, he refused to give in to self-pity.

Some of his children noted that he was developing his more feminine side, a quality that he had earlier depended on Esther to provide. One of his "feminine" tasks was remembering the birthdays of his thirty-two grandchildren. He also took pride in accomplishing domestic chores, including cooking.

As Nevin visited his other children he was also affirming of the choices they had made. He had enjoyed his role as a minister and, as many Mennonites his age, had encouraged his sons to consider the same vocation. He once asked Merlin why he had chosen not to be ordained since he had extensive training in theology. Merlin responded that he felt it would be a "monkey on his back" in his efforts to build understanding between Muslims and Christians. Nevin came to understand and affirm that some of his children had made a clear decision to be other than ministers because they felt their calling was different.

In August Nevin participated in the wedding of his son Don to Judy Harak. Judy had been a Franciscan Sister and the wedding included aspects of the Mennonite, Catholic, and Quaker religious traditions. A Catholic priest participated by giving the homily and Nevin performed the ceremony and also read the Prayer of St. Francis. This whole-hearted participation in his son's wedding demonstrates his remarkable pilgrimage from his early narrower view of the church to a more inclusive view of God's work and God's people.

During the visits with his children, Nevin made a point of helping with child care, preparing meals and washing dishes, as well as helping with food purchases. His special treat was to buy steaks to barbecue. When he visited Titus and Ann in New Orleans he took care of Mike while Titus was in school and Ann was at work.

Ann called home one time to ask how things were going and Mike answered the phone. When she asked who else was there Mike said, "Just my big cousin." Ann asked what his name was and Mike replied, "Some people call him Grandpa." At first Mike was a little uncertain about staying with his grandpa, but his uncertainty vanished when Nevin won his heart by taking him across the street for an ice cream cone.

Nevin visited Miriam and Elmer and their family in winter 1969-70 in Ohio, for what was intended to be a two-week stay, but turned out to be longer than expected. When Nevin developed a pain in his abdomen, Miriam made an appointment with their physician, Dr. Linscott. After checking out his chest, the doctor went around to his back with his stethoscope and announced that Nevin had pneumonia. Nevin good-naturedly asked how he could tell that from his back when the pain was in his abdomen. Dr. Linscott gave him some medication but after several days Nevin was worse. Nevin returned to the doctor, who immediately sent him to the hospital for tests. Since Nevin was feeling quite sick at the admissions desk, Miriam began looking in his wallet for his medical card. Nevin informed her that he could still handle such matters. After seeing the X-rays, the doctor had him admitted to the hospital and changed his medication. Within a few hours he began to rally and soon went home to be with Miriam and Elmer.

A paragraph from a letter to Mildred shortly after his return to the Jantzi home from the hospital demonstrates Nevin's ability to keep perspective and a sense of appreciation for those around him, as well as his sense of humor, even in difficult experiences.

"I might say that I am feeling real well, almost as fine as "frog's hair split in two.' Last night I lay down to sleep without taking anything to help me but I didn't seem to take off. I was a bit like a jet that is unable to get off the ground, so at 10:00 I took a Megadon and slept straight through until about nine with just a few intermissions in between. Being in the hospital, all considered, was a pleasant experience. I did have such good care and I feel that it added to one of the dimensions of my life. I am, of course, receiving such good care here at Elmer's."

By the time Nevin's recuperation was complete, the visit had extended to seven weeks. He enjoyed a visit from Elmer's brother Jerry and sister Matilda with their spouses. Nevin entertained them with stories from his life, possibly including tales of excitement such as his World War I experiences, motorcycle escapades during his 20s and civil rights work in Mississippi in the 1960s. Nevin appeared to relish these conversations as well as the activities at Rosedale Bible School.

Miriam frequently took Nevin to see his brother Earl in Shipshewana, Indiana, about 230 miles from the Jantzi home. Miriam drove and Nevin paid the way. They would spend an evening and night at Earl's, returning the next day. They always received the royal treatment from Uncle Earl and Aunt Katie despite the age difference of twelve years. They also tried to find Willie Stoneburner, who had lived with the family when the children were young. They stopped at different places inquiring about him and finally located his son, but not Willie. Shortly after, they heard about Willie's death and went to his funeral. Another day they went to visit Mary Ann Grassmyer, a friend who had lived in the Greenwood area earlier and who was now in a retirement community in Indiana.

Emma remembers that Nevin was in Mississippi when Beth was born. Emma and Glenn left at night to go to the hospital and Nevin, who lived in their home, spent the rest of the night in their room so that when the little girls, Milli and Sheila, woke up, they wouldn't be alarmed at their mother and father's absence. When Emma was ready to bring Beth home from the hospital, Nevin went with Glenn, who had taken time off from school to pick them up. After Glenn and Milli went back to school, Nevin prepared oyster stew for Emma. When she offered to help he insisted that she rest while he cooked. He seemed anxious to care for her. Those weeks after Beth's birth were a time of particular closeness between Emma and her father.

Because of Nevin's mild heart problem he was supposed to go for a two-mile walk each day. He sometimes waited until almost dark. One time night fell, so he paced back and forth through the kitchen and living room until he calculated he had walked two miles.

Nevin frequently visited Greenwood during the years he was headquartered in Mississippi. He had many friends there including his sisters Lucy and Nanna, who had always been close to him. Equally important was his deepening relationship with his sisters, Amelia, who was widowed by this time, and Savannah who was not well but was always loving and helpful. Savannah's daughter Elizabeth often helped bring different ones together when Nevin was in town.

RETURN TO BEIRUT

It was time for one final sojourn in the Middle East. Nevin had been visiting with different ones of his children for both longer and shorter stays during the past several years. So when Mildred wrote to her father in spring 1971, inviting him to come and spend several months with her in Beirut, he needed little persuading. He looked forward to returning to this country that he had come to love. After Mildred spent much of that summer with him in Mississippi, they traveled back to Beirut together in the fall.

This time there was a familiarity in the arrival although there were no grandchildren to welcome him. Hilda and Merlin, with their children, had returned to New England the year before and were living near Boston. But there were dear friends who were ready to welcome Mildred's father and who had come to value his wisdom and open spirit.

Mildred was a part of a small but diverse group who had been growing increasingly close. For the past year they had been getting together informally each week for spiritual sharing and worship. Just as Nevin entered the picture, a few of them, including Mildred, were exploring living together "in community" and had decided to be more intentional in sharing their lives. This commitment and effort to share worship and daily living in a deepening way grew out of renewal happening within the Eastern Catholic Church as well as in the broader church, both ecumenically and internationally. The circle included a young Lebanese couple, Peter and Najwa; David, a Lebanese/American professor at AUB; and Marie who was a 68-year-old widowed American and the house director at a nearby women's college. This diverse group, along with Nevin and Mildred, moved into a three-storied stucco house near the university. With its great front room the house fairly begged to have people gather there, which they did for a weekly evening of sharing and worship and often for the hospitality offered around the dining room table. A diverse group of people visited and some occasionally stayed for a few days or weeks.

It was an interesting experiment in community living, and Nevin adapted to this new situation with his usual grace and "grand sense of humor," as Marie described it. She recalls that he "fit in so beautifully; he stayed who he was and took it all in stride." No one was a more helpful or committed member of the household than he was. He assumed his share of the work with joy. Having experienced a lot of loneliness since Esther's death, he took special delight in sharing life this intensely for a little while. He felt loved and needed. He learned to know a retired couple, David's parents, and in them found kindred spirits. Esther, David's mother, was an unassuming, gentle woman, and they developed a warm relationship. They, with Marie, provided more "mature" friendships for him.

His simple room with an adjoining porch provided a place of privacy, always so important to Nevin. He again went to occasional classes and lectures at the Near East School of Theology and renewed friendships with professors and students he had met during his previous stay. He resumed the strolls along the Mediterranean and sitting on "his rock" to rest and reflect for a while during his walks. A treat for both him and Mildred was to go out occasionally for a special dinner together—to talk theology, to remember, to look ahead, or simply to enjoy this time together.

Mildred, who was teaching at the American University of Beirut, was concerned at times because he was so far away from all his other children and grandchildren. But although he must have missed them a great deal, he did not dwell on that. Rather, he gave himself to this new experience, to the people he was with and to those he sensed needed a little extra understanding. Many came to love him like a father. It's interesting to read again an excerpt from a letter he wrote to Mildred soon after leaving Beirut in March. Adnan, whom Nevin had learned to know, was a brilliant student struggling to break free of drugs. "It is really nice that Adnan can be at the Community House again," Nevin wrote. "I do trust that he will be receiving real deep healing. Tell him that I love him and I'm continuing to remember him in prayer."

A number of experiences were unique to this second stay in Beirut. Several events stand out. One was the communion and foot washing service that Nevin planned with Mildred and Jerry Dines, a Church of the Brethren college teacher who spent time with the community. As Nevin was always open to participating in some of the more Catholic ways of the group, it meant a great deal to him to share with his Catholic friends the simplicity and beauty of this Anabaptist practice. It was an intimate and unforgettable evening for the little circle.

These few months also provided an opportunity to see more of the Middle East. He and Mildred traveled together to the lost city of Petra in Jordon. It was an awesome experience to go by mule the last leg of the journey, where the brilliantly colored rock formations barely allowed passage, then suddenly opened upon the remains of this ancient hidden city.

A journey to Turkey after Christmas provided more contact with biblical sites as well as other historical places. Nevin found Istanbul an amazing city, so rich in architecture, in history, and in the friendly people who were always ready to help a foreigner. He also enjoyed, in a profoundly quiet way, walking through the remains of the city of Ephesus, which brought many reminders of the apostle Paul's ministry there. No guide was needed that day. The place and the atmosphere spoke for itself.

Mildred remembers her father's sensitivity toward her on this trip to Turkey. She was feeling particularly vulnerable as she struggled with a decision to end an important and difficult relationship. She knows she was not as present to him on that trip as she would like to have been. Nevin was supportive and accepting and in his gentle, nonintrusive way, willing to be there, to listen and talk or to be silent with not a hint of judgment. He also did not shortchange his own enjoyment of experiencing this unique country.

A silent weekend retreat, which they took together at a simple, lovely convent in the mountains near Beirut, was probably a first for Nevin—to be in silence at a convent or monastery. Taking retreat had become a part of Mildred's life in the last couple years, a part she felt her father would appreciate. And he did, more than she could have dreamed. It was a shared experience that she will always treasure. It was in this experience, as well as in community times of shared prayer and worship, Mildred believes, that Nevin came to a still deeper forgiveness and peace about the events in the last years at Greenwood. There was a profound letting go, although he did not speak many words about it.

He had come for three months, and he stayed six. Everyone who learned to know him wished it could have been longer. But it was time for him to get back to his grandchildren and the rest of the family. Mildred recalls that it was difficult to see him leave, but his spirit among them continued. He was a vital part of the beginning days of this little community which continued to grow and became a bulwark of love and stability during the civil war that soon followed.

BACK TO MISSISSIPPI

It was March 1972 when Nevin left Beirut and headed back for the United States. When he arrived in Boston, Hilda and Merlin with their family were there to meet him. With their previously shared experiences in Beirut, it was good for

Nevin again to have time with them and share some of his new experiences. After visiting some other members of the family, he headed back to Mississippi.

As he again settled into life with Glenn and Emma and their children, there was an unspoken change. In the earlier two years, their family was living with Nevin who was head of the home and sat at the head of the table. It was still Nevin's house, but it was now Glenn and Emma's household with Glenn at the head of the table. There were obviously things to work out, but it was a growing and enriching time for each of them.

Milli, Sheila, and Beth loved having Grandpa back again. Beth and Grandpa spent hours playing together with her toy garage, and for years after he died it was hard for Beth to let others play with it. The garage belonged to her and Grandpa. Nevin still went for long walks often accompanied by Sheila. When they were late getting home, Emma could assume they had stopped to have a visit with someone. He tried to get home from these walks before dark, but sometimes his ideas of dark and Emma's were a bit different.

Even though Nevin was now 80 years old, he still had his keen sense of adventure and was always ready to try something new. He enjoyed the roller skating parties with the Pearl River Church and began to think maybe he should learn to skate. The voluntary service unit in Pearl River was very impressed with his adventurous spirit and encouraged him to try, but at the counsel of Glenn and Emma he decided against it. He also enjoyed swimming and camping at Choctaw Lake in Ackerman, a favorite campground in Mississippi for both the Myers and the Benders. Nevin enjoyed diving in the lake, and would come up after a dive with a handful of dirt to show he had been to the bottom. Some of his adventures weren't quite as amusing to Glenn and Emma, because of their concern, as they were to him.

During this time, while going through some of his papers and letters, Nevin found a letter he had misplaced earlier. It was the last letter his sister Cora had written to him before she died, and he had always treasured it. He was thrilled to find it and reread it many times. Sometime later he was having stomachaches and the doctor put him into the hospital for tests. His writing materials, a new roll of stamps, and the letter from Cora went with him. After several days of tests he was diagnosed as having gall bladder problems. He was put on a special diet and allowed to go home. He wasn't home long when he realized he had forgotten to clean out his desk at the hospital where he had put Cora's letter. He and Emma rushed back but the desk had been emptied and no one would admit to having found anything in it. He assured them he didn't care about the stamps but only wanted a letter that was important to him, but it seemed useless. They referred him to the basement where he and Emma spent time going through garbage, but to no avail. This loss was difficult for him and he wondered aloud many times why he had taken the letter along.

Nevin always enjoyed visits from his other children. Emma and Glenn felt fortunate to be part of these visits. He would go to the butcher shop and look carefully for the very best steaks when family came. He also became interested in learning to cook a few favorite dishes, especially spaghetti.

During this time, Nevin again visited his scattered children, but not as often as he had before his second trip to Beirut. He spent some time with Don and Judy in Atlanta while their son Chris was in the hospital. Chris had been adopted with a birthmark on his forehead and was having it removed and skin grafted in its place. He was an active little boy but needed to remain quiet while the skin graft took hold. Nevin spent days in the hospital caring for his grandson and trying to keep him from being too active and run the risk of bumping his forehead. He also took his granddaughter Anneke on daily walks to the park in her stroller.

Nevin began to think and talk about what he should do when he "retired again," as he put it. He had come to Mississippi feeling he might possibly live out his life there, but he was experiencing a growing desire to be back in Delaware where he had lived so much of his life and where three of his sisters still lived. He weighed the various issues carefully. He spoke to Emma and Glenn about their earlier move to Mississippi to help in the Choctaw work, because if he returned to Delaware he would be leaving them alone. As he was working through this process, he talked with all his children. They encouraged him to think about what he really wanted to do and what would best meet his needs, both in nurturing and being nurtured, at this stage in life. Finally he decided to move back to Delaware.

At first, he questioned how he would feel going back to the Brick Church after the difficult experiences there, but time had brought deep healing. Surely with so many people with needs and hurts, he could find a place to plug in. So the decision was made.

As Nevin began making more definite plans, he decided he would like to buy a trailer to live in. He accepted Lura and Millard's invitation to move on to the home place with them and selected a trailer with careful deliberation. Emma remembers the job of going through some of his boxes with him as he decided what to keep and what to throw or give away. The fairly regular coffee breaks helped make the job fun.

After packing was completed and school was over for the year, the little caravan set out in May, 1973. Glenn pulled a Nationwide trailer behind the Rambler and Emma and Nevin followed in Nevin's car. Sheila, Beth, and Milli took turns riding in the two vehicles.

There were mixed emotions for all of them as they realized that the years of working and living closely together in Mississippi, years of trauma and amazing victory and grace, were coming to an end. After two days of travel with an overnight stop to see Don and Judy and family along the way, it was good to drive in the lane toward the home place and see the trailer Nevin had selected waiting for them.

Fourteen

RETURN TO GREENWOOD

Going home.

—In a number of ways, Nevin's
return to Greenwood was going home.

FOR BOTH ESTHER, WHO LEFT THE FAMILY in 1967, and for Nevin, who left in 1975, coming to the end of life on earth without the pain of prolonged illness or loss of mental abilities was a gift from God.

But there was a negative side to this. They and the family were not able to say good-bye to one another as they would have liked. Good-byes have always been important in the Bender family. Farewells have often stretched out for many minutes, even when leaving each other for only a month, or perhaps for a year and on occasion for several years. No one in the family was able to say good-bye to Esther or Nevin when the moment to leave this earth had come.

Nevin came closer to bidding farewell than Esther. During his last two years at Greenwood he came more completely to terms with the paradoxes of both the exhilarating and deeply painful experiences of his life. In a sense he experienced these two years as an extended leave-taking while staying very much alive. This occurred in a number of ways.

First, he had come to terms with Esther's passing.

It would be a mistake to see Nevin's life after Esther's death as a painless journey. It was clear to his children that he missed Esther to a degree that words cannot convey. After her death he turned his attention to being with his children and their families and to becoming involved in the everyday activities and concerns of their lives.

In spring, 1973, shortly before moving to Delaware, he visited Titus and Ann and their family in Norman, Oklahoma. Nevin made clear he would like to go north on Interstate 35 to the place near the small town of Perry, Oklahoma, where Esther had died nearly six years earlier. They found the place, near an overpass and stopped. He repeated the details of her death. It was here he had looked over and had seen she was unconscious. At this very place he had tried to rouse her and the crushing truth had begun to sink in—she was gone. He had driven quickly to a small cafe to call for help. So Titus and Ann took their father on to that cafe and Nevin told an attentive waitress of his eventful stop there six years before. They went on to the funeral home where the director had taken Nevin under his wing. The director had helped make arrangements for the return of Esther's body and stayed with Nevin at the Oklahoma City airport, waiting until his son Titus arrived.

On many occasions Nevin had worked through the loneliness of Esther's leaving. Yet for him this "journey back" was important in completing this chapter of his life. The next time he visited Titus and Ann he felt no need to return to Perry.

After several years Nevin considered remarriage. With his gentle ways and a reputation to match, a number of widowed women came into his life as close friends. For him this was healing and invigorating. As always, Nevin valued his children's insights and concerns. All of his daughters remember serving as listening ears and looking at potential joys and problems that might follow. Nevin's sons and daughters had one concern: whatever choice he would make he should be treated with kindness and respect in his need always to be growing and learning.

One event, for which all of his children are grateful, occurred at the 1974 family reunion at Springs, Pennsylvania. There, as a group, they made clear to Nevin they would support him in whatever decision he would made about remarriage. Mildred remembers walking back with him to his sleeping place for the night. He told her he did not know that he would go further in plans toward remarriage but the affirmation of the family meant much to him. As time passed and Nevin's life became filled with the lives of his children and grandchildren, the "just friends" relationship with these older women had become enough. It seems significant that the accident that took Nevin's life happened while he was providing transportation for one of these friends, Sylvia Mast, whose friendship meant a great deal to him.

Second, these two years were a time to get more deeply in touch with his siblings' and his family's roots. There was time to deepen relationships with three surviving sisters, Lucy, Amelia, and Nanna. He invited them to his trailer for food and conversation, and visited in their homes. As their older brother he had always been special to them and they to him. During the last couple years the relationship between Nevin and his sister Amelia became particularly close, especially after her husband Eli died, as they shared each other's loneliness. Both before and after his sister Lucy and Ted Beachy were married in 1974, the three of them spent much time together.

Nevin's guest book shows that he and his sister Nanna also were together on a number of occasions. Visits from his children and their spouses became opportunities for inviting his sisters for supper. And there were others who ate at his table— children and grandchildren as well as other friends from the community and from a distance. At mealtime his specialty was spaghetti, which Nevin prepared with the confidence of a chef.

One crucial event was the pilgrimage to Springs, Pennsylvania, in summer 1974. In retrospect it was especially appropriate that about a year before Nevin's death the family had their last family reunion with him present, near Nevin's boyhood home. This provided a sense of completion that symbolized the deeper acceptance of Nevin for his own history and that of his parents and siblings.

For Nevin it must have been a "Trip to Bountiful." They walked over to the home place where Nevin had grown up. The barn, especially, had a look of history about it (ancient history, perhaps, since it needed repairs). They even dreamed of the possibility of buying this old home place. But deep inside they knew it was just a dream.

Don remembers his father pointing out a tree and saying, "I used to sit under this tree." They walked across the bridge, down the road, and up a hill to the area which had been the entrance to the mine that Nevin's family had operated. Ginny remembers the bounce in Nevin's step that day as he shared with his children and grandchildren the memories of his experiences on the home place.

Nevin pointed out the field which the family of his grandfather, Wilhelm, had walked across one fateful day in the 1830s. Wilhelm had come from Germany as a 16-year-old lad to avoid being drafted into the military and to prepare for his family to come to America in several years. He had not heard from his family for a long time and feared they had been lost at sea. Not knowing they had arrived in Baltimore and were on their way to Springs on foot, one can only imagine Wilhelm's sense of relief and exhilaration when his family came into view. Across the field he counted the distant figures. "One is missing," he told those who were with him. His father had died before the family could make the journey. Titus recalls, "To see the field across which they came into view to be reunited as a family, our family, was to look at holy ground."

Nevin showed us the area where his father, Valentine, had operated a still and told us the story for the first time. In an incident many years earlier, an Internal Revenue Service agent had been searching for, but had not been able to find the still. He promised Valentine if he would disclose its location he would not arrest him. When Valentine cooperated he was fined what was an enormous amount for those days. The openness that enabled Nevin to share this bit of history never before shared, touched his family deeply. This brought to mind the family history that shaped Valentine's and Nevin's position related to alcohol. Valentine had kept homemade alcoholic beverage in the basement until some young lads close to him became intoxicated one day. From that day on Valentine stopped keeping or using alcohol.

Nevin's brother Earl and his wife Katie were also present for a day during the reunion near Springs. Because of Earl's tendency, during his youth, to think for himself and to practice a significant degree of independence he had been somewhat isolated from the church community at Greenwood. He married Katie and moved to Indiana. Although he and Nevin had kept in touch through the years, the relationship had not been as close as Nevin would have wished. This had been changing in the last several years. As Nevin and Earl sat and talked at the family reunion it was clear they were becoming brothers in a profoundly deepening way. Emma remembers that time with Earl as a healing experience for the brothers. Earl was obviously moved that Nevin saw fit to include him and Katie in this family reunion at Springs.

Nevin and Mildred made a pilgrimage to Juniata County, Pennsylvania, that same summer. They visited the place where Esther had been born and the house where she was living when he was courting her, and even the place where he had proposed. Mildred remembers the hours they spent with Roy and Mary

Graybill who had been married in a double wedding ceremony with Nevin and Esther. The two couples had taken their honeymoon together. There in Juniata County they sat reminiscing about the wedding and the honeymoon at Niagara Falls.

Third, during these two years Nevin experienced an ever-growing appreciation for the potential of building community within community—in the ordinary events of everyday life. When they were young, his children were all conscious of Nevin's efforts as a pastor to help people find faith and find each other in public events. They remember his handing out bread and grape juice during communion as he spoke the following words in a quiet voice, as though Jesus were next to him, "As you eat this bread and drink this cup, you do show the Lord's death till he comes." The family remembers his carefully organized sermons spoken in words some people believed were focused too much around love rather than appealing to fear. They remember his bass voice as he and Esther sang with gusto. Many of his efforts to help create community were related to public life during their growing up years.

Those last two years, unfettered with public leadership, he celebrated around his own table and other informal settings with great enthusiasm. He overcame loneliness in his own life by helping drive the loneliness from the lives of others. For example, while Mildred was visiting him in summer, 1974, they invited to supper the following persons who had lost their spouses: Sylvia Mast, Polly Schlabach, Vernon Zehr, and Nevin's sisters Amelia and Lucy, along with the spouse of Lucy's remarriage, Ted Beachy. His sister Nanna one time jokingly voiced her jealousy at how tight the bonds were among this group who had lost their spouses. Lura remembers that Nevin met monthly in his trailer with Sylvia, Polly, Amelia, and Lucy. Toward the end he visited Lucy and Ted in their own home after she became less able to get out. This celebrating around the table was no radical change from Nevin and Esther's way of celebrating in earlier days. The family all remember the call,

"Look what we got," when oysters or ham were brought in from the grocery store or when trout arrived from the "fish man" in his pickup truck straight from the seacoast. But now informal celebrations shared with a few friends and family took center stage as a means of building community. Eating spaghetti or pancakes was a medium for celebrating life and faith with elders and youth alike.

Fourth, these were two years of bridge building. For both Nevin and Esther, bridge building had been a major theme of their lives. But now, without official church leadership responsibilities at Greenwood, Nevin, with little thought of political consequences, reached out to youth who were alienated from the local church. Ginny and Paul remember when her nephew was part of a group of youth who fell out of favor with the Greenwood Church. Nevin discovered that they were in danger of being purged from membership and invited them in for lunch. The youth were deeply impressed that Nevin invited them in as equals. Ginny's nephew spoke for years about that occasion. This was in stark contrast to a remark which Don, as a young person, had overheard a number of years earlier from a member of the Greenwood congregation, "We don't kick enough people out."

At Nevin's funeral one member of the Greenwood Church told the congregation of his appreciation for Nevin who had reached out to his daughter. As an unmarried mother, she had been in danger of being isolated from the church community where such "embarrassment" was usually avoided by a quickly arranged wedding.

Don and Mildred remember accompanying Nevin on his regular Sunday morning attendance at Tressler's Church where Millard was pastor, then to the Brick Church in the evening where he had pastored for decades. Don went with Nevin to the Brick Church one Sunday evening. Since Nevin's hearing was somewhat impaired they walked to the front. He remembers entering the church with a sense of warmth and openness that evening. One thing that strengthened Don's ability to forgive and be forgiven was Nevin's spirit of openness with the people. There, where his widely appreciated ministry had come to a painful conclusion one and one-half decades earlier, he was now asked to speak occasionally and was accepted with warmth. At Tressler's he had a standing invitation from Millard to speak when he "felt up to it."

Fifth, during these last two years Nevin was coming to terms in a deeper way with death as a part of life—a new chapter. Just before moving to Greenwood he visited the church in Oklahoma where Ann and Titus were members. After the Sunday school discussion about the importance of facing death ahead of time, Nevin talked with Titus and Ann about his sense of relief in being able to look death in the face. This attitude was also evident during his last two Greenwood years. Don remembers visiting Nevin during this time. Paul and Ginny brought to Nevin's trailer a film that told the story of a man who was nearing the end of his terminal illness. The film included conversations between him and his family. Don recalls that his father "was very much into the discussion."

It would be a mistake, however, to see Nevin as drawing back from life. Just before he moved to Greenwood, Ann asked Nevin what he dreaded most about getting older. His answer was immediate, "Losing my independence such as my driver's license." Millard remembers a near-accident as Nevin turned left off Route 13 to come home to his trailer the back way. The car behind him ignored his signal and sped around him on the left. Nevin described with satisfaction how he avoided the accident by slamming on the brakes at the last moment. However, knowing the concern of his children, Nevin reluctantly agreed with Millard and Lura that he would confine his nighttime driving to going to the Brick Church on Sunday evenings.

Titus remembers a conversation with his father just before he moved to Delaware. He wanted Nevin to locate the trailer against, rather than several hundred feet from, Lura and Millard's house so he would be closer in case he needed help. Nevin resisted vigorously and successfully. Independence and the ability to stay active were crucial to him.

Sixth, these last two years were a time to say good-bye to his children and grandchildren. For Nevin, the final two years at Greenwood were devoted to sharing his home with family from near and far. Nearly all of his children and their families spent a week or part of a week just being with their father and grandfather. Following are several memories from each of the nine children and their families about their times of visiting or being visited by Father/Grandfather during the last two years of his life. The memories begin with those living nearby and continue in order of age.

Living in his trailer just several hundred feet from Lura and Millard provided the support that was necessary while giving Nevin the space for a significant degree of independence. Lura remembers him asking regularly when she would be doing laundry, then bringing his over to be done together while they talked. Frequently he came to their place for supper. Millard remembers discussing theology with Nevin around the supper table. Lura recalls how he "flowed with" the grandchildren. For example, he would kid granddaughter Carol about her sizeable earrings. She would respond in kind. He accepted all of the grandchildren, even if some of their decisions were different from decisions he might have made.

Lura and her family checked daily to make sure Nevin was okay and just to talk. Millard usually walked over to chat with him for a few minutes when he saw Nevin backing out to leave. The morning of Nevin's accident, granddaughter Phyllis kidded Nevin about "taking Sylvia out."

Paul and Ginny lived near enough to stay in close touch with Nevin. Paul helped Nevin build the steps to his trailer. Sometimes Nevin went to Dover to visit them, returning that evening or staying overnight. Paul recognized that Nevin was "sometimes lonely, but not desperate. He knew what to do about it," such as relating to other people, including his family.

Paul particularly recalls time in Nevin's trailer, which captured for him the importance of his frequent visits with Nevin. They were talking about how it felt to live alone. Exhausted, Paul fell asleep in the living room chair. When he woke up and apologized Nevin said, "That's all right; it's just nice to sit here and be together." Sometimes there was a lot of conversation, but for both of them, being together was more important than the specific activity.

Miriam visited Nevin twice for an extended period of time during those last two years in Delaware. Soon after he arrived in Delaware she helped him clean the trailer. In spring 1975 Miriam again went to visit him by bus. She was in the process of looking for a table and chair set, so they made a day trip to Pennsylvania. Nevin "knew the right places to look." On the way they stopped to see two of Nevin's nieces, Margaret Schrock Eby and Mary Lou Lauver Blank, who lived in that general area. They traveled as usual, with her in the driver's seat and Nevin watching the map and the road to keep them on course. It was a good trip.

Miriam remembers the oyster stew which they enjoyed together several times. Nevin explained to her how to wait until the ends of the oysters began to curl just the right amount, then to take them off the heat and immediately put them into the milk. Oyster stew needed to be made "just right." Miriam again helped Nevin clean his trailer. She was hoping to return with some of her family that same summer to give it a "spring house cleaning." However, he died in June.

Hilda spent almost a week with Nevin in spring 1974 while Merlin kept the children. Nevin invited the uncles and aunts for supper. He wanted Hilda's help in making the meal. He decided he would like to have an old-fashioned home-cooked meal of Swiss fried steak and potatoes. Maybe Esther used to cook it this way. She warned Nevin she was not used to "fancy cooking" but it turned out to be a great evening. Hilda remembers frequent evenings of talking around the table.

Out by the milk house the daffodils were just coming into full bloom. She and Nevin picked a beautiful bouquet, put them in a pint jar with water, and took them to Esther's grave. Nevin was so pleased to be "giving her this gift."

Nevin's first visit to Titus and Ann after they moved to Oklahoma was in spring 1973. He went along to one of the classes taught by Titus at the University of Oklahoma. After being introduced Nevin made a few comments. Following the class period a number of the students gathered around him, talking and asking questions. Because Titus had moved from pastoring into teaching, it was heartening to have Nevin tell him he could now understand how he felt about teaching. Being a pastor had always been special for Nevin whose roots were deep in that vocation. To his credit he encouraged each of his children to do what they believed they ought to be doing.

Titus, Ann, and their family were the only ones who did not get to Delaware to see Nevin in his trailer. Ironically, plans were nearly complete for them to move to Harrisonburg, Virginia, to be nearer Nevin and the extended family, as well as Ann's family. But the timing was off.

Mildred was able to spend much of summer 1974 with her father. Together they took a pilgrimage to the scene of Esther's childhood years. Mildred remembers he was totally absorbed as he relived his and Esther's earlier years. He pointed out the house where Esther spent many childhood days, even recalling the specific room where he proposed to Esther. As Nevin reminisced with Mildred and Roy and Mary Graybill (the couple with whom Nevin and Esther had shared a double wedding and honeymoon) about these events, Mildred remembers his deep belly laughs. The "young" in Nevin that all of his children had seen came through frequently.

"Mildred, you have learned to know me well these last several years," Nevin told her. "I have found a place of deep peace."

He hoped she would communicate this to others who knew and loved him. As he said good-bye he mused, "In case anything happens before you return, know that everything is well."

Emma remembers a week she and Beth spent with Nevin in spring 1975, several months before he died. They had a wonderful time visiting Nevin, Millard, Lura, Paul, and Ginny. When Nevin made spaghetti she kidded him, "I think you are enjoying this more than when you were living with us." He responded, "You know, Emma, I do kind of like my independence." She found herself hoping he could stay in the trailer as long as he lived. It also seemed important to Nevin to drive when they went places. Emma was impressed with how careful he was, admitting that his reflexes weren't as sharp as he grew older, and trying to compensate. Nevin told her that he had quit driving at night because his sight was failing him somewhat. Emma was glad she could tell him in all honesty that she was relaxed with his driving. .

Nevin Jr. remembers discussing with his father efforts to develop a covenant at the church Nevin Jr. was pastoring. He also recalls discussing sermons he had preached there. His father had always been interested in reading sermons Nevin Jr. had preached, especially when he dealt with an issue of deep interest.

Nevin and Lourene and their family spent time with the older Nevin in November, 1974. Nevin especially remembers the pancakes, no doubt eaten with maple syrup they had brought with them. When their father was ready to cook, he remarked, "There are two things I can make—spaghetti and pancakes." Lourene recalls the care and delight with which Nevin fixed supper for them. Standing over the electric stove, he measured everything carefully, looking at the recipe and then taking the next step. This carefulness was probably both the perfectionist in him and the cook not quite secure in his new skills. She remembers him looking up with a big smile as he wondered if she wanted to taste it.

Don and Judy and their family visited Nevin soon after he moved back to Greenwood. The relationship between Nevin and Judy had developed into one of extraordinary closeness. An affirmation of this was something Judy shared with the family at their first communion service after Nevin's death. She had become a Franciscan many years before to find the spirit of St. Francis. There she did not find it, but ten years later she knew she had found a kindred spirit of St. Francis when she met Don's father, Nevin.

One evening during Don's last visit with Nevin in 1975 Don offered to rub Nevin's tired feet. Concerned that feet are often associated with bad odors, Nevin said, "That would be great if you would not mind." What began as a simple gesture became a much greater gift of love because Nevin saw it as so special. Don's took his father to the greenhouse one day to buy several plants. Nevin wanted to know the name of each one and was particularly intrigued with the prayer plant. At the time of this writing, Don and Judy still treasure this plant.

And seventh, these last two years were for Nevin a time for expanding his understanding of a phrase he used so often in his prayers, "Finally take us to heaven without the loss of one." No doubt, early in their marriage he and Esther were thinking primarily of their own. Heaven without the family would lose much of its appeal. It became clear in his church leadership role that the members of the church were included in his and Esther's plea. Then there were the excluded church members whom others could not see as "real children of God." Nevin and Esther pleaded for their future, sometimes creating controversy for themselves and their family. In Mississippi it was clear that Nevin and Esther needed to find broader definitions of how God might include a wider circle of people than they had envisioned earlier. In the Middle East Nevin's honesty pulled him toward recognizing God's work in the hearts and lives of Muslim friends, even though they worshiped quite differently. During Nevin's last several years he frequently said to his children, "God may have things in mind we do not begin to understand."

One event that symbolizes Nevin's acceptance of all who came presenting a need, occurred one evening while he was spending the night at Paul and Ginny's home. Their daughter Joan was also there. There was a noise on the back porch about 11:30 at night. A man had come on the porch, looking for a place to spend the night and fell to the floor intoxicated. In gentle tones Nevin tried to get information about his needs. Nevin thought it might be feasible for him to spend the night on the porch in that condition. Joan was frightened and, with Nevin's permission, called the police. When the officer arrived to take the man to the station for the night, Nevin offered to bring coffee and breakfast to the station next morning for the inebriated man. The officer hardly knew how to respond. It appeared this was the first time he had received such an offer. He assured Nevin they would take care of the man's breakfast. Joan remembers a deep sadness within her that the world no longer seemed to "work that way." For her this event remains as a "hallmark of Grandpa."

How Nevin and Esther worked out the details of an ever-emerging theology, to believe God wanted to take care of us all "without the loss of one," we probably will never know. But one thing is clear, they were never able to find satisfaction in the demise of anyone, even outcasts, whether these outcasts were seen by their peers as God's children or not.

Although all of Nevin's family knew his time could be short, none of them was prepared for the news that came that fateful day of June 9, 1975. Their father had died. He was taking Sylvia Mast to pick up her car which had been repaired and to leave his for repairs. As they entered Route 113 near Milford, the car Nevin was driving was hit. Marvin Nicely, a nurse from the Greenwood Church came by and stopped. Nevin, though critically injured, was conscious. Consistent with his usual concern that no mistake of his cause others to suffer, Nevin asked

Marvin, "Was it my fault?" Judging with a quick glance, Marvin assured him it looked like it was not. Nevin was relieved. He was not to know before his death that this information was not entirely accurate. The occupants of the other car were not seriously injured. Sylvia was rather seriously hurt but soon recovered. Nevin's injuries also were serious. At the hospital Paul and Ginny, who were there for a doctor's visit, saw attendants rushing someone from the ambulance on a stretcher, not realizing that on it lay their father near death. (A recollection of this appears below in the Appendix.)

Most of the family's tears were shed in the presence of those who knew them well and had cared deeply about them and their parents. All of the sons and sons-in-law wanted to help carry their father's body to the grave. Nevin and Esther had wrapped their love around their children and their families, then gave them room to grow. Symbolically, the family wanted personally to carry Nevin's body to the grave to say to him and Esther, "Thank you for being there for us."

Nevin and Esther encouraged their family and the people whose lives they touched to dream, but not of winning battles against others. They encouraged them to struggle for what they believed in, but not in such a way as to forget to celebrate. They encouraged them to be themselves, yet to be in relationship to all of God's children and God's creatures.

Step by step they widened the circle of people with whom they hoped to spend eternity "without the loss of one." They walked in the shoes of Native Americans and fundamentalists. They walked in the shoes of Christians and people of the Jewish faith. In Beirut, Nevin walked in the shoes of Muslims. They walked in the shoes of persons coming into the Conservative Conference and persons whose journey was taking them from the Conservative Conference or from the Mennonite church. They walked in the shoes of those beleaguered by struggles from within and those who were rejected or oppressed by other people. While they were not swept from the central core of their own faith, they recognized authentic spiritual journeys by persons from diverse theological perspectives, even when they did not fully understand those journeys. However, one kind of journey that disturbed them was a journey in which persons found it "necessary" to hurt other people or to draw circles that excluded others from their lives.

Without realizing it Nevin left for his family a present from him and Esther—a pint of oysters in his refrigerator. After his death, they discovered this symbol of the way they brought together the deeply spiritual and the everyday physicalness of life. Oysters, as indicated throughout the book, were one of Nevin's favorite family treats. Little did he know that it would be his children who would make this pint of oysters into stew and eat them together when they gathered a month or two after his memorial service. For many of them, perhaps all, it was the most sacred communion service—communion with oyster stew— they had ever shared.

AFTERWORD

It is a soft summer day in early June. The late afternoon sun shines on the heads of those gathered in the room, lighting the varying shades of gray. The pace of the conversation picks up and faces, reflecting lives that have traveled many paths, relax and soften.

In their opening to the flow of stories the lines they share in common begin to come into focus. The laugh lines around the eyes shared by an older sister and younger brothers deepen with stories of children's misadventures. The deep belly laugh shared by those separated by years and place in the family echoes around the room.

There are others there too. Spouses who have become part of this original family through years of shared celebration, common meals, common losses. They gather also, their love for their own spouses but also these "adopted" siblings apparent. This is a family that holds its members close, that values membership in the clan above what are sometimes painful differences. That holding includes those who join by marriage, by birth, or even sometimes by friendship.

My husband and I were there too that day and the next morning, honorary Benders, privileged to share this moment in a family's life as they gathered to once again share stories that had been shared before, to remember, to mourn, to celebrate and to reclaim their collective history.

I am a lover of stories. It doesn't matter where the stories come from: around the world, imagination, people's lives, or a family's legacy. No matter where the story comes from it holds the possibility of connecting us to each other, of reminding us of the collective human experience, and of allowing us to look in at the unique way we each choose to use the resources we have been given.

Listening to these Bender stories on those magical days in June reflected that collective human experience. We all grow up in families, we all learn through the people we love. Sometimes those lessons are painful and sometimes they come easy. This particular family's experience connects with any family's experience.

They are unique as well. All families have rules, spoken or unspoken. The Benders were no different except that their unique rule was spoken and is represented in the title of this book: *without the loss of one.* Listening to their stories, being invited into the inner heart of a family to observe the story's evolution, provided an opportunity to watch the stories unfold. Stories of missed connections with each other or of misunderstandings, stories of conflict, and stories of coming to new understandings around the family story. In every aspect of the storytelling, through pain and joy, the commitment to hold onto each other, without the loss of one, was evident. At one point in the morning I had that sense I often have when people gather to tell their stories, that the Author of all our stories was walking in the room and the ground of that basement room had indeed become holy.

In the sharing of stories recognition grew of how different they were in the middle of their connection to each other. How does a family love into a next generation, especially in the context of children who represent increasingly different cultures and expressions of faith—and thus ones who, without a family connection, would never connect? Story doesn't make those differences disappear. But somehow in the context of a shared history, the differences diminish and the strengths in that shared history become apparent as a legacy that can nurture future generations no matter what their differences.

So the Bender's story results in a book you have now read. The book was partly motivated by that family rule of "without the loss of one." One of the siblings gathered to ponder the stories clustered around that rule said, "My siblings are the stones across Niagara Falls, I want to bring my children across those stones." There was a recognition that one of the ways we hold onto each other in an increasingly geographically spread community is through sharing what has gone before. We need to know the soil from which we grew. We need to carry within us the stories of grandparents, great aunts and uncles who we may not have known. They are flesh of our flesh, bone of our bone in literal and figurative ways.

So how do we tell our stories to each other? How do we capture and hold onto those stories of our past and of our present? I suggest these ways:

First, face-to-face storytelling takes some intentionality but the contexts can be created. How often do children ask their parents about the day the child was born, about a time when the parent did something wrong as a child and got into trouble? Every request for a story is an opportunity for sharing. Take advantage of such opportunities. Tell the stories at bedtime, in the car, around the table. Create family storytelling evenings at family reunions. Once one person starts, others will follow. If the storytelling lags, use a prompt. Tell about a time when.... Or ask, "Do you remember when...?" Once the tradition begins, it will carry on with each gathering or become an accepted practice around the table.

In these contexts listening is key. Stories need to be listened to in their totality so whether teller are four or 40 or 80, whether they are expert tellers or ones who give too many details, their story deserves to be born and respected. In this context of respect safety grows and even the shy ones at the table will enter in.

Modern technology has provided us with wonderful opportunities for storytelling. Informal video captures moments in a child or adult's life that will never emerge again and then become grist for the mill of more family storytelling.

Video can be used in a more formal way to capture the family story. Particularly for older people, sometimes an afternoon with a loved child or grandchild and a video camera is a wonderful way to capture their stories of their parents and grandparents in a way all will treasure in the years to come. This form of storytelling is also enhanced with a listener who comes prepared with a list of questions. A good listener makes the camera disappear.

Through the magic of e-mail, written stories are accessible to extended family spread across the country. Family letters a generation ago chronicled the first steps of a child, the funny phrase from the lips of a four year old, the joy of a new home, all the normal transitions of life. Those letters were limited by their inability to be easily shared with the whole family. E-mail allows for that sharing to happen easily and spontanously. Stories can be started, shared, added to, and archived. The stories shared between visits can keep that storytelling connection alive so that when life finally brings us to each other's door, we are picking up in the middle of the conversation, not having to start a whole new one.

When we reached the end of our days together, I looked around the room again. Now I saw the people differently. Now I saw people who had been loved by two now gone, people who had been asked to step into life fully by parents who didn't live halfway. All had taken the story their parents had given them and shaped it with their own life experience and culture. The story of each one's life was different than the story of their parents, but running through each story were indeed Nevin and

Esther, whispering to each to hold onto each other, to let no one be lost. Their lives reflected that commitment, not just to each other but to the world they each serve in their own way. Each had loved others on the road, drawn them into that incredible Bender family, surrounded them with love and in very real ways kept them from being lost in the rush of our culture.

I hope each of you who read this book learn your story, hold those you love dearer, and write new stories each day of faith, of risk for a better day, and of love.

—*Joan K. King, Telford, Pennsylvania, is a family therapist, a nurse consultant, and a professional storyteller.*

APPENDIX I: REFLECTIONS

REFLECTIONS

The reflections that follow were included in the first (family) edition of this book. At that time children and grandchildren were invited to share with the larger family their reflections and concerns. These are the responses that were received. The family thinks it is important to include them again in this revised edition.

Thoughts on the day my father died
Written March 13, 1983

Ginny and I had been at the hospital for X-rays of her wrist and a fresh bandage, following a fall a week before. Just as we were ready to walk out the door of the emergency room we stood aside to allow the emergency team to enter with the two people whose identities we did not know.

We watched the stretchers come in through the alcove of the emergency entrance. First came a woman, white-faced, appearing dead. She was followed by a man of medium build, unconscious, but without that death-like appearance. We recognized neither of them as the attendants wheeled them through the door and down the hall.

On the way to Ginny's sister's house we detoured to the scene of the accident and saw a square back Volkswagen that looked very much like the one my father drove, but I was sure it was not his because I felt certain he did not have his roof rack on as the wrecked car had. (Denial is a powerful defense against the reality of things we find difficult to accept.)

We found a phone and immediately I dialed the number of my sister, Lura. Then I knew that the car on the side of Route 113 was my father's car, and the man on the stretcher was my father.

A few minutes later we were back at the hospital. That man on the stretcher had been my father. It was the last time I saw him alive and I had not known him as they rolled him by.

Three hours later, as we waited to go in to see him for just a few minutes before he went into surgery, the doctor came out to report that "Mr. Bender did not make it." I was devastated; my father had died!

—Paul Bender

My Grandpa and Grandma Bender Bender and the meaning of faith

I feel blessed to have had the opportunity to come to know Grandpa and Grandma Bender as well as I did. My memories of Grandma are not as numerous or as vivid as those of Grandpa, and yet I feel that I learned to know her spirit. I can imagine her being in this room with me today. I can picture her facial expressions, imagine what she might say, and feel the warmth of her presence.

One of my clearest memories of Grandma goes back to the Mississippi reunion of 1967. I remember her optimism and compassion and her patience with the grandchildren, even when we were crowded into her kitchen while she was trying to prepare meals. I will never forget Grandma's gentleness, her soft spoken-manner, and her ability to make everyone feel welcome and accepted. My last memory of Grandma is of her waving good-bye to our family as we left New York harbor aboard the *Michelangelo* in 1967. Grandma's wave made us feel loved and cared for unconditionally and my memory of this event is all the more precious since Grandma was waving good-bye to us for the last time. As I looked down on Grandpa and Aunt Millie arriving at the airport in Beirut in 1968, I was profoundly aware of our loss.

I have many vivid memories of the time which I spent with Grandpa. To me he was grandparent, mentor, role model, and friend. He was a friend who accepted me without conditions, who was there when I needed him, who was patient with me, and who spent time listening and talking to me. I can recall almost as if it were yesterday our many walks along the Mediterranean Sea during his year in Beirut. Grandpa loved to walk and he so much appreciated the beauty of the Mediterranean. I can picture him taking in a deep breath of the breeze off of the sea and the expressions of satisfaction on his face. Grandpa truly loved being alive, and he loved the process of life, and he reveled in its details. I remember him saying on one occasion that he believed he could make it to live 100 years.

Grandpa's love of life and its details went hand in hand with one of his most wonderful attributes, his empathy. I always felt that Grandpa wanted to get to know and understand me, to feel with me. As he immersed himself in the lives of others he became able to support them, to help them, and to empathize with them. Grandpa met you where you were and accepted you for what you were.

I remember an example of Grandpa's support and empathy which meant the world to me at the time. During one of his visits to Cambridge, Grandpa and I shared a bedroom and, on one occasion, misbehavior on my part meant that I would go to bed early on that evening. I explained my predicament to Grandpa and asked him if he would join me at this earlier time.

He agreed to be my companion and turn in early, thus easing the pain of my situation. Grandpa was never above it all but able to understand individual people at many different stages of life and with diverse needs.

Grandpa's immersion in the lives of others stood at the very core of his faith. Grandpa's faith brought him closer to people and to their lives and this may be the greatest lesson I learned from him. Faith and the spiritual experience should bring people closer to one another rather than separate them, as often happens. Religion should not place us on a lofty plain and isolate us from others but rather should bring us into closer contact with others, even though they may not share our values and faith. Religion has the ability to separate people because of the universal scope of the principles involved.

For Grandpa, the Christian faith was an invitation to become involved in the lives of others, to empathize with one another and to present an alternative to others through the example of one's life. The teachings of the New Testament involve universal principles, but the fundamental message is as simple as it is beautiful. God became flesh and lived among us and in so doing taught us how to love God and how to love ourselves and one another. My memory of Grandpa has been so important in my grasp of this message. Grandpa's faith and belief in Jesus kept him down to earth and led him to touch the lives of many people in ways that are so numerous and deep that they could never be adequately expressed in words.

I have a very special memory of a conversation which I had with Grandpa when I was 12 years old. Grandpa and I were on a walk together during one of his visits to Arlington. We were discussing the life of Jesus, his crucifixion and resurrection. I asked Grandpa why the crucifixion was such a sacrifice on the part of Jesus if he knew that he would be resurrected and return to heaven. Grandpa stopped in his tracks, looked at me intensely and earnestly and quietly said, "the pain and suffering." For me this conversation beautifully revealed the focus of Grandpa's faith.

Grandpa treasured his relationships with people and he valued the concrete manifestations of these relationships. Aunt Millie gave him a harmonica as a gift on one occasion and I remember the meticulous way in which he cared for the harmonica. For Grandpa, it was a symbol of an important relationship. I do not have any vivid memories of Grandpa relating to Grandma, but I do recall something he said about her at a Lauver reunion several years after Grandma's passing. Grandpa introduced me to Uncle William Lauver and said to me, "This is Grandma's brother, the only brother she ever had." Grandpa's expressions, words and dispositions at this time spoke volumes to me of the depth of his love and appreciation for Grandma. He cared about everything which was important to Grandma in a way that was not possessive.

One of the greatest gifts which Grandma and Grandpa gave to all of us is the example of their relationship to each other. I know that Grandpa and Grandma would consider our knowing and appreciating this to be a most meaningful tribute. Their lives gave us hope while they were with us and our memories of them are a beacon and still give us hope today. I believe this is why my memory of singing "Lift your Glad Voices" at Grandpa's funeral still brings tears to my eyes.

—*Daryl Jay Swartz*

Refugees
>My sisters and I
>Used to play
>"Refugees"
>By wrapping up
>In an old holey red blanket
>And stumbling through the desert
>In the living room.
>People laugh when I tell them
>But I hold it close to me

Because I've never met another person
With that memory
—*Jean Bender*

"You Have Considered"

My mother and dear friend, Lura, has reminded me of a part of the following song when I have tried to "carry the weight" myself instead of relying on God. I've been awed by her stability and down-to-earth understanding of life. I'm thankful to Grandpa and Grandma who nurtured this understanding that has been passed on through her. I'm also thankful for their love of music and God. I'll never forget Grandpa's deep bass voice.

You have considered your needs
Against the balance of your power
And know that their weight is great, their weight is great
You have considered your pain
And tried to erase what you suffer
Until there seems no way of escape, no way of escape.

Chorus:
Have you considered the force of the wind
Or the abrasion of the river falls
Under many tons of ocean water living things survive
Beneath the weight of it all
Have you considered all that I have made
Have you considered my awesome strength
I can make your little bit of faith to move a mountain tall
Be not afraid. Be not afraid. Be not afraid.
You have considered your fears
Against the balance of your courage
And know that their weight is great, their weight is great
You have considered yourself
And tried to die to sin in your own strength
Until there seems no way of escape, no way of escape.

Bridge:
Listen to the voice of my Spirit. Be still and wait

The balance of your needs are no match
to the greatness of my love and strength.
—*Phyllis Benner*

To Mother
You're standing at the ironing board.
I hear you now, as we talk of Papa's going away
to hold meetings. I am complaining,
not wanting him to go, missing him already.
"I have to step on myself," you say
"when Papa is called to go, and I wish
he didn't need to, and we both feel he should.
I step on myself, then I can go on."
That breaks my heart as I remember—
rips me apart. I get this image—you, pushing
yourself down, making yourself small enough,
obedient enough, to step on.
Unable to bear that picture
I reach out for another one.
You're sitting in your apron
at the table, laughing
until your plump belly shakes
and the tears roll down your face.
You use your apron
to wipe them away.
We all laugh
loving your laughter
laughing with you
loving you
and grateful to see the worry lines
gone for a little while.
Both of these are you.
You held too much within your being—
whole centuries when being a woman
meant marrying and birthing children—
as many as God gave you.
And yet you chose.
Remember when I asked you,
"Are you glad you married Papa?
Would you do it again?" (What nerve!)

And you answered, "It's been hard and wonderful—
and yes, I'm glad,
and I'd do it again."
And then you added, as we talked
about Papa—and men—and we were teasing, asking
was it more important to marry a good man
or a handsome man?
Your answer lies deep in the warm places of my heart.
With your mischievous look, your eyes twinkling,
you said, "If you can't have both, what matters most
is to have a good man. But I am lucky—I got a man
who is both very good and very handsome!"
You meant it and you were right.
Sometimes we'd tease again
"Don't you wish you'd have stopped sooner
having children?"
And you'd smile and ask,
"When do you think we should have quit?
Before which child?"
We couldn't agree on that one
and we'd laugh and talk
glad we had all been born.
Remembering
tears me open
heals me
I stay with both
It's the journey of women.
Mother, thank you
for what you taught me in your quiet way
about being a woman
about loving—
how much you knew.
Thank you, too, for what you couldn't teach me
that I've had to learn in other ways.
I walk a different path. Yet
we share our sisterhood, its pain and joy
passionately, fully.
For it surely is a lifetime work,
this learning to be a woman. So says the poet
Yes, and it's not learned in a lifetime, even

many lifetimes, perhaps. Your story continues
in me
in all your daughters
in all daughters and mothers
so totally different
so totally the same.
Many years since your death—
and even yet, your spirit's strong within
beautiful, free
You laugh with me
and cry and love passionately
and grieve the loss
trusting the pain
birthing the passion
the passion birthing
Creating new life—
Is this what is meant by eternal life?
—Mildred Bender

My garage buddy

I wonder, Grandpa, if you ever wonder about me, about the dreams I've discovered, the beauty I enjoy and the people I love. Do you wonder if my childhood love of our toy garage has transformed into an imagination that can create new worlds and new lives? That remains my only memory of you—taking the cars and pushing them down the ramp over and over again as the magic never faded for me with watching the elevator move up and down. Did the magic exist for you, or did you know that the elevator only moved because of springs and levers? But somehow in my heart I know you weren't just humoring a three-year-old granddaughter—you too wondered if the car would make it to the top and knew with certainty that the noise of the elevator was not springs that needed oil but the grunting of the little man inside who ran it.

My memory has faded with age. I can no longer remember how often we played or what we would say to each other. But I pull out the worn yellowed remembrance and dust it off occasionally and try to touch you in the visions of my mind. But you were my pal, my garage buddy, and something about that time lodged itself deeply into my subconscious so that no other child could dare touch that toy. But then my rational mind increased with age and decided that I was being too unreasonable. I think I would have been 17 when that milestone was reached.

What would you think of me now, Grandpa? I would have been so easy to love then with my simple childhood wonder and excusable immaturity. But now I'm older and excuses are harder made for the choices of my life. Would you still appreciate my imagination and free mind when hooked to a 22-year-old body? Would the love flow as freely now that I'm older?

But perhaps the memory of our garage joy would be most prevalent in your mind. I now know who you are, my closet garage pal—the great preacher, teacher, missionary, and pioneer. Other people's memories struggle to replace the only glimpse I had of you. But I still think of you crouching on the floor and rolling the cars down over and over and over.

Please don't be angry with me that I can only remember you through the unblemished eyes of a child. You tricked me though, buddy. I never realized you were older than me until much later when I saw you the very last time asleep. Your body didn't know what I knew with complete certainty—that your soul belonged to childhood and toy garages.

—*Beth Myers*

A tribute to Nevin from his daughter, Miriam
(Reprinted from *Brotherhood Beacon,* by permission)
Dear Dad,

I can still feel the pain I experienced that summer day in June when word came that you had been killed in an automobile accident. I felt such deep loneliness and emptiness.

During my last visit with you in your trailer in Delaware, you were making the most of life as you then experienced it with your usual enthusiasm and enjoyment. You always loved life, and whatever the situation, you rose to the occasion and found reasons to rejoice and be glad.

You showed us the way to God by precept and example. The words and instructions you spoke with your lips corresponded with what we saw and lived out in daily life.

Loving, gentle, and kind are three words that are very descriptive of you, Dad. There are several examples especially that I think of in which these manifestations of the Spirit were demonstrated so well.

I do not ever remember receiving a punishment from you that was not preceded with an explanation of why you were doing it. You also assured us children that you were hurting as badly as we were. At the time, that did not seem real, but after nearly 42 years of parenting, I understand that you were indeed speaking the truth in love. You always took time after our punishment to assure us of your love.

Another example is the way in which these words were demonstrated by you toward Mother. You so joyously did the little things for her and were free in showing her your affection. One incident stands out vividly in my mind. Mother somehow got her dress shoes very muddy. You gathered all the needed equipment for cleaning them and went outside to work at those shoes till they were ready for church wear. I recall thinking, "Dad, you really seem to be enjoying that." You did because of your love for Mother.

You had a way of making small events seem special. The many trips we took to our grandparents in Pennsylvania were highlights of our time spent together as family. We were a crowded bunch in the car. To help prevent any boredom and stress that might come, you would often start singing. As soon as the rest of us picked up on it, you would go to your deep bass, and we would sing-a-long as we traveled. You and Mother singing "Silent Night" as a delightful awakener on Christmas morning is a cherished memory.

Thank you, Dad, for all the things you meant to me as a father; also for allowing me a glimpse into your imperfections, which are a part of all of us. That has made my way easier in accepting my own imperfections as a parent.

I love you, Dad,
Your daughter, Miriam
—*Miriam Jantzi*

Nevin's final family circle letter
Greenwood, Delaware
April 9, 1975
Dearest Family,

I just got through reading the C.L. [circle letter] in which each of you participated in writing, including Paul Lynn and Daryl. Thanks.

It seems to me it was the best letter yet, each of you speaking deeply which I did enjoy. Each of you touched spots which I have been feeling deeply about, some more, some less. Space won't permit me to touch on everything.

At this point I felt I needed a rest. I read all your letters without a magnifying glass, which tells something about the new lenses that I now have. They are quite an improvement. My blood circulation of course is a bit at a minus. Age tells a bit of the story. But I'm really pleased and thankful for what I have. I have much to be thankful for.

I believe I can understand at least in part, the love, the caring, the understanding and even the hurt that each of you feels. What I experience is very similar. I believe that finally truth and right will triumph. Many, many people feel the deep hurt. And it seems a bit dim as we seek to analyze what we see, to see triumph. I am pleased with the effort each of you makes. I share your desires deeply. Not a sparrow falls without our Father's notice. He does care deeply for people. He does desire our caring and what we can do. I am with you. The last chapter is not written.

I was real pleased and felt encouraged with the visit of Hilda, Miriam, Don, Emma, and Beth, and Saturday I'll be pleased to see Nevin's and their family. Paul's have been here to add to my joys. Paul and Doreen and then Ann and Brad added so much. The Lord bless each of you. Millard's and their family are close and they do mean so much to me.

Last Saturday morning Donna Carol and Wayne and Uncle Ted's were with me for breakfast. We had pancakes and country sausage. At about 10:00 a.m., they left from Milford for home by plane. It was one in which Wayne's have a share. When they came near Wheeling, West Virginia, they hit a snowstorm and decided to land. They were held up for some time. Later they landed at Donna Carol's brother in Ohio (Willard). They picked up a third passenger there and left for upper Michigan at 7:30 p.m. That was our last word that evening. Uncle Ted's kept vigil and I did, too. At 11, I believe it was, I decided to rest. The next morning we learned that they had reached home safely. It must have been around 11:00 p.m. Eastern time. I did enjoy that visit very much.

I want to have John Swartzentruber's and their family some evening, and later Elmer Hostetler and his children and his mother, in each case for supper. There are others I have in mind. I desire to do, in a small way, what I can. MCC doesn't escape my interest. Last Saturday evening was when Miriam and Elmer came, and left for Virginia Tuesday morning. Their being here filled a big place.

I had company from Dover for about an hour, a Jehovah's Witness. We didn't seek to destroy each other, but we took a brief look at Christianity from the time of Christ, then Constantine, Mohammed, Luther, Anabaptists, Charismatics, and so forth. We both felt many teachers muddy the waters for others to drink. I believe we both recognized Christ as central. He leaned more toward Jehovah. We had a nice visit.

With all my love to each of you,
—Daddy

APPENDIX II:
Documents

MILFORD CHRONICLE ARTICLE

...Y, FEBRUARY 24, 1928

MILFORD CHRON

SCHOOL CHILDREN MUST SALUTE FLAG OR SUFFER SUSPENSION

State Board Acts When Mennonite Children Fail To Salute Emblem At Greenwood.

SEE FLAG WAR EMBLEM

Pastor Of Their Church Says It Is Against Their Religious Belief. May Build School.

Alleging that in their belief the American flag is an emblem of war and that there could be no peace except that which comes from God alone, children of the Mennonite faith who attend the public school in Greenwood have refused to salute the Stars and Stripes as is required by law in this state at the patriotic exercises held every morning in all the schools in Delaware. If they persist in this attitude they are to be suspended and if further persistence is evidenced they will be expelled, according to the decision of the State Board of Education, the members of which took official notice of the incident at their meeting at Dover last Friday afternoon.

The school board officials made no effort to conceal their contempt for and impatience with those who cannot have reverence for the American flag. Rev. Nevin Bender, a minister of the Mennonite Church at Greenwood, appeared before the school board to explain the position of the members of his flock in this matter, but, after hearing his arguments, it was the unanimous decision of the board to instruct the school teachers to strictly enforce the state law requiring the flag salute from every pupil in all the public schools in Delaware.

Dr. H. V. Holloway, state superintendent of public instruction, a few days ago received a letter from the school teachers at Greenwood in which it was stated the Mennonite children had refused to salute the American flag. When the children had been reprimanded for this attitude they told their teachers their parents had taught them that it was a matter of conscience with them; that they were not allowed to salute the flag because it was an emblem of war; that they were peace-loving people and believed only in that peace which comes from God.

This stumped the teachers and they asked Dr. Holloway what they should do. He brought the subject to the attention of the State Board of Education at their meeting last Friday. Rev. Nevin Bender knew the subject was to be discussed and he asked for the privilege of explaining the Mennonite side and this was granted him.

He reiterated the statements of the Greenwood children as repeated from their parents. He said the Mennonites are peace-loving people; that they are opposed to war; that

[Continued on page 7]

SCHOOL CHILDREN MUST SALUTE FLAG OR SUFFER SUSPENSION

[Continued from first page]

they could not fight against their fellowmen in any cause; that they could not kill and that in the light of the dictates of their consciences the American flag is a symbol of war and therefore they could not salute it and they would not permit their children in the public schools to salute it.

Members of the school board took issue with Rev. Bender and asked him if the American flag is not as much an emblem of peace as it is of war; they demanded to know it the flag was not in fact the only real emblem of peace and no matter what it stood for they wanted to know if every American did not owe it allegiance. They declared it is the emblem that protects Americans at home and abroad and as such they declared it must be honored and respected. They wanted to know why the Mennonites, now that this country is at peace, could not salute the flag, but Mr. Bender replied that to the Mennonites the American flag bespoke militarism and therefore they had to regard it as an emblem of war and could not salute it.

President Williams of the state board insisted the flag is a flag of peace and that this country is at peace and not at war and he demanded to know why the Mennonites could not salute the flag as an emblem of peace. To this Rev. Bender evidently failed to see sufficient light to make reply.

The board members refused to enter into the religious phase of the argument insisting that part of it had nothing to do with the law requiring the allegiance of all to the flag.

The debate ended with the adoption of a resolution by the State Board of Education instructing the secretary, Dr. Holloway, to write to the Greenwood school teachers and direct them to strictly enforce the law requiring the flag salute. If any of the Mennonite children or any other children refuse to comply they will be suspended. Persisting in their refusal they will be dismissed from school.

Rev. Mr. Bender stated that if all the Mennonite children were thrown out of the public school for their failure to salute the flag then the Mennonites will build their own school. He gave no indication that the children would be instructed by their parents to salute the flag.

Joseph S. Wilson, a member of the board, suggested that if the Mennonites wanted any special privileges or relief under the state law requiring the flag salute that they should take their case before the next session of the Delaware Legislature.

In other parts of the state where there are Mennonite colonies they do have their own schools.

FOR THE PURPOSE OF GETTING THE VOICE OF THE CHURCH REGARDING ISSUES CURRENT IN 1958

all members counted.

QUESTIONAIRE *given to Congregation on my own*
July 20, 1958

1. Would you appreciate to have our people continue the practice of wearing the plain coat and the cape?
   yes ⋯
   no ⋯
   no answer //
   not clear //
   choice ⋯ — 77% yes

2. Do you feel that the wearing of the plain coat and the wearing of the cape should be enforced?
   yes ⋯
   no ⋯
   no answer ⋯
   not clear ⋯
   Enforced — 75% No

3. Do you feel that television should be made a test of fellowship?
   yes ⋯
   no ⋯
   no answer /
   not clear ⋯
   yes Conditionally ///
   not sure // — 62% No

4. Do you approve of our general policy in discipline?
   yes ⋯
   no ⋯
   no answer ⋯
   not clear ⋯
   Generally /
   yes Conditionally ///
   12 / — 75% yes

5. Do you favor ordaining one or two ministers in the near future?
   yes ⋯
   no ⋯
   no answer ⋯
   not clear /
   Preference. /
   — 92% yes

6. Do you favor ordaining a bishop in the near future?
   yes ⋯
   no ⋯
   Exert influence — No.
   Clear on what we vote.
   Those not present.
   yes Conditionally ⋯
   no answer ⋯
   not clear /
   Preference ⋯ — 53% yes

THE JOURNEY TO EGYPT

(Reprinted from *The Casselman Chronicle*, by permission)

I remember as a boy in school I used to study about the Sphinx and the Pyramids of Egypt, about the Nile River and the crocodiles. During Christmas vacation this year the history of this ancient country came alive for us as my two daughters and I spent a week there, seeing perhaps most of what I had studied about—except the crocodiles.

Near the city of Aswan a number of experiences stand out: a simple buggy ride one evening through the narrow market streets which were filled with people, and one couldn't imagine an automobile getting through, but occasionally one would wind its way through. The sides of the streets were lined with fruits, vegetables, breads, and nuts of almost every description. The people were very friendly and seemed to be happy to see strangers visit their marketplace. A sailboat ride on the Nile around two interesting islands was relaxing and enjoyable. The huge Aswan Dam, which is claimed to be one of the largest dams in the world, is nearing completion and is already being used in part. It will furnish electricity and irrigation and will make a great difference to the country. It is a source of deep pride to the Egyptians.

The different tombs and the ruins of temples near Luxor built around 3,300 years ago reveal a masterpiece of work. They did not have the use of modern inventions and machinery which we have today, but they did have tremendous skill that enabled them to carve out huge pillars in one piece and construct huge temples close to 1,000 feet long. Some of the tombs were dug into the mountainside through solid rock 1,000 feet long. The carvings and the paintings inside the tombs revealed preciseness in skill which they possessed. This was done to help the king in his long journey into the afterlife. It required an enormous amount of work. It required dedication to a task. The men who worked no doubt felt that they would be rewarded for thus being devoted to the king.

Around Cairo pyramids instead of tombs provided burial places for the kings. The oldest of these dates back nearly 5,000 years. One is impressed with a pyramid like the one of Cheops. This pyramid originally was built to a height of 481 feet. More than 2,300,000 blocks were used, each block weighing around two and one half tons. This required engineering skill which staggers the imagination.

One evening we took in the *Sound and Light* program given at the Pyramids of Giza. It was intensely interesting and challenging to the imagination as the lights played on the Sphinx and the pyramids and the voices of the kings boomed out, seeming to come from within the pyramids. We were carried away into the ancient past. We could almost see the laborers at work, the shouts and the singing, the clashing of armies, and the rise and the fall of kings. It was most impressive.

The area of Old Cairo is filled with churches, synagogues, and mosques representing Christians, Jews, and Muslims. It was heartwarming to meet a Coptic priest with whom we could converse and feel in him a love for Christ and humanity that seemed to leap barriers, and experience genuine fellowship as he showed us around the "Hanging Church" dating back to the fifth century.

Evenings along the Nile were unforgettable with the palm trees and buildings on the opposite bank and sailboats on the river being silhouetted against the flaming sky as the sun set. In the midst of poverty, of uneasiness, of distrust, it made us feel that this should be a land of peace and beauty.

OUR JOURNEY TO PALESTINE (PART 1)

(Reprinted from *The Casselman Chronicle*, by permission)

During Easter vacation my daughter Mildred and I had the pleasure of taking a journey to Palestine by plane by way of Nicosia, Cyprus, as this was the only way open for us. The Palace Hotel, where we stayed, was located at the lower side of Mt. Scopus, which is really a part of the Mount of Olives. This was outside of Jerusalem at a very quiet place which provided circumstances favorable for thoughtful meditation. On a number of occasions I would walk down to the Garden of Gethsemane in the early morning before breakfast, and several times we went to the Garden Tomb and the place of Ascension on the Mount of Olives. We loved to linger in that area.

I can give only a very brief sketch of this journey. At Bethlehem we visited the Church of the Nativity which is built where the stable is supposed to have stood where Jesus was born. This was a touching scene to us. The shepherd's fields where the angels gave the message: "Peace on earth good will toward men" are not far away. We walked through the narrow winding streets of Nazareth, the town where Jesus spent his boyhood and manhood days. We visited the cave-like home where it is claimed that the family lived. The Church of the Annunciation stands close by. A well at Burith marks the place as one day's journey from Jerusalem where Joseph and Mary may have become conscious that Jesus was absent when they were returning from the feast when he was twelve.

Bethel a bit farther north is where Jacob used a stone for a pillow and where he saw in a dream the ladder stretch from earth to heaven. It is also where Abraham and Lot parted. Shiloh, which is about five miles east from the road to Samaria, we did not get to see. The road to Shiloh would need to be traveled by foot quite some distance which time did not allow. It is here that the ark of the covenant was kept for 200 years and the place where Samuel served in the temple. Jacob's well and "the well is deep" is not far from the two mountains Gerezim and Ebal. We both had a refreshing drink drawn from this well by a rope and pail.

The places around the Sea of Galilee are interesting. The Hotel Tiberias, where we spent one night, is located a small distance above the city. In the time of Christ this was a pagan city. We sailed by motor boat from Tiberias across the sea to the ruins of the city of Capernaum. The mountains from where the demon-possessed swine plunged into the sea could be seen across the sea. The places of the Loaves and Fishes and the Mount of Beatitudes where Jesus gave the Sermon on the Mount are close by. The Mount of Transfiguration at the foot hills of Mount Hermon is some distance from here. We could see the snow-capped peaks in the distance.

Coming back to Hebron we saw the burial place which Abraham bought near the "Oak of Mamre." Six of Abraham's family were buried there. A memorial to Joseph stands in that area, since his bones were buried near Shechem. Rachel's tomb is located near Bethlehem. Solomon's pools, which have been repaired a number of times, are close by. We stopped at Bethany where Mary and Martha lived. The tomb where Lazarus was supposedly buried is close by. The inquisitive person would no doubt descend into the tomb perhaps 25 feet to see the place from which Lazarus came forth. We missed seeing the place where Jesus was baptized because fighting had erupted at that place just the day before. Qumran, the place where the Dead Sea Scrolls were found and the way in which they were found is an interesting story.

OUR JOURNEY TO PALESTINE (PART 2)

The part of our journey to Palestine that I desire to give in this last article refers to the closing days of our Savior's life on earth. What is now thought of as the "upper room" is really a memorial built by the Crusaders. A Byzantine pillar is found in the wall of the building. This is the area where Jesus spent the last evening with the disciples before going to the cross.

The Kidron Valley is just a short distance away, across which Jesus went to the Garden of Gethsemane to pray. A beautiful garden in which olive trees are growing marks the place where the three disciples waited. The Basilica of Agony, the Church of All Nations, is recognized as the place where Jesus withdrew alone. A large stone stands in the center of this building.

St. Peter in Galligante or Caiaphas Hall, also called "The Crowing of the Cock," is where Jesus was tried after being taken to Annas. Underneath Caiaphas Hall is a deep pit where some feel that Jesus spent a part of the last night in confinement. This is a solitary place. The place where Jesus appeared before Herod and Pilate is the area of Herod's temple which was destroyed in 70 A.D. We were shown a part of what is claimed to be the original floor in Herod's temple. This may have been the place where Jesus was tried and then taken to Pilate where he was condemned.

The Way of Sorrows, known as Via Dolorosa, was indeed a painful way. The present street is from 10 to 30 feet above the original, but it leads to two places where it is claimed that Jesus was crucified: the one to where the Church of the Holy Sepulcher now stands, which was built by St. Helena after her son made Christianity the state religion, the other which leads out through Damascus Gate. To the side and below we could see a much smaller gate, through which Jesus may have carried the cross.

Not far from here is a beautiful garden in which is a tomb hewn out of a rock. This was discovered and excavated just about a hundred years ago. Close by is a huge rock bearing the resemblance of a human skull, the eye sockets and nose. On top of this is a Moslem cemetery. This would seem more like the place where Jesus made the supreme sacrifice and bore our sins in his own body on the tree. This is called the Garden Tomb. We attended an Easter morning service in this garden. I bought a tape recording of this service. Whether it is from this tomb in the garden that Christ arose or the one mentioned before is not the big question, but we know that he arose and that he is alive today.

During th 40-day period following Christ's resurrection he made many appearances. At one time he appeared to the disciples at the Sea of Galilee which is about 75 miles from Jerusalem. He then returned to near Bethany to the Mount of

Olives. On this mount is the Pater Noster Church or Church of the Ascension. In this church the Lord's Prayer appears in 42 languages. It is evidently from this mount that Christ ascended into heaven, and at which time two men in white stood by and told the disciples that he would return as they saw him go. This is a blessed thought for the blood-washed saints.

TALK GIVEN BY NEVIN AT NEAR EAST SCHOOL OF THEOLOGY (NEST)

It is a real pleasure to me to be associated with you as a student body as well as with the faculty here at (NEST). One thing that makes it especially interesting is to be with so many from so many different countries. It makes one feel as though a large family came home.

In this devotional period I desire to quote from a few statements that Jesus Christ made to John when John was on the Isle of Patmos, which was directed to the church of Philadelphia as follows (King James): "Behold I have set before thee an open door and no man can shut it; for thou hast a little strength and hast kept my word, and hast not denied my name. Because thou hast kept the word of my patience I also will keep thee from the hour of temptation which shall come upon all the world, to try them that dwell upon the earth" (Rev. 3:8-10). This is a wonderful testimony from Jesus Christ and it contains a wonderful promise.

The church of Philadelphia was one of the seven churches of Asia which Jesus Christ addressed in his message to John. Many students of the Word believe that the message to these seven churches also refers to the Christian church in seven periods of time, placing the church of Philadelphia in the period of time from about 1517 A.D. to the end. Whether this is true or not I sense a beautiful parallelism here. If I have the proper concept, God was moving among men around the early part of the sixteenth century for men to write and to study the Word, which changed the course of church history. There was a great awakening, a period of evangelism, a period of a great missionary movement. Doesn't it seem like an open door?

I am especially interested in noticing what Jesus Christ had to say about this church. I quote in part: "Thou hast kept my word and hast not denied my name." This is the part that I am interested in, no matter to whom it may refer. It is a part that we should ponder very carefully. What is involved in keeping his word and in not denying his name? To answer this question fully would no doubt require the Holy Spirit's message in the whole New Testament. But I would like to notice especially the basics, or the major thrust of the New Testament, truths which Jesus Christ emphasized strongly.

First: Jesus said in John 8:31 to those Jews who believed on him, "If ye continue in my word then are ye my disciples indeed." True discipleship stood high in the thinking of Jesus and is one of three major areas which identify a person as one who keeps his word. To adequately define true discipleship would cover a large area, but if my concept is correct let me confine myself to three statements:

1. To be a disciple of Jesus means to be a learner or a follower.

2. To be a disciple means to live as Christ's children live, or to allow Christ to live his life in us, to live in victory over sin, to live in holiness.

3. To be a disciple of Jesus means to live in obedience to his will. This covers much territory.

Second: Jesus said in John 13:34, 35, "A new commandment I give unto you, that ye love one another as I have loved you, that ye also love one another. By this shall all men know that ye are my disciples if ye have love one to another." Under the Old Covenant we were to love our neighbor as ourselves, but in Christ we are to love as he loved. In Ephesians 5:1-2 we read, "Be ye therefore followers of God as dear children, and walk in love, as Christ also hath loved us and hath given himself for us an offering and a sacrifice to God for a sweet smelling savor." Christ laid down his life for us and we are to lay down our lives for one another.

The history of the church is a sad story when we compare the love that Jesus taught with the love that the church practiced through the centuries even to the extent of taking part in the shedding of human blood. But I believe that a vision of Christ's love was recaptured in the early sixteenth century when thousands gave their lives for their faith in Christ. Let me give just one illustration: A man by the name of Willems confessed his faith in Christ and when the authorities learned of it they immediately put a thief catcher after him to bring him to judgment. Willems fled, and in fleeing crossed a river frozen over with ice. The thief catcher pursued him across the river, but in so doing he broke through the ice and fell in. Willems, sensing that the man was drowning, turned back and rescued him. At first the thief catcher would have left Willems free but, remembering his oath, he took him back to the authorities where he was tried and then was burned at the stake. Willems must have possessed divine love.

Third: Jesus said in Acts 1:8, "But ye shall receive power after that the Holy Ghost is come upon you; and ye shall be witnesses unto me both in Jerusalem, and in all Judea and in Samaria, and unto the uttermost part of the earth." This was Jesus' closing message to the disciples who were present when he ascended up into heaven. It is claimed today that only 25 percent of the earth's population profess to be Christians.

The challenge facing the church today is to be true disciples of Jesus, to love one another, and to witness the love of God to the world.

THE AUTHORS

Don Bender, Atlanta, Georgia, is the owner and president of Neighborhood Commercial Redevelopment, Inc., which has, with its investors, bought, renovated, and leased commercial properties in three in-town Atlanta neighborhood shopping villages. It has turned these formerly run down commercial districts into viable, revitalized destinations. A central part of this revitalization has been creating space for the arts, including the adaptive re-use of two former boarded up movie theaters into live music and live theater venues. Don is in the process of turning his work over to younger associates and is beginning partial retirement.

After graduating from Eastern Mennonite University, he taught elementary school for one year in Grottoes, Virginia, and beginning in 1966 taught three years in junior high and high school in Atlanta, Georgia. He lived at Mennonite House, located in an African-American neighborhood, as a volunteer under MCC for the first two years. In addition to his teaching, he was also active in the civil rights and peace movements there. In 1969 he married Judith Harak, whom he met in Atlanta. Together they served for two years as the program coordinators and residents at Quaker House with a primary emphasis on draft counseling.

Don received his M.Ed. degree in adult education from the University of Georgia in 1971 and worked in adult education part time for 10 years, while also serving as homemaker while Judith taught at Atlanta University. Beginning in 1977, Don began his business ventures, starting with a restaurant and gathering place before focusing on real estate redevelopment.

Inspired by a core belief in the inclusion of all segments of society, he has been committed to neighborhood activism and community building, This has included leadership in neighborhood organizations and business associations. He was active in opposing a proposed expressway through his community and later served as president of Freedom Park Conservancy as it turned 200 acres of land intended as the expressway into a major linear city park.

He was a leader in the early 1980s in the decision of the Atlanta Friends Meeting to declare itself a Sanctuary for Central American refugees. His family hosted a Salvadoran family for six months while they waited sanctuary in Canada.

Mildred (Millie) Bender, Sandy Spring, Maryland, began her teaching and counseling vocation at age 20 in Greenwood, Delaware, with one year and a summer of college. After later graduating from Eastern Mennonite College and two more years teaching at Greenwood, she moved into what was to become a unifying theme in her life—reaching across to work and share life with other cultures and religions. First there was Newfoundland with the Mennonite Central Committee for two years, then a move south to Neshoba County, Mississppi. When Martin Luther King Jr. marched, she was teaching English to Choctaw youth, a minority within a minority and working closely with her father and mother in their life among the tribe during the turbulent 1960s.

Graduate study at the American University of Beirut (Lebanon) earned Mildred her master's degree and opened the door to seven rich years of teaching—mainly Arab students, many of them Muslim—at the university. During those years she had the rare privilege of traveling with her father in the Middle East and Europe, exploring, among other things, the sites of Anabaptist history as well as Bender history.

Washington, D.C. became home for Mildred in 1975. Besides teaching at Georgetown University, she joined Sojourners Community in the inner city. Further graduate study in pastoral counseling (at Loyola College, Baltimore) while serving as a pastor and counselor in the community called for constant deepening in her own spirituality. A sabbatical in California's Bay Area studying creation spirituality was a feast of imagination, truth, and storytelling that led her to integrate a body-mind-spirit focus into her counseling. The greater Washington area is still home for Mildred as, retired from teaching, she continues her work at a healing center near Sandy Spring, Maryland.

Titus Bender, Fort Defiance, Virginia, is retired from Eastern Mennonite University, where he taught social work in the fields of human behavior and social policy since 1976. He remains active in one of the fields in which he had specialized—a program of working with men convicted of substance abuse-related crimes to help restore them and their communities rather than just getting even.

After graduating from Eastern Mennonite University and one year of seminary he and the person to whom he is married, Anna Yoder Bender, spent 11 years, including the 1960s, in Meridian, Mississippi. There they led a voluntary service unit. Titus' work included pastoring Fellowship Mennonite Church and working as the Peace Representative in the South for Peace Section of MCC. He worked at issues of racism, unemployment, literacy, homelessness, and poverty at the personal and institutional levels. When over s70 church buildings burned in the mid-1960s, he became a part of a statewide church-related group, Committee of Concern, which raised money to help rebuild these church buildings and to organize volunteers to work alongside members of some of the churches in rebuilding their sanctuaries.

Feeling the call for continued involvement at the community level, he earned his masters and doctoral degrees in social work at Tulane University in New Orleans. After four years of teaching at the University of Oklahoma, he returned to Eastern Mennonite University. There, as in Mississippi, it was clear to him and his family that standing with excluded persons was for them the only valid option, unless these persons were exploiting or excluding others. They have learned to live with this decision.

Printed in the United States
33381LVS00008B/109-117